THE BUDDY PLAN

Don L. McCorkle

Long after the battles are over, other struggles persist. War never goes away. It drags the unsuspecting into its ugly fog and refuses to let go any victims. They are forever trapped.

♦

A number of seemingly *unbelievable coincidences* occurred during the experiences of the main characters in this book. At times, it seems to be the imagination of a Hollywood script writer, but it is not. It is far too improbable for that.

♦

The major part of the book is dedicated to a young soldier who "lost his life" in Vietnam, only to be revived from an embalmer's table and eventually after miracle after miracle lives today to tell of his faith, family, and circumstances which allowed him to survive.

Don L. McCorkle

Copyright © 2018 Don L. McCorkle

All rights reserved.

ISBN - 13: 978-1539632214
ISBN – 10: 15396332210

Linda Harris McCorkle
27 September 1944 – 18 October 2012

I was honored to have served with some of the finest soldiers I could have known. All soldiers who fight battles don't wear uniforms. I had the distinct honor to have witnessed the relentless bravery of one such individual.

Linda, I remembered something you said a long time ago: I knew the flowers would bloom and the butterflies would come to display their beauty as they hovered around the bushes and gently lit.

Table of Contents
Chapters

01. Misty Images
02. Howey's Store
03. Mr. Luke, Jack Ghent
04. Slagle's Happy Acres
05. The Buddy Plan
06. Brief History of Vietnam
07. O C S
08. Mothers Everywhere
09. Fort Sill
10. Tour of Duty
11. Cry for The Children
12. The Coma
13. The Medical Journey
14. A Mother's Faith
15. The Medical Journey Continues
16. Jacky Meets Another Angel
17. The Adoption
18. The Wedding
19. Lieutenant Ron Dunn, USMC
20. SFC Bruce Logan
21. Jacky's Faith
22. In Memory of Scout Dogs
23. Epilogue

Thanks!
Hope you enjoy -
[signature]

Acknowledgements

Wanda Mayhugh for her editing skills and her continued encouragement.

Louise Pettus for information about local characters and history.

Pat Threatt, Harry Slagle's niece, for her information and insight into the story about her mother and her uncle – the intricate details.

Ron Dunn for information and providing real documents. And a very special thanks for his role and efforts in finding SSG Bruce Logan.

Bruce Logan, obviously, thanks to him for first saving Jacky and setting in motion the series of miraculous events that led to Jacky's recovery.

Patsy Bayne for the information she gave – her role in the story – and especially for her unrelenting care for Jacky throughout the years.

Jacky Bayne for the information he shared about his life and his inspiration to others.

A special thanks for those people whose wonderful stories made all of this possible.

Photo credits: Mandy J. Hill – Back cover and About the Author.

Back cover photo – Veterans Day celebration, 2016, Indian Land High School, SC.

PREFACE

There is little doubt that the impetus for this book is the desire to tell *the beyond amazing* story of Jacky Bayne, my high school friend and buddy with whom I enlisted in the Army. His story merits special recognition because of an extraordinary series of miracles and *coincidences* which took place since the day he was pronounced "dead" from wounds he received while on a mission in Vietnam.

Although the main story is about Jacky Bayne, other stories which are of great interest appear within the book. Some had a strong influence on my thinking in my formative years and later in life when I began to write seriously. The narratives are both informative and heartwarming and well worth reading. Two of these stories are heartbreaking. Early chapters provide the background and setting for the book and build up to the main story.

The reader is also given an historical background about Vietnam and other events happening in the U.S. at the time which helped shape the mindset which eventually determined the fate of Americans and others in Vietnam - and other places in the world.

Much of the information was collected from personal interviews with knowledgeable sources or actual persons. Other information came from news stories or research previously done while teaching the subject of History.

A special thanks again to Louise Pettus, Professor Emeritus at Winthrop University, for her contribution of local history.

Part of the book's format might appear somewhat different from other books. I have done this to provide emphases on important lines or paragraphs and/or to allow a short pause for the reader to think. Hopefully, the reader will not only accept the style but will find it to be a refreshing change.

> **There is a break in the main story which is noted by a text box before chapter nine. The reader can make a choice as to how to proceed.**

Introduction

"Coincidence is God's way of remaining anonymous."
Albert Einstein

♦

In my youthful days, I often sat and marveled as the older folks told stories of which they were a part. Quite frankly, some of the tales seemed beyond what reality would afford a normal person. But I have since learned that reality can be much stranger than fiction. Oftentimes, reality far exceeds even the best imaginations.

♦

Perhaps roles are cast for people to play. Those chosen to play certain roles should to do so with the best of their abilities. We must learn from the experiences and pass the lessons on to those who follow. Hopefully, what is learned will benefit everyone on their life's journey.

Don L. McCorkle

"My generation is exceptionally fortunate to live at a time when we will not be affected by war or the threat of war."

My thoughts, September 1962
(Shortly before the Cuban Missile Crisis)

♦

"It's an insignificant event. The little country is foolish for attacking our big ships. It will be over in a short time... if there is a bigger conflict."

My thoughts, July 1964
(After President Lyndon B. Johnson announced North Vietnamese gunboats had attacked American ships near the Gulf of Tonkin)

♦

"Greetings..........."

August 1966

THE BUDDY PLAN

"I heard a strange noise coming from his body. It was not the ordinary type of sound that you hear. I grabbed his wrist as tightly as I could. There was a beat. It was a faint beat, but it was a beat."

Bruce Logan, graves registration specialist, Vietnam, July 1967

♦

The young soldier was given up for dead twice in Vietnam. As his contracted body lay woefully in a coma, the best trained medical professionals at Walter Reed Army Hospital, who had seen thousands of horrendous wounds, gave him no chance of recovery. "Your son may live fifty years. He will not improve. We believe he will always need constant care."

Head of Medical Staff – Walter Reed Army Hospital

♦

A strong faith mother who refused to accept the grim prognosis as she stared down the medical staff at Walter Reed Army Hospital, "I believe my son will get better. You are not the final authority. I believe in a higher power. I believe he has come back home for a reason."

Bunia Bayne, August 1967

Chapter One

Misty Images
(July 1967)
(Partly Dramatized)

"Hit it!!!" The chorus of shouts from the company commander to the squad leaders came. The explosion possibly meant many more to follow along with the pop-popping of the AK-47s, the roar of the machine guns, and the eerie sounds of rocket propelled grenades whizzing by their heads.

Within a split second of the dreadful sound, the soldiers blended as much with the rice paddy as they possibly could. Adrenaline heightened the senses and they listened intently while their eyes scanned the tree line for any movement or weapons flashes.

There were no more explosions or other sounds. It was probably a mine.

"Check for your buddies and fellow soldiers!"

The explosion had come from the direction of the point man, the young Specialist 4 with the dog.

"Check out the dog handler!" There were no signs of him or his companion.

Two young soldiers, possibly risking their lives, ran to where they thought the explosion had occurred. They came upon the unthinkable. The awful smell of burned flesh and rice paddy mud churned their stomachs and made them want to discharge the morning's breakfast. They did not.

"They're gone – no hope!"

Such a pronouncement meant the soldier and the dog both had met their final fate.

"Get them out of there! Don't leave anything behind! Take them both to a clearing nearby so we can load them on a chopper!"

It was just one of several hundred similar scenes which had taken place in Vietnam, and it would continue over the long course of the war.

A helicopter crew would extract the remains, take the soldier to a battalion aid station, and from there he would go to a graves registration unit located nearby to be processed for the long sad trip back to the United States. His friend and companion's remains would be taken to a special burial site set aside for service dogs.

They all knew the routine. But the routine for this particular "dead soldier" would be dramatically different. In fact, there would be nothing ordinary about a long series of events from this time forward for the young combatant.

It was personal to me, extraordinarily personal. We had been on the same sports teams in high school. I had sat with him and marveled at his wonderful sense of humor on numerous occasions as we conversed with our friends. We had enlisted in the Army and had gone through Basic Combat Training together. We had shivered together on freezing October nights as we shared a small tent during bivouac at Fort Jackson. We had both planned to go to OCS. We had made plans for "after the Army". *But now, everything had changed... forever.*

♦

The most valued of our treasures lie within our memory. Our experiences affect us in ways we may never realize. We are changed. The soft slate on which memories are scripted cures with time and they are forever embedded there. For better or worse, the recorded events remain.

♦

A wise man once said there was no such thing as time, only changing circumstances. At times, it is hard to adapt to such changes and maintain sanity.

♦

Thoughts of My Youth
(1980s)

As I stood looking out over the now empty student area below me, the rays of the warm August sun sank deep into my body and lent comfort to my soul. The tensions of the long difficult day were easing and my senses drifted to thoughts of more pleasant things.

Just how many wondrous outings had the old concrete bleachers ringing the field below me witnessed over the years? They were times when students casually gathered, sat, talked, and basked in the glow of friendships each shared with one another.

Thoughts of my own youthful days began to creep into my consciousness. I drifted farther away and felt at peace with all of Creation. Faces from my past, now only misty images, popped in to say hello and then dashed away as though they were children playing a *peek-a-boo game*. Trying with all my might to keep them there, begging them to stay for just a short while longer, was to no avail; they still flickered away and were gone in an instance.

The images were the faces of the wonderful, wonderful times when there was nothing but the carefree pleasures of the day - faces and moments etched forever into the deepest creases of our being. It was the time of our own splendor in the grass. Spring breezes blew softly across our laughter and the looks and the unspoken thoughts we shared unconsciously with one another brought pleasures yet to be perceived.

Those were the days my friend, but I always realized they would end.

Psychologists tell us that the most impressionable time in our development is the early years of our childhood. There is no doubt of this truth. The experiences are written upon the still soft slate of our being and we are forever affected, whether it is for the better or not. The most important things which happened to us are remembered until the inevitable fading of all our memory with time.

I would also point to the years of our transition from youth to adulthood as a time when we establish bonds which affect us throughout our lifetime as well. It is our first chance at independence; we pick, choose, and do things we have never done before with new people who just happen to cross our paths, or isn't it better to say, people with whom our paths intersect, perhaps for a purpose?

Too often, we mistakenly go into the world thinking we need only ourselves and one or two others, but the reality of it all is: The love we have for so many we knew isn't realized until the autumn of our lives begins to set in. Moments to be cherished forever revisit us. They reach from deep within and tug painfully at our hearts.

Anxiety, frustration, sadness - it is all there as the images slip away. Where are those faces now? Where did it all go? It was a time when all of the smallest particles of our being came together just perfectly in the already miracle in which we existed... and it extended into something even greater. Now, it is gone forever. *The only remnants left are misty images.*

What would we give if we could go back? How many tomorrows might we trade to be able to do things once again that we so dearly cherished? Relive it all again? Or perhaps, pick one special moment and live it forever. What would we do differently? Would we be able to say the things we wish we had said or maybe take back some words or actions we now regret... or would it end up all the same? Was it all that wonderful or have the lines been rewritten by time? I truly wonder. But we did have the certainty and security of our youth. At least we thought we did.

Physics deny us the return to our dearest times. However, we need the dreams, the fantasies. We need them for our own sanity. Although at times, the pain... the heartache of looking back holds capture our emotions. We can still smile as we wipe away the laughter - t*he tears, the bitter sweet tears.*

Even in my state of almost total disconnect from the present world, I could sense someone coming close to me. For the moment, it was so grand. I was almost there – in another world of my own making, the perfect escape.

In spite of all I have ever read and studied, I have never been able to answer the haunting question of "why, in the moments in which we are dreaming or consumed by the most pleasant thoughts of all our mind games, we are interrupted?" We are about to achieve life's most fantastic moment... and it never happens. I wish I knew the answer. Maybe it's Nature's way of preventing us from bidding reality a total farewell and drifting off to never return. I don't know, but I do know there is a reason. I'm just not quite sure what the reason is.

Kenny Griffin

Wayne Beard, a fellow football official, was approaching. That's why we were all there. We had assembled to talk about football and the many complicating situations that violations of the rules can produce just when everything seems to be going along "just dandy".

Something much more important than football was on Wayne's mind at the moment. I had heard some news and suspected he wanted to talk to someone. Maybe "the news" was another reason for my own melancholy and the attempt to escape reality for at least a short time.

"I lost one of my people today," he began in a low painful voice. He sounded too attached to the situation. More than likely, he was. Wayne was the local Veteran's Affairs officer.

It is strange how the system works. Those who are overly concerned cannot seem to help those in need of care as much as they should because they become part of the problem rather than providing a solution. Wayne was simply too wrapped up in his work for his own sake and for those he wanted to help. He was violating the rules by becoming emotionally involved.

"He fell in the hospital and hit his head and before the nurses could help him, he was gone," Wayne continued in an even more solemn voice. "Did you know Kenny Griffin?"

"Yeah, I knew him," was all I could utter at the moment, and maybe that was a good thing. It had not been a particularly good day emotionally for me in other respects. I'm not sure I could have said anything helpful to either of us.

As more fellow football officials approached, the short conversation changed to other subjects. The interruption was good for Wayne. I'm sure his day had been much worse than mine. The usual hellos and greetings took place. For the moment, Wayne and I stopped our private conversation and suppressed the thoughts of Kenny and so many others we had known and continued our small talk with the group.

We soon adjourned to the meeting room upstairs in a small nearby building where the topic once again was football and all the rules involved with the game. So many people think they know the rules. This is especially true of the fans. We who have studied the details know differently.

It's similar to life. You have to really study the rules to begin to understand it. Even then, mistakes are made. Sometimes, the mistakes are game changing.

The session was a good one and, for a time, the adrenaline raised my spirits. After the meeting, we all left. Most of the guys had worked the day and were tired. Short goodbyes and we were on our way. I didn't get a chance to talk further with Wayne. Perhaps just knowing I knew about what had happened and sensing something of concern in my voice helped in some way.

On the ride home, I felt myself sink again. I guess it was because I was emotionally and physically drained. It felt as though my car seat was dragging the roadway. I really hate such a feeling for all sorts of reasons. It allows the most unpleasant thoughts which are all stored away and hopefully locked in a safe place a chance to wiggle their way into the conscious mind.

As I looked off to my right and across green cropped field, the last remnants of the setting sun were glistening though the trees. The sky was tinted in shades of pink and azure. It was reminiscence of the beautiful sunsets I had seen in former times and places far away. Memories of times, which were best forgotten, began to find a way into my consciousness. It was a time of sunsets whose beauty gave way to anxiety about the impending dangers of the nights.

I was once again reminded of times when I felt that there had been a roadblock placed in the pathway to my living happily ever after. Not only had it been a hurdle for me, but it had been the same for thousands and thousands of others. Sadly, not just for my generation, but for many of the generations before me. Too many never cleared the hurdle and too many others who got over it were permanently impaired.

The bastard human powers who could not stand for the generations to be happy and enjoy life in its fullest had to start something for their own personal gain. There had to be something to disrupt the pleasures of the time. The older I get, the more cynical I become as to the causes of wars and our involvements. I don't doubt evil exists and needs to be confronted, but we must always reflect after it is over to be sure we were not the cause of it and ask ourselves, 'How can such nonsense be prevented in the future?'

I can never overstate the importance of this obligation. It is our debt which we must pay forward to the future generations. This must be done so they do not become the victims of events orchestrated by but a few and which consume the lives of so many innocent people.

Can the good of the earth ever overcome the sins of greed for wealth and lust for power?

No doubt our involvement in World War II was necessary. *Evil incarnate* walked upon the face of the earth and would have controlled all of mankind in unimaginable ways had that generation, our fathers and grandfathers, not suffered the great sacrifices they did. There is no way possible for us to have ever thanked enough those who are gone or the relatively few who remain from that era. They saved for us a way of life that is unparalleled on this earth. Perhaps the greatest monument of all would be to preserve the ideals for which they gave so unselfishly. No doubt the greatest disrespect we could show is to tarnish those ideals with our own selfishness and greed.

Korea was a worthwhile commitment. Other involvements I question more critically. President Eisenhower was more spot-on in his farewell address than he might have wanted to be. There is a Military Industrial Complex which shapes our political commitments, and hence our military involvements, more than we can imagine or care to acknowledge.

None of this in any way diminishes the men and women who have served or continue to serve in any of the conflicts. They have gone and still go to serve with the best of intentions and have made and continue to make sacrifices beyond expectations. We must always maintain the thread of patriotic service. There can be nothing short of honor for all who have given or continue to give of themselves. We must always appreciate the sacrifices borne by their loved ones as well.

Perhaps questioning the causes of our military commitments might not be so unpatriotic after all. Proper concern might help us to prevent more outright criminal acts by our leaders. Blind allegiance to political powers in charge has caused wars for which there was no purpose other than to serve the political and financial fortunes of a few. The critical skepticism of man's motives in all situations seems to have been missing as the patriots donned their battle garb and marched away to places unknown and to circumstances yet to be determined. Never forget... *the politicians who call the shots of war are not among the dead and lame.*

A story published in a local paper (*The Herald*, Rock Hill, S.C.) on December 7th, 2011, the 70th Anniversary of the Japanese attack on Pearl Harbor, quotes a local survivor of that attack who makes an excellent point. Platoon Sergeant Retired, Army, L.C. Rice: "We assisted any way we could - helping the living and collecting the dead," said Rice. "You could say World War II was born that day. The devil was born. Wars are no damn good. This was no movie."

"Had I known Kenny?" Yes, as a matter of fact, I had known him quite well. He and I had attended the same high school. He was younger than me. It was a rural school of the mid-1900s design. The long brick building housed all the grades from first through twelve. Grand oak trees in the front of the main building and in other places on the grounds, as if Nature had planned it all for the students to enjoy, made the setting even more picturesque. A long concrete walkway from three steps near a parking area led to three more steps into the main entrance.

There was innocence to it all, even though it was not completely so.

The small school setting allowed each student to know most of the others. No one was lost in the crowd. We thought it to be an ideal situation. It wasn't Heaven and it wasn't Iowa either - but it was a wonderful experience of bonding closely with friends - bonds to be cherished forever.

To be honest, I was sort of jealous of Kenny. He was a tall, thin, All-American looking boy. He was handsome and mannerly and had a pretty older sister and an older brother who would later become an officer in the U.S. Army.

Kenny, like so many of the youth of my time, had joined the service in 1968. Young men get caught up in the ideal of patriotism. We were taught such when we were in school and anyone who doubted what the

THE BUDDY PLAN

country's leaders did, especially to "make people free," was unpatriotic. *We were naïve to the fact that real motives of our leaders at times were camouflaged better than the combatants who we were convinced to believe were our enemy.*

The suffering, the sorrow, the killing, and dying are all done by those who are most innocent of the human crimes of greed and lust for power. Those who lust for power create in the minds of those they choose to use for their dastardly deeds the idea of a mission which is glorious and purposed. "A vile enemy that oppresses all that is good and just must be ridded from the face of the earth." This mantra is propagated and finally accepted as truth.

Perception is reality, but reality has a way of changing perception. Perceptual changes are slow and require well-thought-out theses and conclusions. Such processes are too often unused. Learning must take place through experience... which, too often, is a brutal teacher.

Kenny had been seriously wounded in Vietnam. Other problems began during his long and painful attempt at physical recovery. Unfortunately, as is too often the case, doses of "pain killers" used to treat one problem become another problem - a very difficult one. His new problem of addiction had to be treated as well

After his discharge from the Army, his care was handled by the Veterans Administration. This is the other side of the war few people want to talk about. These veterans are the ones who are supposed to fade from the mainstream and go quietly away so the war which caused their misery will be forgotten by the new political powers who might repeat the same misadventures as their predecessors.

Kenny had been assigned to Wayne as one of his veterans in need. I had learned about some of his difficulties from conversations on a golf course from a mutual friend who was also a veteran of the same conflict. He wasn't kind in his assessment of Kenny's behavior. He told me some things which are best not discussed. Maybe he lacked understanding as to what really can control someone's behavior. I think down deep he had compassion but, perhaps, was unable to show it in this situation.

Strange things happen to people. Some do unusual things without ever having gone through extraordinarily painful circumstances. If there is such a thing as an excuse for questionable behavior, maybe Kenny had one. Maybe thousands of others like him had an excuse, too. Could we ever be so kind as to call it a reason? Maybe we should?

To be sure, like so many others, he was a casualty of war, but the better question might be, "Was he also a *victim* of the war?" That might require more thought. Wars have a far greater number of victims than casualties. We have been conditioned to accept what happens and move on as though all is well. To those directly affected, it is not well at all. Wars produce hells which don't stop when the last shots are fired or the last rounds explode and soldiers leave the battlefield.

Kenny's name will not appear on the Black Marble Wall in Washington, D.C. Nor will many other names whose youth were stolen away by the Vietnam War appear there. Just as surely as dawn turns into day, their lives were shortened by their service. There were so many before them in so many other wars that were all fought under the guise of *noble causes*. There are many more like Kenny and similar others yet to be. We have known but a small number of them

THE BUDDY PLAN

The ride home was just long enough to get my thoughts back together. I could package it all away, get a good night's rest, and have more energy tomorrow - things would be okay.

Chapter Two

Mr. Luke and Jack Ghent
(1950s)

♦

War is among mankind's greatest failings – perhaps second only to the greater failing of total indifference to the plight of masses of others who suffer needlessly because of circumstances.

♦

That anything could be wrong in the world was incomprehensible. Although we didn't have much money, I thought everything was fine and in my naïveté, all people cared for one another and each had the other's best interest at heart. Such an idea was an easy assumption when the people about you displayed those characteristics and the scope of your world was limited.

Obviously, I can understand now how ignorant I was to the facts of history and the evils of some men - as most children are. Unfortunately, there doesn't seem to be a better environment today. Hate and greed are still fostered by ignominious politicians and politicos. The babble on the media is fetid with bias, half-truths, and downright misrepresentations of the truth. It is done solely for personal gain so that some selected persons and their cohorts might grab an undeservedly larger piece of the mythical pie.

THE BUDDY PLAN

Mr. Luke Williams

The autumn Saturday morning was cool and to this day the comfort of the warm quilt is indescribable. I pulled the cover up and was safe in my own little cocoon - protected from any of the harms of the world.

When you are lacking maturity, most problems you might incur will go away if you just hide under the bed covers, or at least you have such an illusion. The security is real to a mind not yet aware of all the harms and challenges the world has to offer. Parents watch over you and provide the support you need. Unfortunately, not all children are so blessed.

Mama and Daddy were up early as usual. She had cranked up the old wood stove in the kitchen. Mama had grown up using a wood burning stove to cook on and was so set in her ways that she would not use anything else.

Breakfast was started. Even the aromas from freshly made biscuits, bacon, and eggs cooking filtering through the crack in the door to the kitchen weren't enough to get me on my feet. It was a day I could stay in bed for a while longer and I took full advantage of it.

Soon, the grinding gears of an old 1938 Chevrolet truck coming around the corner of the house signaled that Mr. Luke Williams, a neighbor from a short distance up the highway, had arrived for the weekly breakfast meeting. It was clockwork. He would park his truck in the back yard, grab his crutches from the passenger's side, place them on the ground, slide out of his seat, and hobble into the house through the back door. Regardless of the struggle he endured, when he first greeted you, there was a glowing grin on his face.

Rather than awakening me further, it cued me to go back to sleep, and I did. The warmth from the freshly stoked fire in the heater was beginning to spread throughout the room and it made sleep all the more inviting.

Mama would open the back door and hold it for Mr. Luke as he placed his crutches "just right on the step."

"Good morning," as he always greeted her with a grin.

He and daddy exchanged greetings and each sat down near the table and soon the conversation on the topics of the day began.

By the time Mr. Luke got to the house, Mama already had coffee made. The small silver percolator pot she had placed on the stove would hold about four cups - enough for the morning's consumption. When it had percolated the right amount, she grasped it with a pot holder and poured a cup each for Daddy and Mr. Luke.

Mr. Luke loved his coffee, and he loved it strong and black, hot, right out of the pot. He always made some favorable comment about the brew. He held the cup with both hands and placed it close to his face before he sipped on it. Maybe the warmth made both his hands and his face feel better. There was some evidence that his arthritis had even affected the muscles in his face as well.

Daddy mixed cream and sugar in his coffee to a point that it resembled a syrupy light brown mixture. After each had taken their first sips, they would sit there in the kitchen and talk about the problems of the world. Mama always gave Mr. Luke a freshly cooked biscuit with real churned butter on it – homemade jelly, too.

Mr. Luke, like so many around, had worked in the cotton mills for a livelihood. It was the golden age of textiles in the South. Most of the small towns nearby had evolved around the cotton mills. Many people from the rural areas were employed there as well.

Daddy worked in Fort Mill and Mr. Luke had worked in Rock Hill where he had grown up. He and his wife, two sons, and a daughter moved to our community years later. They lived less than a half mile from us.

The death of his father when Mr. Luke was a young boy had left an unfillable void in his life. He would never miss a chance to mention him if he could associate it with a conversation.

By the time we all knew Mr. Luke, rheumatoid arthritis had crippled his hands and legs. His fingers were twisted and knobby. One wondered how he even held a coffee cup, but he managed. He had lost his left leg below the knee to the disease, and the right leg required a brace at times to allow him to even hobble on his crutches. Nevertheless, he managed to drive his old straight drive truck and do it quite well.

Despite all of life's problems, Mr. Luke was a man of extraordinary faith. He was a self-made Bible scholar. Quoting scripture and verse had become second nature to him. There was hardly ever a conversation in which he was a participant that he did not do so.

His condition became a testimony to his faith. Never once did I hear him complain about the hardships he constantly encountered. His struggle was evidenced in each small move he would make, even to adjust himself in his chair, but the grimace caused by the pain of movement soon became a grin. He made certain of that.

Little did I know at the time that years later I would see a painful parallel to his condition brought about by totally different circumstances; nonetheless, the condition would be evidence of another person's extraordinarily strong faith as well. The circumstances which caused this person's hardships were, by far, the biggest reason to give even more credibility to his witness.

That same Saturday morning, for some unknown reason, I awakened just as Mr. Luke was quoting a particular Bible verse.

"There will be wars and rumors of wars until the end of time," he stated in the matter-of-fact voice he always used when quoting scriptures.

Even though I had been groggy, his profound statement further awakened me like a bolt of lightning striking nearby. How could such a proclamation be true? It was incomprehensible that people would not want peace in the world.

A child's mind, ignorant to all the evils of the earth, I suppose, was to blame. I thought the wars we had just been through, WW II and Korea, had solved all the world's problems and maybe there would be everlasting peace now.

"Surely this is not destined to be," I thought, but Mr. Luke said it came from the Bible. Thus it had to be true. "I'll go back to sleep and when I awaken, it won't be so." When I awakened again and the fuzziness of the moment rubbed off, I knew it really was true.

In spite of my young age, from that point forward, I looked at life somewhat differently and the words still ring true in my ears today. But for the time being, it was filed neatly away and posed no problem. After all, I was safe in my little cocoon.

THE BUDDY PLAN

Mr. Luke loved to fish. For safety reasons, he would always get someone to go with him. Many of the ponds around the area were accessible and he could drive his old Chevy truck near the banks and then find a favorite spot, bait his hook, and sit patiently on the bank in a chair he took along with his prized bamboo cane pole which was rigged just right with a bobber, small hook, and piece of lead.

It was fishing in one of its most simple forms. A favorite catch was a small pan fish called a bream. More often than not, patience paid a reward of at least a few fish large enough to keep. He might incur some difficulty in releasing the fish from the hook. Whoever was with him always watched and gave assistance if needed. As a young boy, I whiled away many afternoons with him along a creek bank or a pond and still have fond memories of doing such.

The Accident

During the 1950s and 1960s, the trucks from a brick factory located in the small town of Van Wyck, a few miles south of us, usually ran pretty fast on their delivery trip to a construction site and drove unusually slow on their return to the factory. Oftentimes when we witnessed this, we would joke and laugh about it.

Normally, there were at least two people in the truck and many times, three. This was before the modern way of unloading the truck with a fork lift. Back then, bricks were, more often than not, unloaded brick by brick on the job site.

The miracle of the accident was quite visible to anyone who saw the actual scene. The truck, fully loaded with brick, broadsided Mr. Luke's old '38 Chevy as he attempted to turn left onto Doby's Bridge road. The impact knocked him into a large ditch. If surviving the initial impact wasn't enough of a miracle, the fact that this large truck then landed upside down on top of his vehicle in the ditch with the full complement of brick scattered all about with many of them on Mr. Luke's truck and some even in the passenger compartment made it more unbelievable.

When we first came upon the scene, we were absolutely convinced that Mr. Luke and others as well were dead or seriously injured.

"Someone will need to go tell his family. Poor Mr. Luke."
"What about the others?"
"Has someone called the ambulance?"

Thankfully, we were all wrong. All of the passengers in the larger truck were standing about and Mr. Luke, who had been extracted from his vehicle, was sitting nearby. He was still in a mild state of shock.

With the exception of few bruises, Mr. Luke was unscathed, as were all the occupants of the brick truck. He had survived the crash, but his ability to properly operate his truck had come into question.

The brick company was eventually found at fault and Mr. Luke did get a small settlement for his few bumps and bruises and to replace his old truck. He took some of the money and opened a small shop to sharpen hand saws and other small items. He had seen the idea in a magazine and thought it would provide him a meager income of sorts. Back then, many people in the area still used hand saws in their work. All of those who worked on houses would hand-cut the finish work such as molding.

THE BUDDY PLAN

I'm not sure if he ever made much money at the shop, but it did provide him with a feeling of being productive and independent.

One Saturday morning, out of habit, I awakened about the same time as usual. I had not yet heard the scrapping of the gears as the old truck rounded the corner of the house. I went back to sleep under the cozy covers. Shortly thereafter, I was awakened again by the phone ringing and was shocked when my mother, as she hung up the receiver, told my father that Mr. Luke had passed away in his sleep during the night.

We were all saddened by the loss of our dear friend. He would be sorely missed. We would miss the Bible quotations and the smiles he always managed even though he must have felt pain with each movement of his body. I would miss riding in his old rattling truck and fishing along the banks of a creek or pond with him. He was a good man. He would not be forgotten and his messages would always ring true with us – especially the one I heard on one cool autumn morning: **"There will wars and rumors of wars until the end of time."**

.

Jack Ghent

One of the jobs my older brother Pete had during his early years was running an establishment on the north side of Lancaster, SC, called Twin Pines. The small bowling alley and restaurant attracted a variety of people and lots of them.

My other two older brothers often set pins at busy times on the bowling lanes and my sister Florence went to work there after high school. One night, she met a young Marine from Lancaster named Jack Ghent. He became a frequenter of the establishment when he was home on the weekends or on leave.

Not only did Jack take a fancy to my sister, but he also became close friends with my brother and eventually our entire family. Over the course of time, it was commonplace for him to visit our house and sit around and talk to my brother Pete and other family members. In modern terminology, he became a part of our extended family.

Oftentimes, he would come by the house straight from Camp Lejeune, North Carolina, where he was stationed as a Drill Instructor. He was big and robust, typical Marine to the core, and exceptionally sharp, especially when he wore his Class A uniform.

Jack, like my brother Pete, was fond of beer. It was not uncommon to see them sit around the house and enjoy a beer or two and, at times, probably more than they should have enjoyed.

Pete had tried to join the military during WW II but had not turned sixteen until near the end of the war. When he finally did reach the magic age, his endless insistence to join convinced my mother to sign for him. He went through basic in the Navy and was about to ship to the still raging war in the Pacific when the news came of a new mystery weapon dropped on two cities in Japan. He soon returned home - as did many other recent recruits.

THE BUDDY PLAN

The long extremely difficult war was over and America could celebrate.

Although my mother didn't want Pete to join the service, she always kept the picture of him in his U.S. Navy uniform on the mantle for as long as I can remember.

On his trips home, Jack usually stopped at the Post Exchange and picked up a full complement of the brewed delight for consumption over the weekend. Schlitz, the popular brand of the day, was also Jack's and Pete's favorite brand, or at least it appeared to be.

One particular night, Jack came to our house from Camp Lejeune, bringing, of course, a supply of beer. We were all glad to see him. My sister had not gotten home yet, so we all sat around the kitchen table and carried on various conversations.

Later that evening, it seems that both Pete and Jack had enjoyed too many beers. Jack's mood changed noticeably. He became melancholic. As he emptied each bottle, he would place it on the old yellow table along with Pete's empty bottles. We each looked at the others and thought it somewhat strange how he was placing the bottles in a pattern.

When there were quite a few empties there, he started to maneuver them around on the table and explain how Marines used "this tactic" against a potential enemy. At first it seemed as though he was telling how Marine battle plans were carried out on the smaller unit level. We all took interest and watched closely as he situated each bottle.

The bottle shifting soon became overly emotional and personal. Each bottle seemed to have a name. Jack's eyes began to fill with tears. If fact, each bottle did represent a person, some of them represented Marines he had lost in battle.

"Damn it, I couldn't help it, it had to be done. I had to do it to save the rest of the platoon!" the painful outburst came.

"I'm sorry," he apologetically said, after realizing what he had done.

He apologized a second and a third time.

Recomposing himself slightly, he pulled the dark rimmed Marine Corp glasses from his eyes, took a handkerchief from his pocket and wiped away the tears which had streamed down his face. He put his glasses back on and further recomposed himself.

We all sat silently for a long moment. No one looked at the others. None of us knew what to say or do.

We soon realized we had seen the inside of someone whose outside always portrayed the façade of a big, tough, unflappable Marine. Maybe we had always taken for granted things we should not have.

Jack had indeed lost Marines in battles in Korea. The barriers men build so well to protect themselves by hiding away the pain of past glories were compromised by the alcohol.

The compassion for others which must be stifled by military conditioning if one is to become a good military leader had given way to the subconscious good that the vast majority of men innately possess.

Although he never vocalized it, he was making the statement: "I, Jack Ghent, human being, am guilty of making decisions that caused other human beings to lose their lives." It was a cry from the heart. It was a sad outcry of a conflict from within – one which would never be resolved.

We all thought highly of Jack Ghent, the Marine, before that particular night. We always would. We thought even more of him now as Jack Ghent the uncommonly compassionate human being.

Jack continued to court my sister until somehow they grew apart. We saw less and less of him. He would still come to see my brother on occasion.

THE BUDDY PLAN

One day, about two years after he stopped dating my sister, we got news he had been killed in a single car accident on the Marine base. Somehow, he had lost control of his car and struck a utility pole.

My mother believed, and made it known to us in no uncertain terms, that he had intentionally taken his own life. She believed Jack had wanted to leave the Marines and his parents had strongly insisted that he had already served too long in the Corps not to make it a career.

Maybe he had a deep desire to get away from it all and put that part of his life behind him. One can only speculate. No one could ever know what haunted him and how bad it was.

Did my mother have information Jack had made known to her? Perhaps she did. If so, along with her great intuition, she had a very plausible argument.

There were, are, and will always continue to be, the Jack Ghents. They will go about cleaning up the messes made by politicians. They will suffer the traumas to their psyches and other horrors while those who caused it all will live with impunity.

Footnote 1:
Before my sister met Jack, she had dated another young soldier from Lancaster whom we all referred to as "Whitey". This was also during the time of the Korean War.

I cannot recall all of the letters she told us about that he had written from Korea, but I do remember parts of a particular one. In it, he had been overly pessimistic about his chances of returning from there alive.

Whether or not it was a premonition he had, I cannot say. For whatever reason, both my sister and my mother gave substantial credence to his writing.

Not long after the letter, the frequent correspondence stopped. Shortly thereafter, my sister was notified by his family that "Whitey" had indeed been killed in action. Even more sadly, it was just shortly before the final truce - one of many which had been called during the war. The "conflict" in Korea officially ended not long after his death. Was it a premonition or had he somehow contributed to a self-fulfilling fate?

Eventually, my sister did marry an older man who had served in WW II. He had received a Silver Star for heroism. He never told us exactly why he was awarded the medal, but Silver Stars and higher medals were pretty hard to come by and required a substantial hurdle of bravery.

He kept his stripes and medals, along with some newspaper clippings, displayed in a neatly constructed wall hanging. He gave me a small Bible he said he had carried in combat. He wanted me to take it with me on my trip to Southeast Asia. I gladly obliged.

George Tinker had served in the Italian campaign against the Germans. He was proud of his service, as well he should have been. He had reached the rank of Staff Sergeant before the end of the war.

Perhaps my sister had been destined to marry someone such as him. It was well that she did. In the last years of her life, she needed constant care for a considerable length of time. George was unrelenting in ensuring she had whatever she needed. He showed the devotion of a loving husband and an outstanding soldier as well.

Footnote 2:

Jack Ghent, the Marine, had once told a fib or had found a way to sneak by the scrutiny of the U. S. Marine Corps. I know. In my research, I discovered he had entered the Marines before the minimum allowable age so he could serve in WW II. Some men are meant to be Marines.

Don L. McCorkle

Chapter Three

Howey's Store
(1950s)

Where I first met Harry Slagle

♦

The noise and bright lights have dimmed our minds so we neither hear nor see the most important things of life - those things that are within us and ought to be. There's a sadness that surrounds us and self-centeredness abounds in us as we all look the other way. Gone are the days of Ozzie and Harriet.

♦

History is what happened last weekend and the future is all about the approaching weekend.

♦

The Change

A hundred years or so, or at least it seems, have passed since my youth in what once was a sparsely populated area of Lancaster County, SC. People who never knew the place existed now call it home and hope others will not find out about it. Some of the newcomers are just as genuine as those who grew up here. Others seem to be lost in a world of self-absorption and "cell babble fast-speak" as they hurry about to places unknown, but are obviously important to their days' plans. I've often wondered "to whom they were talking?" Fact is, it seems as though no one listens anymore or thinks before they begin to babble incessantly.

So many of the "newbies" walk right past you; they are seemingly lost in a world protected from any outside contact. Some never seem to want to speak.

THE BUDDY PLAN

Eye contact is forbidden. Perhaps they have been conditioned over time, for whatever reason, to behave in such a way. I cannot judge the behavior outright. There could be so many causes. It still seems foreign. The grocery store conversations still take place, but it is within small groups. The monstrous grocery stores are a far cry from the country stores which dotted the highway in years past.

Narrow roads of yesteryear have given way to four lanes with traffic flows often resembling an interstate highway. Stoplights, which were non-existent in the early times, aggravate those who speed through as they hurry to work. The simple courtesy of a signal as people weave their shiny vehicles in and out of traffic is randomly, if ever, extended. There's sadness about it all. The "bright lights of progress" now hide the glow of the night's stars and lightning bugs that fascinated children who held them on fingertips. It is an age lost forever and a place raped of its innocence.

Time, the archenemy of mortality, has exacted its toll on the older generations of my youth. Those remaining, who fit so well into the old scheme of things, have become lost in the crowd of new faces. There are so many new faces. Those who lived through the horrendous times of the Great Depression capped off by World War II are scarce and the memories of their existence fade more as each day's sun sets.

Their predictability was as sure as the light of a new day. Weekdays saw them up at dawn to begin their chores or go to their workplace. Sunday meant church. A particular pew was filled by familiar families. Sometimes now, if you look at the pews where they sat, the memories are vivid, and for a moment, they are still there.

Each gave what was affordable in money and time. The values of truth, honesty, dignity, and all other good things that made man a noble creature were not only preached but were practiced as well.

Neighbors were neighbors in every sense of the word and most of the people knew each other and what was going on with them. Each had a sense of community which entailed responsibility of charity for those in need.

Grownups sat on Sundays at family gatherings and conversed about the topics of the day after a delicious home cooked meal had been consumed. Children played in the yards and barns and wherever else they chose. "Just don't bother Grandpa's king snakes in the hay; they keep away other snakes and rats."

The fellowship was real and the memories made were everlasting. There were no digital devices to waste away the time. Human connections and interactions lent a reality which seems to have disappeared in modern time.

The people were still connected to the land. Many had farm animals and large gardens from which they canned fruits and vegetables. Some still processed their own meat from the animals they raised. But even then, it was a transition time from the field to the factory. The surety of a steady job made possible more money and increased the buying power which was novel to people who had sacrificed for so long.

Howey's store was typical of so many such businesses that lined the Highway 521 corridor in that period. It sat in a prime location on the corner of the main highway and Shelley Mullis Road. A single stop sign located on the opposite side of the tar and gravel secondary road was all that was needed for traffic.

THE BUDDY PLAN

Howey's Store in the 1950s

Fancy asphalt was not common around the area in the 1950s. Secondary road beds were scraped, tar was put down and on top of the tar, layers of rocks were spread. The first layer was packed down until the tar oozed through the rocks and then another layer of smaller rocks was placed on top and packed.

The original main road (Hwy. 521) was modernized back in the 1920s. My father told me about working on it with animals and drag pans. It was slow and difficult for all, especially the poor animals. The area was not well-developed and machines were not plentiful.

By the 1950s, the main roads were concrete. Alongside of the road were the sidewalks consisting of an additional two-foot wide strip of tar and gravel. They were paved over when the asphalt craze began in the 1970s. Our little walking strips were gone. I've walked many miles using them. Back then, the traffic was such that an occasional car was all one might need to worry about while walking beside the road.

Pepsi and Coca Cola were in a race to see who could be the number one in soft drink sales. The two companies were quick to put as much advertisement on a store, and anywhere else for that matter, as possible. Moore's Store, which was just down the road about 500 yards from Howey's Store, had a giant Pepsi bottle cap hand-painted on the side. It was visible to all north bound traffic. The local playmates were amazed as we stood watching the sign painters display their own special talents. Bottle caps which had to be pried off from glass bottles with an opener went their way and were replaced by the pull tab can or screw tops on plastic bottles.

Hot summer days often found us playing stopper ball at the back of Moore's store. We had a pretty sophisticated league set up. Score was kept in spiral binders complete with names and positions. Games were either 3, 5, or 7 innings. In reality, the only positions were pitcher and hitter. The back of the store was perfect. I guess the wall was about 30 feet from the batter's box and about ten feet high. Any stopper hit to the top of the store was out of the park and a home run. It was simple, but at the same time, somewhat elaborate.

Stoppers could be pitched any way one desired, except real hard. Curves, drops, and even knuckle balls were common, just no fast balls. Believe it or not, some of the outs were made by catching a fly ball - well, a fly stopper. If business was slow at the store and not enough drinks were consumed, we had to collect stoppers off the ground. If there had been an onslaught of homeruns, we would get out the ladder and climb on top of the store and collect as many bottle caps as we could.

THE BUDDY PLAN

Other entertainment was as good as the imagination, and the imagination was good. It's sad that technology has given us so much at the expense of some things greater.

Howey's Store was adorned with metal Coke signs. White enamel with neat green letters seemed to be their basic offering. There was a personal version of their bottle cap. A big bright red metal disk with Coca Cola scripted on it hung in the most visible location. If we were lucky enough to find an old one, we might use it to slide in the snow - that is, if it ever snowed. I don't see how they made enough money to pay for all of the advertisement. Cokes and Pepsis cost a mere six cents at the time.

The dark green screen doors on the front of Howey's store were adorned with Merita Bread logos. Actually, in addition to the Merita name painted on the actual screen itself, the hand guard across the door bore another Merita logo. Evidently, they had provided the doors as well. The screen doors were a necessity because there was no air conditioning. In the summer time, a large fan circulated air (literally) through the store. Usually, the back doors which connected into the feed room were open to make this possible. Most of the people still had farm animals and chickens, so it was common for all of the stores to provide livestock food as well.

Only a few vehicles came through the intersection in a day. Then too, there were not many cars on the main road either. The faces of the drivers were familiar and the times they ventured to and fro were as predictable as sunrise and sunset. One could feel the warmth of their wave as they slowly turned the corner.

There was no shortage of friendly conversation if the people stopped to purchase gas or grab a few items they might be running short on. Oftentimes, when chairs were not available, patrons would pull up a coke crate and balance on it. Back then, cokes came in 6 ounce bottles, 24 to the crate. If anyone was good at handling the crates, he could grab a bottle in each of two crates and carry them up along by his side for transport.

Many times as people sat and talked, a deaf mute who lived across Shelley Mullis Road would be present. To make sure he was included in the fellowship, someone would think of an innocent joke to play on him. The limits were understood and it always turned out well so it ended with a smile on his face. He was also cared for financially by the Howeys who owned the land and building where he lived. He did odd jobs in order to feel he had earned his way.

One of the regulars at the store was a lady who walked three miles (round trip) every third day or so to get a few odds and ends. Winter or summer, she trekked along from her old dilapidated wooden framed house on Doby's Bridge Road where she and her brother lived with her parents. Her "vagabondesque" appearance was complete with a small cloth bundle tied to a stick carried over her shoulder. She adorned herself in long sleeves and a man's dress coat whether it was warm or cold.

She always sat for a spell when she first arrived at the store. Snuff dripped from the corners of her mouth, and perhaps she could have used a bath several days ago. Her words were few, but when she spoke, her voice was coarse and deep. She pulled her change from a small handkerchief or her folding money from her sock, bought her goods, wrapped them in the cloth on her stick, placed the stick on her shoulder and was on her way. She was a kind and gentle soul like her parents and brother. Her clothes were frazzled.

I guess she and the deaf mute were just some of the ones of the "never known by many and forgotten too soon by those who did know them." I would pray that the Gracious God of all things would have something special in store for them and those like them who were so seemingly insignificant on this earth. I will always believe that every piece of the Great Puzzle is extraordinarily significant. It's just that we cannot seem to figure out much of it at all.

Earl Howey had inherited the store after the death of his brother Zelf. Long before we understood such things as depression, we asked questions as to why anyone would take his own life. Zelf had walked into the woods just across the main highway from the store, and not too far from his own small framed house, placed a gun to his head and pulled the trigger. He left a wife and son. His wife was a tall slender lady who taught English at the high school within walking distance from the store.

Jimmy, Zelf's son, would frequent Moore's Store and Grill just down the road (visible from Howey's store and just across the road from where I lived). He would stand and wave at the traffic which passed from time to time. I guess he had acquired some of his necessary people skills through this. He later attended law school and joined the Air Force, which he made a career. I think ROTC helped him pay his way through the University of South Carolina.

Moore's Store in the 1950s

After Jimmy had become successful in his own right, Food Lion paid him a tidy sum for the land on which his small house sat. As best I can recall, he married and retired somewhere in Colorado - quite a switch from the migration pattern we now have in the community.

Earl ran Howey's store until his own death and because I was no longer connected closely to the community, I don't know other details of the place. I do know it was torn down in the name of "progress" when the main road was widened to the present four lanes.

The small frame house in which I grew up was also claimed by the same "progress". Many of the older dwellings disappeared in my period of absentia. I wonder what exactly happened to them. Time changes the face of the landscape as well as other things.

THE BUDDY PLAN

Face to Face with Harry

In the summer of my twelfth year on this earth, I went to work at Howey's Store. My fishing friend, Frankie Kennedy, had worked there previously and he had told me about moving on to bigger and better things and that his former job was open. I walked the few hundred yards or so from home to ask Earl about working for him and was hired on the spot and thus joined a list of young boys who went through a right-of-passage of sorts by working at Howey's Store.

It was my first major responsibility. I could handle it though. The pay was two dollars a day and the work week was six days – Monday through Saturday. The money was fine. A few dollars in the 1950s would buy a lot of things for a youngster.

As with most growing children and older people as well, the only problem I experienced was getting out of bed early enough. The store had to be open in time for at least some of the early workers to stop by and get gas or some other supplies for the day. Earl liked money and was eager to get as much of it as he could from each day's efforts.

Predictably, when there was no traffic, he would sit and count the money in the cash register. This was his twice daily routine.

My job consisted of the regular chores which needed to be done during the day. The first order of business was to get the oil products out front. Back then, the oil racks were between the gas pumps. Even in those days, there were the different grades of oil. Only today, the prices are much different.

The price on the gas pumps usually ranged from 13.9 cents per gallon to around 17.9 cents per gallon. Between the gas pumps was also an oval Amoco sign located on a 15 foot high pole. Curiously enough, most people purchased gas in 5 gallon quantities. Maybe it had been a carry-over from the war years when people had to use rationing stamps to get certain commodities.

I once heard an argument, well a discussion, regarding a man who had promised to take some relatives shopping in exchange for 5 gallons of gas. Instead of choosing regular, he decided to get "high test" (premium). The cost was only about 2 cents more per gallon, but money was not plentiful at the time.

I have actually seen gasoline sell for as little as the taxes on the gallon. If I recall correctly, that was less than 10 cents per gallon. No store owner was about to be outdone by the other. The prices were usually posted on a small "A" frame sign somewhere near the main road. Oftentimes, store owners would have someone ride around the countryside to see what other gasoline prices were.

During the hot and not so busy time of the day, I would find a nice shady spot around the back corner of the store. Earl would usually catnap during that time so I knew it was safe to sit and let my mind wander as well. The awnings on the store usually provided shade during much of the day but I wanted to be sure I was out of sight so I wouldn't be called on to do anything. I usually stayed caught up on the work anyway

One particularly hot sunny day as I sat around back of the store, my eyelids were growing heavy, and as I was about to venture into another world, the unmistakable loping of an old flat head Ford engine at the gas pumps startled me. Half out of my senses, I still knew I had to get to the front of the building to do my job. I hopped to my feet and was on my way. By the time I arrived at my duty station, one of the occupants of the car was already pumping gas into the tank. It was an old black '49 or '50 Ford. Black was the basic color for that particular model.

THE BUDDY PLAN

The loping engine sounded as though it needed a good tune up. Many men did their own mechanical work. Engines of the 1950s didn't have all the extras they have today. They were fairly easy to work on with just a little knowledge and a few tools. No diagnostics beyond "it sounds like" was necessary.

I later learned that the gentleman who was pumping gas was Joe Blackmon. He was tall and thin. Smokeless tobacco, as it's called today, oozed out of one corner of his mouth. Snuff, as it was called then, was used by many and was sold in small cans. Everyone had a favorite brand they bought. No one knew of the health hazards it posed. It was also used for all sorts of minor maladies to include bee stings and other insect bites. Usually, it was applied to an injury straight out of someone's mouth.

Joe wore blue jeans and his white t-shirt had something turned under in one of its sleeves. Unlike today's scams, blue jeans were the most economical dress then - probably less than a couple of dollars a pair. They weren't all damaged either. They were worn clean and neat. Patches and holes in jeans usually indicated you didn't have enough money for new ones.

As Joe was busy putting gas in the Ford, I noticed someone get out of the passenger side and start to walk around the back of the car to go inside the store. He was shirtless and it was obvious that he had been in the sun for some length of time because he was darkly tanned. His thick black hair combed straight back brought to mind someone of Native American descent.

I was only going to glance at him as he rounded the back of the car, but as I did, I realized he was looking directly at me. When we made eye contact, I was mesmerized for the moment by his inexplicable stare that seemed to look right through me.

"What was this about?"

"Had I done something wrong by not being there to put the gas in the car?"

"No... that's not what it's about at all. It's a different look altogether... an extraordinarily different look."

"Why didn't he just say something out loud?"

I was bothered, but not at him. I was bothered because what had just happened was puzzling and frustrating beyond my ability to comprehend.

The moment was broken and he continued on his way into the store.

"Dear God, what happened to him?" was the unspoken question I asked myself as his back came into view.

Shock is not an adequate word to describe what I felt as I looked.

"How was he even alive?"

"What in this world has caused such injuries to his body?"

He was slightly overweight or out of shape, probably some of both. The fat tissue was evident and it made what I later found out were wounds look all the more worse. Across his back were several deep scars from gashes which I thought would have been enough to surely have killed any man.

"And was that where a hole had been in his back?"

What I didn't know - that at the time when the wounds had been inflicted, he would have had scant little flesh on his body. His bones would have been exposed. How awful it would have looked is not imaginable.

THE BUDDY PLAN

Frequently, when my dog Jamey stared at me, I could almost swear that he knew my thoughts. Maybe dogs are much more connected to us than we have ever supposed. I'm almost smart enough now to know what he wanted. Nature blessed him with a special way of communicating. How much more can humans convey with thoughtful looks?

"What had I seen in this man's eyes?
"Was he trying to convey something to me? If so, what?"
"Did he have any degree of satisfaction that he had accomplished what he wanted to do?"
"What had he seen in my puzzled look?

His eyes... his eyes... Now that I have the tools and experience to begin to analyze what I saw, I realize it was just a peephole into a troubled soul, and rightfully so. It seems so much clearer now than it did then. To totally comprehend it, someone would have to have been a part of the suffering he must have encountered. I was only given a glimpse. Perhaps his misery is somehow linked to the misery of countless others who have endured such painful experiences.

What about remembering what was in Harry's stare all these years? But I have and when it comes back to me now, it is haunting and troubling. Perhaps I am yet to know all I am supposed to about that moment. Explaining it to someone else in the manner in which it should be explained is a totally different matter. But I know I am supposed to try my best to achieve that goal.

I would like to think that somehow I conveyed to him I was aware that he was trying to communicate with me. I sincerely hope that somehow he knew that he would be remembered.

The moment from seeing Harry until he and Joe left the store is all blank. My mind needed the time to attempt to make sense of it all. I still had to deal with the shock of what I had witnessed.

After the two had gotten into the car and pulled away, I wasted no time going into the store to quiz the owner about the man. I don't know whether or not he had anticipated the questions. From the look on his face, maybe he had.

"Who is that man and what happened to him?" I blurted out almost as soon as I was within earshot of the owner.

Half smiling, he looked at me and quizzed back, "You don't know 'Ol Harry Slagle'?"

"Obviously not" was my thought, but I dared not make such a remark to a grownup.

The moment was interrupted by others before I got an answer and the questions were filed away, but I knew I could ask my mother when I got home. She could explain it all to me.

Finally, the work day was over. I finished my chores and stayed around for Mr. Earl to gather up his money, place it a bag, and with his small pistol in his pocket, we locked the several locks and cage steel gate on the front door and left the store area. He got into his Oldsmobile and headed toward his house a short distance away and I started my own little journey home.

The walk was long enough to get my thoughts together about what I had seen and let my subconscious store away the important things for future reference. I pulled some of the long grass growing by the side of the road and bit the ends off. It had a unique sweetness to it. The habit was common for people who lived in rural areas.

THE BUDDY PLAN

About 10 minutes later, I reached my destination. Mother would start supper about dark and we would sit down and eat. Daddy worked the second shift in Fort Mill and would not be home until after eleven p.m. or later. My brothers and sisters would not be home for a while. I would have a private audience to ask any questions I chose and my mother would know the answers.

Since there was daylight left, the usual routine was to go across the road to see what some friends were up to. Moore's Store was less than a hundred yards away and my best friend's daddy ran the store and my best friend was usually there so we might throw and catch baseball or do something outdoors.

It was soon time to return home for supper. As my mother and I fixed our plates and sat down, I finally got my thoughts together. There was a special question I wanted to ask her. *How important it would become, I could have never known.*

"Mama, what happened to Harry Slagle?"

"Son," she started.

With such a beginning, I knew whatever followed was serious, especially since I saw the expression on her face change dramatically. I knew then she had a story to tell about Harry Slagle... and it would be from a mother's perspective.

Chapter Four

Slagle's Happy Acres
(1950s – 1970s)

♦

The vast majority of people on this planet have an obscure beginning, live a life unnoticed except by the closest of friends or acquaintances, die, and their memories go silently into the dusk of the days. Tomorrow dawns and the people are forever forgotten. It is as if they never walked upon the earth.

Many led storied lives. They and others like them were the fibers which held the fabric of the nation together - the labor, the soldiers, and whatever else was needed in their time. So many made great contributions - even to include making the ultimate sacrifice.

May God be most merciful to those who went away and did not return at all and to those who loved them? Some who went away are buried in the remotest regions; others not buried at all - the final insult to their existence. Soon forgotten but to the God who created all the living things and all other things that go along with them. Perhaps in the end, it is all that can matter. Everything will pass away except God's memory and we pray He will show kindness and mercy for everyone who has ever existed.

♦

There are so many stories about people which should have been written. There are so many stories that will never be told. All great people aren't written about in History books. All people written about in History books aren't great people. Those who come after them may never understand why they enjoy the pleasures of their time. They may not even care. Unbridled pleasure is a birthright.

So many gave so much and yet received so little in return. Others exacted so much from the bounties of the land, yet gave so little. It all seems so unfair and imperfect, but perhaps what makes the world a perfect place is all the "imperfectness" about it.

Wasn't it meant to be, after all, a place where struggles create greatness which is measured in ways we don't always understand?

Maybe it is just as well. Normal people want to be left alone and would be forever happy to go to work, do their job, and squeeze whatever pleasure they can from the time they have for themselves. But too often, too many in some generations are never afforded such a meager opportunity. At times, the world spins wildly and the evil madness reaches its tentacles out and grabs the unsuspecting and exercises control over lives of which it has no right to do so. For the sake of mankind, good people rally and confront the evil. Men must leave the comfort of their surroundings and go to strange places where they are forced into situations unnatural to civilized humanity. Survival demands they act in ways contrary to all the goodness they were ever taught. Some return home safe and sound. Some return with parts damaged or missing, but mobile. Others return with crippling injuries. Crippling injuries are not always visible. It is for sure, all who return will never be the same.

Upon the slate of their being are written experiences which will haunt them forever. Memories are etched so deeply and painfully that nothing short of passing beyond this earth will be enough to console them, perhaps not even then.

♦

Sugar Creek

Sugar Creek, whose name itself is somewhat of a misnomer, originates about 30 miles north of the point in Lancaster County, South Carolina, where it becomes quite formidable before it empties into the Catawba River. It meanders lazily along most of the time unless there is a big rain upstream. Then, the torrent of red rushing water pulls and grabs at whatever is in its path.

Magnificent trees lining its banks reach out to the Heavens to praise God with their wondrous splendor - all the while begging to be spared yet another day from the waters that once nourished their rise to glory.

"Oh Master, have we not served you well and shown your beauty to all who would but notice?"

Their twisted naked roots reach and grab with all their might to hold on to whatever they can to give them a last bit of hope. The circle of life is closing. Their fate is inevitable. What has been given for so many years is now being taken away.

Perhaps for thousands of years, the waters were pristine. It was part of the lifeblood for Native Americans who fished and trapped along the undisturbed banks.

Listen... be still, the twigs are snapping and the leaves rustling, hear the gentle splash in the shallows. Is it a creature of the woods? Could it possibly be the Native American spirits returning to feed on the bounties of the water? It was their life source, their existence. Perhaps it's only the wind. Perhaps?

Oblivious to it all, water bugs perform their magic as they skate atop the brownish glistening waters to the rhythms choreographed by Nature. They have not a care in the world as they glide effortlessly along.

THE BUDDY PLAN

I've sat along the banks with Connie Brown on several occasions and waited for the catfish, or whatever else, to take the bait. He told us if the water was rising, or was it if it was falling, the fish would not bite. I think the latter, but not to wager on it. I do remember... if you did catch a catfish and were careless disengaging the hook, it was painful. If there was a bounty for the day, Connie Brown would put it in a "tote sack" to carry it back to a small branch near his home-place where the fish swam until he was ready for a "mess" of fish. He said the swim in his branch got the "taste of the creek" out of them.

Connie Brown was a contradiction in many respects. At times, he was impeccably dressed, clean, shaven, and a perfect gentleman. At other times, he let his appearance be prey to the demon spirits of the bottle, yet, "he was always a perfect gentleman."

"Brown", as people called him, lived in a small single room cabin built for him on my grandmother's and Uncle Bud's place. It was a short distance through the woods from the creek. Brown walked most of the places he went. The stores were close by, but if he needed to go to town, my uncle would oblige or he might catch a ride with someone else. Connie Brown was mostly self-sufficient, which then actually meant self-sufficient. He earned his keep and spending money by working at times with my uncle on home repair jobs.

The waters flow on and just south of our fishing hole once stood an old wooden bridge. The original one was built back in the 1800s. It was so named for the family who was responsible for its construction. John Miller Doby had moved here in the mid-1800s. He built a flour mill, worth - according to the census of the day - $4600.00 for tax purposes. He cleared a road and built a bridge so York County customers could get to his mill. The site was acquired in an agreement with the Native Americans in the area at the time.

My early recollections of the old bridge were that it was a thousand feet long and a hundred feet high. At least my boyhood illusions made it seem so magnificent. Each crossing lent itself to the wildest imaginings of horror. *Surely this would be the day that disaster would strike.* "Yes, this had to be the day. How could it stand one more crossing?"

The grinding roar intensified as the drivers shifted to the lowest gear to creep along in order to stay on the lane made by two boards placed where each wheel on the vehicles would be. The warped grayed oaken timbers moaned and groaned. Metal rods and plates which held this strange configuration together added their own unusual notes with their eerie creaks. The macabre symphony had begun. It grew louder with every rotation of the wheels. It would all end with a thunderous clasp of cymbals as we crashed to the rocks below. Then, there would be silence, the peaceful silence of the waters flowing about us.

But it never happened. The engine revved, the gears roared again, and we lunged up the hill out of the jaws of certain death. The hallelujah chorus was singing and it was delightful. Indeed, it was a thankful occasion.

The sigh on the driver's face turned to a "possum's grin", as the elders would say.

"Was there ever a doubt?" the look on the driver's face questioned.

"Yes, there was a doubt," the thankful stares replied.

THE BUDDY PLAN

Doby's Bridge in the 1920s. It still looked similar in the 1950s. The roads were better on the approaches.

The Homestead

About a hundred yards up the hill on the Lancaster County side of the bridge off the roadway 75 feet or so was a small green cinder block building - not much to look at in the way of a dwelling. The door was usually open in the summer, as were the small screen-less windows. A few twigs of sparsely spaced wild grass sprouted in the otherwise bare clay yard. In the summertime, there were hammocks randomly hung between trees.

The yard sloped down to a bend in the creek. Along the wood line, old "junkers", as people called them, were turned upside down. It was easier to cannibalize them for spare parts from their exposed underbelly. "Shade tree mechanics" was the proper term for those who kept their old cars running. Of course, again, it was before the age of the need to hook up to a computer to get a readout diagnosing seemingly insignificant problems. Most mechanical problems then were solved if it "sounded good".

If the fear of crossing the bridge had subsided enough, one might take notice to wave at the people in the yard. If you did, they were neighborly enough to return it and then go about their way. They were courteous and friendly like all country folks were thought to be. A couple hundred more yards on the old dusty road and all was forgotten, including the little green hut and the people seemingly roaming about.

Years later, another road was cut for a new bridge up the creek from the ancient wooden dilapidation. The old bridge did eventually fall, but there were no cars on it when it finally gave way. It died of neglect and slipped unnoticed into the waters. If you make your way along the deep ruts of what once was a passable road and look carefully, you can still see the remnants of the bridge abutments. Like so many things which existed in its era, it is known but to a few.

The little green building along with its patrons was now isolated and forgotten except for a small wooden sign hung from a post along the intersection of the old road and the new paved road. Hazel Griffin, a local sign painter extraordinaire and frequenter of the place, adorned it with "Slagle's Happy Acres". The name was a bittersweet irony that would live on long after the inhabitants and frequent visitors had given way to the perils of time and fate.

For some curious reason, a large timber was placed "smack dab" in the middle of the old road that gave access to the happy acres. Anyone who desired to go there by vehicle needed to actually drive on the side of an embankment to maneuver around the obstruction. The best information I got about the reasoning for placing the timber was that the proprietor of the property felt it necessary sometimes to "run from the law."

THE BUDDY PLAN

Joe Blackmon

It seems that when the county sheriff was bored, he and a deputy might give chase to some of the residents of the happy acres he saw driving out on the road. The lawmen were positive they would be able to confiscate some illegal whiskey. Joe Blackmon, the proprietor's chauffeur and all around handyman, was rumored to have the skill, during any of these hot pursuits, to aim the old black Ford directly at the timber in the road and at the last minute put the car in a controlled slide up the bank and back down which allowed them to safely reach home base before the sheriff could stop them.

It was also rumored that the law was so embarrassed from hitting the obstruction or sliding out of control that the pursuit ended abruptly once Joe successfully completed the feat. It was another small victory for the guys from the small abode. It's hard not to imagine a possum grin with a trickle of snuff out the corner of his mouth on Joe's face. And maybe, just maybe, there was a hint of laughter deep from within Harry.

"We showed 'em boss, didn't we?" Joe might grinningly ask Harry.

"You done good, son," Harry might reply. "You done good."

Another story told on Joe concerned the issue of the new Kennedy half dollar. It seems that Joe had been given the coin in change from a local store. Realizing it didn't look similar to the other coins he had received before in the same denomination, he was sure that it was a fake. Instead of confronting the store owner, Joe, in a gentlemanly manner, took the coin and when he got back to the happy acres, he walked down to the old Doby's Bridge area. While venting his displeasure with a few choice words about someone having taken advantage of him, he tossed "the counterfeit piece of metal" into the creek.

The Gatherings

Then there were the infamous gatherings at the happy acres. This usually occurred around the end of each month and lasted for no special length of time. It was from these "get-togethers" that an unsavory reputation of the place grew. It was not uncommon for rumors to circulate about stabbings and shootings and that some patrons lay dead or mortally wounded.

About the same time condolences were to be extended to the families of the poor departed, or even afterwards, surely enough, the "victims" reappeared unscathed except for the wear and tear of the lengthy binge. They would clean themselves up and go back about their business until the next month.

Connie Brown was also familiar to the happy acres crowd. He was among the cast of characters who were beyond the imagination of a Hollywood writer. They all gathered for the common kinship they shared, albeit a kinship most outsiders might never understand.

Jim Moore

Another regular at the happy acres was Jim Moore. From our front porch, we could witness the stooped figure make his way from the small house he shared with his elderly parents to his brother's store about 50 yards away. His body, with slumping shoulders, was bent from the waist as he walked, but somewhere in his step was evidence of a small spark of military mannerism. Usually, he had a day's growth or more of stubble on his face. Although he was still in his forties, he resembled his father who was in his 70s at the time.

THE BUDDY PLAN

Many of the houses in the area were torn down to widen the main highway. His small house escaped destruction. It still stands and each time I pass by it, which is often, the warm thoughts of the times when my friends and I were young and played football in his front yard are awakened. Even the adornment with salmon colored paint and palm trees along with the sign which identifies the real estate company that now occupies it doesn't take away the valued memories.

One of Jim's favorite places was an old chair in the front corner his brother's store. In the winter time, it was the place to be. A kerosene space heater kept the area warm. Sometimes, he would grab the small children and tickle them and rub his whiskers on a bare place.

I still remember the times and even now, I can sense something bothered him. There was something missing... even when he mustered a laugh.

"Deanie Lynn", as he often teased me, was not my real name. I'm sure he did it to get a reaction. I never minded at all.

Jim often visited us. He would sit in the yard under the shade trees at the back corner of our house in the spring and summer time. He talked to Mama as she shelled beans, cleaned corn, or prepared other vegetables from the garden.

How I wish I had listened more closely, but at the time, there were things to do.

"Sis", as many called her, had a special capacity for understanding. I suppose she had been chosen for the role of the neighborhood counselor. She listened intently and was very empathetic. People knew this and were greatly appreciative.

Jim might raise his pant leg or the bottom of his shirt to scratch and as he did, the physical wounds he had received during the war (WW II) were revealed. They were very substantial. Such injuries carry other serious scars as well.

I remember on more than one occasion, Jim's brother, Rone, who ran the grocery store/gas station across the road from us, telling us that Jim had been killed in a fight during one of the infamous bashes at Slagle's Happy Acres. However, it never happened. Jim died of natural causes at age 62.

Harry Slagle

The most obvious question still remains. Who was Harry Slagle?

The answer to that question could have been as simple as "Ol' Harry Slagle was nothing more than an alcoholic who minded his own business and was nice to everyone with whom he had contact." That would be the truth. But to those who knew about Harry, he was certainly more... much more than that.

(From local Historian and college professor, Louise Pettus)

"Harry was reared on the old Slagle farm near Van Wyck, SC, where generations of Slagles' country boys all and proud of it, had been reared. Harry was taught to go to church every Sunday morning and to give a tithe of his earnings to the minister and to be a good boy.

But good boys can also be restless. He took up reading Zane Grey. Perhaps that set off the yearning for adventure. He traveled all the way from Lancaster County to Orlando, Tampa, and St. Petersburg in Florida. That was not a small feat for a country boy at that time.

His adventurous spirit and probably limited financial resources led him to enlist in the U.S. Army. That would allow him to see parts of the world he might not otherwise be able to see. Surely enough, he traveled to the islands of the Pacific. He had ventured far, but country boys do get homesick.

THE BUDDY PLAN

Only when he had spent four years on beautiful Oahu and beautiful Luzon did he realize that he wanted to be back among the simple peach trees and the pines with his feet firmly on the red soil beside the Catawba River. He wrote home to his father to clear a patch of land, set out some fruit trees in straight rows, and some pines to hold the soil, and in a while, he would retire and come there to build a home."

Unfortunately, there was an interruption in Harry's plans. Before any of his well thought-out reunion with the Carolina soil could take place, the Japanese had attacked Pearl Harbor and WW II was raging full scale in the Pacific. Harry and all the many soldiers, sailors, and Marines in the Pacific found themselves right in the middle of the deadly conflict.

As fate would have it, Harry and numerous others would also later find themselves in a military situation for which they were ill prepared. The Japanese were superior in numbers and equipment and a heavy cost would be exacted on American servicemen. For fear they might be slaughtered in battle, American servicemen were surrendered to the Japanese.

On April 9, 1942, 78,000 American and Filipino soldiers and officers became captives of Japanese forces on the Bataan Peninsula, the Philippines.

Whatever humane rules of war supposedly in place were somehow forgotten by the cruel captors. Americans and Filipinos were marched, starved, beaten, and slain to satisfy the evil egos of the captors.

Hell had made its way to earth.

Harry spent 39 months in a Japanese prisoner-of-war camp hell hole following the Bataan Death March. He would bear the scars for the rest of his life.

The deep lashes on his back might well have been secondary to the scaring of his mind. You can't helplessly watch your comrades suffer and die and be otherwise!

On Aug 20, 1943, a *Lancaster News* headline , and article, read: **"Slagle Writes from Japanese Prison Camp"**- "It was the first word the parents had gotten in two years. The typewritten card sent from Japanese Prison Camp #1 was signed by Slagle. The card said Harry was sick in a hospital but his health had been fair. He sent his love to the family with best regards to his brother Robert who was serving overseas."

Hell hath its propagandists.

His loved ones who had suffered the agony of not knowing anything now knew he was alive. Why had it taken so long? Acts of humanity demand more than was given. At least there was hope among the new questions which now abounded.

The End to "The Happy Acres"

When the war ended, Harry was 32. He came back to Indian Land, but not to farm or to get a regular job. The small green cinder block building became his mansion and the small plot of land near the creek became his happy acres that he loved so dearly.

He was free... free to roam and smell the fresh air. There was no stench of filth in the mud and the smell of death was gone. It was Heaven.

Compared to the hell he and others had lived, it was indeed Heaven.

Playing cards with the regulars at nearby "Rose's Cantina" seemed to provide his only other pleasure. He didn't talk much. People who knew him back then describe Harry as a "loner". He was soft-spoken and polite but rarely smiled. He was usually barefooted, even in very cold weather. No one remembers seeing him wearing a jacket - and doubt that he even owned one. If he had a shirt on, it was usually unbuttoned.

Harry was set to live out his days in his kingdom by the small creek. But such was not to be.

Late in November of 1979, three young men paid an unsuspected visit. Their intent was evil from the beginning. For whatever reason, they believed Harry had hidden away enough money to make their scheme worthwhile. He would forfeit the money or else.

The headlines of a local newspaper (*The Lancaster News*) read: **"Former War Hero Slain; No Suspects"** -

"The bullet riddled body of a World War II hero was found Tuesday morning in his little two-room house in the Indian Land Community."

The article continued: "As officers worked in the crime area, several of Slagle's relatives and friends came to the site, including a sister, who said, 'He was happy here. He wanted to be where it was quiet.' 'He loved it,' another relative said, 'This is everything he wanted in the world.'

Slagle's house, without running water or a toilet, was bare of modern conveniences. His primary source of heat was an old wood stove, but he did have a gas range and electricity.

His lifestyle was primitive by modern standards, but an officer said, 'It was of his own choosing.'"

Perhaps Harry had died where he wanted... but what a cruel twist of fate that he should die at the hands of those who seemed to be no better than his captors were some thirty years before.

No one seemed to know who had done the dastardly deed. There were all sorts of possibilities - maybe some of the very ones who had been a regular at the binges were to blame.

Many people in the area felt the crime might never be solved - in spite of one of the criminals confessing his role in the crime to his minister.

Two years later, an anonymous tip led to a suspect and a subsequent search of his home provided enough evidence to arrest him and two others. Each of the three confessed to their role in the crime.

Each perpetrator initially faced the possibility of the death penalty. Perhaps the three would have suffered such a fate had it not been for Harry's beloved sister, "Babe", as he so affectionately called her. She was his confidante and caretaker. She watched over him as he stayed in a small trailer near her home in the winter time. She cooked his meals. She was his Angel.

It was with her that Harry had sat three weeks before his death and planned his own funeral. It was to her that he had given all the instructions about what to do when he died. He was insistent even though she didn't want to hear. She needed to know what to do with the land and the money he had stored away in a bank.

"Babe, you know how much I love you, so I need to tell you what I want done if something happens to me," Harry told Babe as he sat in her house one day. "I have money in the bank. Here is my book to get it out. If something happens, this is what I want done. These are the arrangements for my funeral. Everything has been paid for."

"Harry, I don't want to hear it, I just don't want to hear it," Babe responded.

"Well, you have to," came the short reply.

The money was in the bank and not hidden away as the would-be robbers thought. Harry was smarter than anyone had noticed.

The answers he gave during the beating were true. There was no money there. Harry's death had been for nothing.

Maybe his killers should all die in prison. The crime warranted it. But an Angel said no.

"Babe" said no. How could someone not want this? The would-be robbers and now killers were deserving of such a fate.

"I don't want such a thing." She was adamant to the solicitor. "Harry would be forgiving. He would not want it that way. We can't have it any other way. I can't have it on my conscience."

The solicitor acquiesced and mercy was shown on the three. Some of the charges were dropped and the sentencing carried a stipulation for parole in time.

Harry would have wanted it that way. The Angel had conveyed his wishes.

Wish I Knew

"Harry, as you lay bleeding and you knew death would not let you escape this time, what were your thoughts?"

"The faces... Harry... the faces... they must have haunted you all your life. Did you see them again... or was the Creator kind enough to let you leave in peace?"

"Harry, how did you know I would remember?"

"How did you know I would someday understand?"

"How could you have known that I would someday

have the experiences to know what it must have been like for you and the others? I can never know fully, we both know that."

"Was it in the eyes Harry?"

"It was in yours."

"Was it all written before we knew anything about it?"

"You do know it is about more than you and me. It's about the others we knew and the others we didn't know."

"It's about all who suffered in all the wars. It's about more than either of us will ever understand."

"Harry, whatever you had to do to cope, we... yes... **we** understand. We've had time to reflect and to learn. We understand."

If you walk down the remnants of the old road and stand quietly in the vicinity where the green cinder block building once stood and listen with your heart, you might just hear the softness of laughter. If you look toward the wood line near the creek, you might catch a glimpse of a misty image. Hopefully, as a sign that all is well, it will bear a hint of a smile.

Heroes of Belair
(Credits to Louise Pettus)

The small rural community of Belair had three other heroes - all killed in action in World War II. There are three roads named for them: the Shelley Mullis Road (killed in Battle of the Bulge), the Henry Harris Road (killed on Iwo Jima) and the Charles Pettus Road (killed in action on Leyte Island, the Philippines).

In his book, Men on Bataan, John Hersey wrote about the fall of Bataan, a Philippine fortress, and the subsequent 'Death March' following the surrender of Bataan to the Japanese on 9 April 1942. The prisoners

THE BUDDY PLAN

were force marched 65 miles to Camp O'Donnell - for up to twelve hours a day for five to seven days - without food, water or rest.

Hersey chose three Americans as heroes: a Texas sergeant, a California lieutenant, and **Pvt. Harry Jay Slagle** of Lancaster Co., SC.

Here's what Pulitzer Prize winner Hersey wrote about Slagle:

"I think you ought to meet the private who, when the flames spread, climbed right up on the pile of smoldering, exploding ammunition. He was Harry Slagle from Lancaster, South Carolina."

General Orders: Headquarters, U.S. Army Forces in the Far East, General Orders No. 18 (1942)

"Private First Class Harry J. Slagle (ASN: 6923543), United States Army, was awarded the Distinguished Service Cross for extraordinary heroism in connection with military operations against an armed enemy while serving with Battery E, 60th Coast Artillery Regiment (Anti-Aircraft), in action against enemy forces on 30 December 1941, in the Philippine Islands. Private First Class Slagle's intrepid actions, personal bravery and zealous devotion to duty exemplify the highest traditions of the military forces of the United States and reflect great credit upon himself, his unit, and the United States Army."

An editorial shortly after his death in *The Lancaster News*: **"We Owe Harry Slagle This Much"** – "There was no parade in Lancaster when Harry Slagle returned home a hero from the war. He probably wouldn't have participated if there had been a program held in his honor. That was Harry Slagle.

Until his brutal murder was told in the newspapers Friday, many people did not know much about the Indian Land soldier, the death march, and the Distinguished Service Cross.

Nothing has ever been done in Lancaster County for Harry Slagle, one of only a few men from here who were so highly decorated during the Great Wars. Now, something should be done. An all-out effort to bring his killer or killers to justice is the least thing that can be done for this man who once put his life on the line to save others."

No road in Lancaster County honors Harry Slagle, who received the second-highest medal for bravery this nation awards, but some of us think there should be. Maybe there should be a marker on the 'Ol Harry "Slagle's Happy Acres" - then again, maybe not. He might not have wanted it that way after all.

If you sit along the banks of Sugar Creek on a warm summer's day and listen quietly while your mind wanders away, you just might hear the spirits of those you never knew. The sounds are all around you, listen, listen and you might know the stories as the peaceful waters flow.
The peaceful waters flow. The peaceful waters flow and join the bigger waters to empty into the sea. Lost amidst the waters are the ashes, the peaceful ashes of Harry Slagle. It was his wish. It was fulfilled. The banks he wandered along - his ashes were set free into the wind there. The peaceful waters flow.

Rest in peace my comrade and though I am unworthy to call you this, I think you would say, "It is okay my friend... it is okay."

And did you think that we'd forget you?

Chapter Five

The Buddy Plan
(1966)

♦

RA 12 84 36 92
RA 12 84 36 91

♦

And do not recite your service number too fast when you take off your mask in the tear gas chamber, if you do, you will have to go back in and do it all over again.

♦

If you have enjoyed the riches of the nation, then whatever the price to be paid might be, it must be given when it is due. Others about whom you have no knowledge determine that cost and exact it in ways they see fit.
The political clubs on either side of the conflict, chosen or not by the people, have spoken and you and others like you were selected to do the deeds of war.
It has become a battle for the minds and they possess the means to propagandize their reasons, valid or not. The basic military training must do more than teach those selected to shoot and move. It must take away the questions you might ever have if you really were given time to reflect. You must be conditioned and conditioned well.

♦

Service to One's Country

Growing up in a small community that had seen so many of its sons go off to war creates a sense of duty in those who have yet to be called. There is a naïve sense of patriotism permeating the layers of your being. Your country will never do wrong. After all,

Good, with the Grace of God, had just defeated Evil Incarnate in World War II and Korea and you grew up amongst those who had returned as heroes.

Somehow, you still believed that war was a thing of the past because, surely, after all the misery and suffering which were caused by WW II and Korea, people would be tired of it all and the "Great Earthly Stage" would see no more evil actors play out their roles and lead their peoples into needless bloodshed.

Then again, I did say my naïveté far exceeded my knowledge of the possibility of human behavior in the extreme. I had not yet been made aware of the stupidity of WWI. If ever there was something which was the best argument against future wars, then WW I was it. It did nothing better than to set the stage for WW II.

Nevertheless, there was hope, just as there must always be, even after knowing different.

Mr. Luke's ominous warnings still ring in my senses and somehow I wish they were not so, but, after all, *they are written.* I've never found a reason to doubt anything he ever said. Even for the most skeptical person, his words go beyond any probability of coincidence. Therefore, they are, to me, "Prophetic Truths" from the "Prime Source" to which we ought to pay attention.

The high school years were great because of all the sense of togetherness a small school setting offers. Close friends for reliance and memories of personal warmth were made – never to be forgotten. The good fortune of people who worked to make things better for the community and schools was abundant.

The community was blessed in the best of ways. We were forced to share, pull together, and were not yet blinded by the bright lights of absurdity which have engulfed too many today. Others had more material things but were not blessed more than we were.

THE BUDDY PLAN

The high school sports teams were good because we each had to put forth our best efforts due to the fact there were so few of us. The facilities were lacking, but we never complained. Those things were of little importance in our zest just to be able to play the games. Many from the small school were able to go to college and further their athletic careers. We even had some to play professional sports.

Jacky

Friends made in high school oftentimes carry over to other situations as well. When two good friends receive letters inviting them to serve their country, they are drawn closer together for all sorts of reasons. Honestly, fear of the unknown is one of those reasons, a very major one. Such was the case after I had finished my fourth year of college. I was not married, so I was eligible to serve and, according to those in charge, needed.

One of my best friends who was also eligible, and needed, had gotten a similar invitation. Invitations of this sort are RSVP required in person.

After we got our notices, Jacky Bayne and I spent more time together. Much of that time was in a pool hall in Fort Mill... and, we became quite fond of the game. Neither of us became proficient enough to hustle, but we were decent players.

It was another game for males and Jacky was a competitor. I guess I was more of one than I thought at the time. We had discussed, with some degree of seriousness, the possibility of having our own pool hall after we got out of the Army.

Jacky had purchased a red 1964 Chevy Malibu convertible. As most young people do, he had "driven the wheels off of it."

Never was there a thought that it would be the last summer he would enjoy his red convertible. Nor did we have any idea that the pool room partnership would never come to fruition.

We still had some options left with the Army. We were certain they would pretty much do with us what they chose, unless, of course, we negotiated with them. There was only one way to negotiate and that was to go see a recruiter and talk with him. Yes, we were still naïve.

The recruiter gave us some choices. He could guarantee our MOS if we joined instead of being drafted. Joining would at least hedge against being assigned and serving in the primary MOS of the Army, 11B, which is Infantry. I'm wise enough now to understand – "regardless of whatever MOS (Military Occupational Specialty) you have in the Army, it is secondary to your unstated primary job title which is always Infantry."

October of 1966 drew nigh and we set about to prepare ourselves for our journey to Fort Jackson, South Carolina, I decided to go ahead and get married. My fiancé and I had dated since high school and so we planned a hurried wedding one week before the induction process.

One chilly October morning, my wife took Jacky and me to meet a bus headed to Fort Jackson. Soon, we would see what the Army was about.

Before we had settled into the routine of basic training, we had camped out in a "holding area" of tents somewhere in the in-processing area at Fort Jackson. Because of the "big build up", there was no room for us anywhere else. October of 1966 was a banner month for recruits, so it seemed. We did have the last bit of freedom to do as we pleased before we answered roll call the next day and were officially inducted.

THE BUDDY PLAN

Jacky, a couple other recruits, and I went to downtown Columbia. There was no particular place to go except to get something to eat before we would have to eat the awful army food. Actually, the Army food turned out to be quite good, but we had heard rumors about how bad it was and we had taken them seriously.

We took a taxi into town and, for some reason on our return trip, none of us could quite remember where we were staying. After riding for what seemed like an excessively long time, the fellas realized we were running up a pretty sizable taxi bill. Just before we panicked, we finally recognized a familiar landmark near where we should be.

Shortly before we located our area, someone had remarked we needed to soon find our encampment, whereupon the taxi driver quipped, "Oh we could ride around all night."

Not to be outdone, Jacky remarked in a half sharp tongue, but as always, tempering the remarks in a manner which brought laughter to all, "Yeah, I don't guess you would mind, it's our money."

I never realized at the time how important those words would become several months after they were spoken - how extraordinarily important indeed.

We later found out that the night's jaunt into town had caused a note to be sent to our soon-to-be platoon sergeant about Jacky and I "lacking military bearing," which could have been interpreted to mean we might be hard to train. Such a statement had the probability of having the sights of the platoon sergeant and cadre set on us, which was not a good idea at all.

In spite of the memo, the platoon sergeant thought we both were pleasant surprises. I even got "Colonel's Orderly" after one inspection. Credit must be given to the recruit whose weapon I had received after he completed basic because the extraordinarily clean weapon was the reason for the special recognition. The day of rest I got sitting around the brigade headquarters was welcomed.

We eventually went to another processing area and got all the clothes we would need for the next eight weeks. We also had a number to write on everything we owned. Mine was RA 12-84-36-91. Jacky's was RA 12-84-36-92. We had to repeat it so often that it is still remembered forty-odd years later.

In roll call, all US (draftees) and RA (volunteers) prefixes felt scorn for those whose prefixes were NG (National Guard) because we knew they were going back to civilian life after they completed basic training.

When we finally got our haircuts, we knew we belonged to Uncle Sam. At least the idea was pounded into our heads by the drill sergeants. No one at the time knew their barks were much worse than their bites. We all worried about their barks too much.

Our recruiter had also made us a deal on basic training. He guaranteed that we would be able to go through the same hell they call basic training together. There was something called the **"Buddy Plan"**. Obviously, it was an ingenious conception of the Army to create a sense of security in a world of uncertainty. We even got to sleep in the same barracks - even the same set of bunks.

In retrospect, it is extraordinarily hard to believe my buddy plan partner was afraid to sleep in the top bunk, so I obliged to do so.

"Don, you're gonna have to sleep in the top bunk, I'm afraid I might fall out," Jacky shyly indicated to me when we saw the sleeping arrangements.

"That's not a problem," I responded quietly in a half laugh.

Neither of us wanted any of the other recruits to know any such thing about either one of us. It worked well. The only problem we ever had was keeping the

THE BUDDY PLAN

windows slightly opened because there had been an outbreak of Meningitis at an army base on the west coast. It also required us to sleep head to foot in the bunk bed arrangement.

Jacky had gotten to the platoon area some time before me. By the time I arrived, he had already been assigned KP duty. I can still picture him there with his head in the forty-gallon mess-can and the somewhat dismayed look on his face.

As I approached him, he told me without hesitation, even though he risked being caught and disciplined to some degree, "Hey, we got to run everywhere we go in this area. Don't let them catch you not running."

The advice was taken seriously. It was all part of the process to assure us they were in complete control. Looking back, the methods are necessary, if they are not carried out to the extreme.

We soon learned "Rank Has Its Privileges". The platoon worked hard to keep the center floor of the barracks spotless, even though we could not walk on it. It was reserved expressly for non-coms and officers.

One of the things some of us wondered about when we first got to our barracks was the long sand pit between the barracks and the formation area. It was about fifty feet long and about five feet wide. Well, the wondering was over the second day there. The cadre took us there and showed us what it was all about. It was called the "Alligator Crawl". For some reason, they wanted us to learn to crawl like an alligator. We had to do it before breakfast. It would probably not have been a good idea to do it on a full stomach.

We met all sizes and shapes of fellow soon-to-be soldiers. They were from all over the east coast of the U.S. Some were country boys and some were from the hill regions of Kentucky and West Virginia and some were from the cities, including New York. It really didn't matter, soon we were all U.S. property.

Bivouac

October is not usually cold in South Carolina, but this one had temperatures plunging into the twenties at night. We had made our long march to the bivouac site where we were going to be camping out for the better part of the week. Each man carried a shelter half, as it was called, which was put together with another to form a tent shared by two soldiers. It stopped the wind, but it did a poor job of insulating against the cold.

Jacky and I shared a tent. We each had a sleeping bag and a blanket. During the cold nights, it was impossible to keep warm. We gathered as much pine straw as possible to put under and around us and everywhere else we thought it might serve some useful purpose. Our efforts helped only marginally. We almost froze, but we survived the outing. Never had army barracks looked as good as they did once we were back in the warmth.

One of our final trials during bivouac was to see how well we had learned our *General Orders*. Jacky had been chosen to walk guard duty on one occasion. Soldiers are supposed to be alert on the one hand to anything suspicious and on the other, oblivious to anyone or anything that has no bearing on his duty.

The NCOs had devised a scheme to test the young recruits. As planned, two NCOs in civilian clothing came up to Jacky as he walked just outside our bivouac area. They began to ask him questions.

Jacky didn't take the bait at first, but as they turned their backs to walk away, Jacky evidently felt he had been too rude to them and decided he needed to make amends for his behavior.

To remedy the situation, he tried to sneak ever closer to the two. All the while he sneaked, he glanced in other directions to make sure no one was watching. His sudden change of attitude even caught the "perpetrators" off guard. They were totally surprised when he finally whispered just loud enough for them to hear, "Fellas, I'm sorry I can't talk to you, I'm on guard duty and I'm not supposed to talk to anyone."

Under normal circumstances, the NCOs would have jumped all over him for not adhering to the proper procedures. They simply walked away. They dared not look back – probably because they were laughing too hard to control themselves. I have no doubt what the topic of conversation was later among the NCOs – especially if they gathered at their club for a drink or two.

Reality Check

The platoon assembled before Christmas. The cadre had hit us for donations and I guess now we were going to see how the money had been spent. Surely enough, their human side was exposed. When we had all gathered in the dining hall, the NCOs displayed a bright shiny new bicycle. It was to be given to a youngster at the Home for Boys in Newberry, SC. I had been by the place many times while attending college in the small town there.

Those who had bossed us, yelled at us, punished us, and seemed to be against us were human after all. Deep down, we already knew they were. We understood the need to be extraordinarily well-conditioned to face whatever we might have to confront in the not too distant future.

At times, there are defining moments. Reality hits home. One such moment occurred in basic training at Fort Jackson. The grizzly old Field First Sergeant stood before us just as we were about to go on leave for Christmas and stated in a solemn tone, "I want you all to go home and have a good Christmas... because it may be the last one some of you will ever have."

It sounds cruel that anyone should have made such a statement and you might think we should have cursed the man for his insensitivity. But had you been there, you would have heard just the slightest crack in his voice. It was, by all measures small, but it was there. I knew there was a soft belly under the armor. After all, I had seen someone as tough as this guy with a very soft under belly.

The silence became eerily more silent. That sounds ridiculous, but leave it at that. He was human after all, very human. He had been in the business for a long time and what images came to him in his weakest hours were probably best left well suppressed.

Amongst the soon-to-be soldiers, the realization of the gravity of our new roles became apparent. It really would be a life and death situation for many in the future. The games were over.

OCS Anyone??

During the course of training, we were asked who might like to become an officer in the Army. The Army was in need of commissioned officers at the time. They had once again set up officer training facilities at different posts around the country. Jacky and I were given an opportunity to interview for the possibility to go to OCS. Jacky had been to college for two years and I had four years of college so we both easily qualified in that respect.

Jacky would have been a fine officer in the military. He could have overcome whatever shyness he had. I did my best to persuade him to commit to attend OCS.

We both went for our interviews which consisted of a panel of officers asking us several questions. Jacky and I were able to answer positively to most of them. We both were accepted. I decided to commit and, for

THE BUDDY PLAN

whatever reasons yet explained, he decided not to go once he got to his new duty station.

We parted basic and the "Buddy Plan" had ended. Jacky went to his assignment. I went to Fort Ord, California. At the time, I couldn't figure why I had to go all the way to Fort Ord for Advanced Individual Training, especially when it turned out to be 11B again - not a good thing at all. However, it was a blessing in ways I only later understood.

Jacky was next stationed at Fort Knox, Kentucky, and probably would have gone to Armor OCS. More than likely, he would have had duty in Europe for the remainder of his active tour.

At Fort Knox, he had all sorts of jobs since he had talked himself out of going to OCS. Maybe he felt uncomfortable being in charge of people. Some very good potential leaders never take the step to become leaders. Some who shouldn't be leaders do. Look around.

After not going to OCS, Jacky somehow found himself in a scout platoon. When he told me about his assignment, I didn't like the sound of it at all. This was something I would not have volunteered for. He told me that he might even be a door gunner on a helicopter. I wasn't fond of that idea either.

Strange Coincidences Years Later

Years after we had gone through basic training, I returned to Fort Jackson as an Army Reserve Officer and was assigned temporary officer quarters for my short stay. As I followed the directions and came upon the old wooden barracks which had been remodeled for TDY (temporary duty) officers, it all looked extraordinarily familiar. I parked my car and went into the building to my room which had been partitioned off. It was nice enough and comfortable.

Years before, it was the same spot where a bunk bed had been. Two people had slept there and one had been afraid to sleep on the top bunk. His name was Jacky Bayne. I had slept on the bunk just above him.

Our platoon sergeant in basic training was anything but athletic. He was pudgy around the middle and looked as though he had enjoyed a good life at the NCO Club. But looks are often deceiving. He was tough. When you are in your early twenties,

THE BUDDY PLAN

anyone over thirty seems to be old. So his exact age at the time, I couldn't say. Jacky had developed a "Gomer Pyle" type of affection for him.

Jacky felt that the sergeant was trying to do his best to ensure we were all trained well enough to survive whatever came our way later. Though some of the training was very strenuous, we all did well.

Jacky was not a perfect physical specimen of a soldier. He seemed a little soft around the middle, but his looks would easily fool you as well. He was as tough mentally as anyone I have ever seen. This would be proven later on in unfortunate circumstances. *His will to survive would rank there with the greatest of stories I have ever come to know.*

Many years later, I had a believe-it-or-not encounter with Sergeant Talley, our platoon sergeant who Jacky liked so well. I was teaching at Chester High School.

"Mr. McCorkle, please report to the office," the voice blurted over the intercom.

It wasn't anything unusual. I was called to the office quite often for all sorts of reasons. I obliged and went where the secretary informed me that the gentleman from the time clock company was. He had come to install a new master clock to control the bell system.

I needed to talk to him regarding how to set the bells. Setting the bells to ring properly was another one of my un-official duties.

Our secretary introduced me, "Mr. McCorkle, this is Mr. Talley from Mid-Land Time Clocks in Columbia."

Real life has a way of being much stranger than fiction. What were the odds of meeting this man under these circumstances? Even though he lived in the same state, chances were, we would not ever have met again, certainly not as we did.

He called me "Sir" as I addressed him.

We made small talk and he told me about all sorts of personal things. We discussed the business he was in and how getting work in his business had become so political. He and his son had started their small company after SFC Talley had retired from the Army. It was good to see he had made it through. I wonder about some of the other cadre. I'm sure each had at least another go at Vietnam.

Of course, he didn't recognize me at all. I had been a face in a sea of thousands whom he had trained during his time in service. Now he was saying "sir" to me.

How I wished Jacky could have been there.

Chapter Six

Brief Historical Background of Vietnam
(With Commentary)
(1940s to Present, 2011)

◆

It's good to be living in a generation which will not be affected by war.
Or, this is what so many of us thought, but the perfect storm was brewing, and it wasn't Nature, it was all political.

◆

"In order to rally people, governments need enemies. They want us to be afraid, to hate, so we will rally behind them."
~Thich Nhat Hanh

◆

Communist Everywhere

For my generation, it all began in the 1950s. The world had not long ago seen the end to the second great war of the machine age. But the weapons of war had changed, or at least this was what we were told. Something much more dangerous now existed as a threat to mankind. The nuclear genie had been forever released from the bottle to play havoc upon civilization. The world looked on in awe as two single bombs had destroyed two cities in Japan and brought the fanatical government of Japan to the surrender table.

Robert Oppenheimer, a genius who had helped bring about this new means of destruction, quipped, "In some sort of crude sense, which no vulgarity, no humor, no overstatement can quite extinguish, the physicists have known sin; and this is a knowledge which they cannot lose."

The problem was not so much the sin of the scientists, but the fact that politicians the world over wanted this new source of threat to use against their fellow man. Enemies must be created in the minds of the populace for the politicians to gain support for their new weapons programs and proliferation.

The ultimate weapon was coveted by those who possessed the ultimate insanity. Maybe the only saneness of it all was the cowardice fear that if such weapons were used, the guilty themselves would assuredly die in the retaliatory attacks.

School children in the United States were now taught to "duck and cover" when there was a bright flash or an atomic attack was imminent.

The Soviet Union, an ally during WW II, but now an enemy due to their land grabs after the war and their conflicting political and economic ideologies, soon had the atomic bomb. The mad rush for arms superiority was underway.

Each side's military industrial complex and its influence on the ruling class saw to it that enough weapons soon existed to destroy mankind several times over. Worse than destruction would be the miserable stone-age existence people who might survive a nuclear exchange would have to suffer.

Even though we had accepted the Stalinist Communists during WW II as a necessary evil (in siding with them) to defeat the Nazis, the geopolitical lines were being clearly drawn in the world to separate the awful communists from the good capitalists. It could never be that simple, but the myth was perpetuated and accepted by the public at large. Each side began their competition for world dominance and each side wanted to thwart the efforts of the other. The

THE BUDDY PLAN

political power clubs on either side had the stage set well for their own propaganda campaigns.

Nowhere was it more evidenced than the division of the nations of Eastern Europe. Part of Germany, along with parts of other nearby nations, now fell under the control of the Soviet Union. The liberating Soviet Armies who had freed Eastern Europe from the Nazi scourge never left until they had established pro-Soviet regimes.

Not only was the communist plague prevalent in Europe, but by the late 1940s, the Maoist Communists had taken over the most populated nation on earth. China had survived the onslaught on the Japanese during WW II but now found it impossible to fend off the internal revolution of the well-led armies and executed plans of the forces of Mao Tse Tung. The percent of people living under the communist flag had increased many-fold. The Chinese seemingly had some sort of plan to expand their own menacing ideology to other nations.

A crazed U.S. Senator from Wisconsin had fueled the flames of anti-communist sentiment in the U.S. when he was elected to the Senate and later began his infamous search for communists in government and in all walks of life. It rivaled the *Salem Witch Hunts* of the 1690s in asinine persecution. "There were communists everywhere. They must be sought out and dealt with." It became character assassination by innuendo. The second *Red Scare* had fully blossomed in the late 1940s and continued through much of the 1950s.

The Korean War was further proof still that the communists in the world were now the major threat to civilization. After all, the armies of the communist north had crossed the 38th parallel in 1950 to conquer the remainder of the peninsula and reunite a Korea which had been previously divided into two opposing political camps.

The communists in North Korea were soundly defeated and driven back across their borders in relatively short time and the Korean Conflict might have been much shorter had it not been for the ego maniacal decisions of a famed WW II general, who had been given command of the situation, in disobeying an order from the President of the United States.

Thousands more Americans were killed and wounded than necessary with the intervention of the Chinese Communists into the war. MacArthur had miscalculated with his push north and the Chinese called his bluff. The eventual outcome of the war was the same - the re-establishment of the 38th parallel as the dividing line between the two Koreas. This had been the original objective of the United Nations mandate authorizing military intervention.

Vietnam

Unbeknown to the high school students in the classes of the early1960s was the seriousness of the events unfolding elsewhere in Southeast Asia. Most of us felt we were oblivious to any military problems in the world. We still had young men joining the military. Most would go off and serve and be back home to tell us about their adventures.

Vietnam was not important enough to be mentioned in school. The first I remember about it was in 1964 when the announcement about a U.S. ship attacked off the coast of North Vietnam was made. I paid it little attention. I was in college at the time and knew for certain that the resolution of the incident would be swift and sure.

In the naïveté of the moment, we failed to suspect we were all being prepared for an eventual quagmire in Southeast Asia. The president and his advisors were miscalculating the communist Vietnamese while at the

THE BUDDY PLAN

same time, they were carefully orchestrating a plan to manipulate public opinion against the communists.

Eisenhower had started the catchy phrase of the *Domino Theory* about communism which purported the notion of: *If one nation fell to communism, then others nearby would surely follow the plunge.* People were quick to generalize the concept to all the nations of the world. This was something the U.S. could not let happen anywhere, regardless of the cost.

Vietnam had a long sad history of occupation and/or colonization along with deadly internal strife. The U.S. involvement with Vietnam increased after the French defeat at Dien Bien Phu in 1954. The French and the United States suffered through somewhat strained relations because of the U.S. refusal to provide enough military assistance to prevent the final defeat of the French at Dien Bien Phu.

The French were driven from the Asian continent in humiliating defeat and Indo China was later carved into political divisions by accords from the various influential nations in the peace process. Vietnam proper was divided into two sovereign nations at the 17th parallel. The communists set up a government in the north and a "democracy" was established in South Vietnam. The United States' involvement in earnest began about that time.

In the 1950s, Vietnam was still off the radar screen in importance. The small island of Cuba, just 90 miles from mainland USA, was grabbing the headlines. A man named Castro had successfully staged a revolution there to bring an end to a regime which had been friendly to the United States and had permitted our financial interests to thrive on the island.

Little thought was ever given to any idea that Castro might become a thorn in the side of the United States by allying himself with the communist bloc nations which had been established throughout Eastern Europe. It was "egg on the face" of the United

States when he declared Cuba a socialist nation and nationalized foreign companies.

Certainly, there was a solution to handle the problems the new regime had created. The Bay of Pigs plan developed by the Central Intelligence Agency, with the blessings of President Eisenhower, was sure to do the trick. It was still in the planning stages after the new President took the oath of office in 1961. The decision to go forward or not was now left up to Ike's successor.

A new era in gamesmanship was about to unfold with the seemingly least likely President of the United States to try such tactics. The tired old beloved General Ike was gone and replaced by a charismatic Senator from Massachusetts who had eked to power in an extraordinarily close election. Without the help of a fellow Senator from Texas, such would not have been the situation. It was to be, and in the election of 1960 was written the fate of the United States and *innocence lost* forever.

John F. Kennedy decided to execute the plan of the Bay of Pigs invasion in Cuba and then he chose not to carry through completely. The end result was another embarrassment to the United States. The exiled Cubans who we had trained and convinced to go back and rescue their beloved homeland were left naked on the beaches at the Bahía de Cochinos in 1961 when the promised air cover failed to show. Capture followed, but surprisingly, many months later, the invaders were released. This gave Castro another victory, a major league propaganda victory.

The next major problem with Cuba in October of 1962 almost resulted in a nuclear exchange between the major super powers. The two nations were literally one small miscalculation away from devastation. Only the most knowledgeable of people have any awareness of exactly how close the

United States and the Soviet Union came to all out nuclear war. It all could have happened as an accident which neither side had calculated into their bluff.

The Soviet Union had placed missiles in Cuba to counter the missiles we had aimed at them from bases in Turkey and other nations in the Mediterranean area. Evidently, the Soviets had failed to gather enough information to know that the missiles we had placed to their south were not very reliable.

This information is first-hand from officers who commanded the missile batteries and later joined our battalion at Fort Sill, Oklahoma, after the missiles in the Middle East, which had played an initial role in the Soviets sending missiles to Cuba, stood down. It was part of the final agreement between the U.S. and the Soviet Union.

Such an agreement could have been reached without the escalation of the situation where all the safety stops to prevent a nuclear war had been removed.

The war mongers on either side could have pushed it a tiny step farther and the world would have been taken back to the Stone Age. Some cooler heads from the intelligence services worked behind the scenes to make sure the Soviets knew they could not win a nuclear war; as if there would have been a winner!

Only Divine Intervention saved the world. I firmly believe this.

The Missile Crisis was over in late 1962 and, within a year, so was the presidency of John Kennedy. With his death, perhaps the role of the United States in Southeast Asia was changed for the worse along with the fate of thousands of U.S. servicemen. Former Vice-

President Lyndon Johnson was now President and some claim that almost immediately after he took office, he rescinded orders for a withdrawal of troops already in Vietnam.

Would there have been a withdrawal of the U.S. Forces before the conflict grew? The real answer is lost in the events of the fateful day in Dallas, Texas, when a crazed gunman named Lee Harvey Oswald who wanted to be "famous" chose the path of assassin and focused John F. Kennedy in his rifle sights... and pulled the trigger. The event may have had a greater effect on the history of the U.S. than most will ever know.

Lyndon B. Johnson was sworn into the Presidency and a new set of Presidential priorities were put in place. Vietnam came to the forefront of those priorities.

The 1964 Presidential election pitted the "war mongering" Barry Goldwater from Arizona (at least he was labeled as such) against the "I'm not about to send young American boys to do what Asian boys ought to be doing for themselves" Lyndon Johnson. Johnson won by a landslide because of the perception of peace he had misrepresented.

In March of 1964, Secretary of Defense Robert McNamara visited the powers in place in South Vietnam and essentially promised them that "the United States would support them at whatever cost." It was the first lines in a political play whose actors and victims would become many. The political situation was anything but stable in the small country. Kennedy had already had his problems there and may have actually had a former leader of a regime assassinated via a coup.

After McNamara's visit, the advice to President Johnson was to increase aid to the struggling regime. We would shore up the sagging South Vietnamese Army with new military aid. There is always a catch when sending in military aid to any nation. You must

THE BUDDY PLAN

then send in troops to train and advise those forces in the proper use and deployment of those weapons. This creates the real probability that our own forces will become targets, which in turn more deeply involves us in a conflict that has nowhere to go except to escalate to a point at which we have to commit a huge number of resources or decide to withdraw.

"A communist victory in South Vietnam would globally damage the credibility of the U.S. according to McNamara and other Johnson policy makers. The fall of this small nation to the communists would weaken the United States' reputation as the chief police against communism in the world and would seriously damage the reputation of President Johnson."

Why and how did the ego of one man take precedence over the potential suffering and sacrifice of thousands - no - hundreds of thousands? What was the strategic importance of a small nation in Southeast Asia? Who were the real powers of influence in these decisions?

The "Gulf of Tonkin Incident" (if it really was like it had been told) was the emotional stimulus that got everyone excited about going to Vietnam and showing the communist that the U.S. would not tolerate her ships being attacked on the high seas.

Strangely enough, during my time in Vietnam, I was told by a U.S. Army Captain working out of the Military Assistance Command in Saigon that the real story of the Gulf of Tonkin incident was considerably different than it had been portrayed. He had access to *real and timely* secret information fed from throughout the theatre of war, so I accepted his statement as fact. Another Army Captain in the same command verified it. In 1995, Vo Nguyen Giap, the retired commander of the North Vietnamese military forces, vehemently denied any such attack on American vessels in the

Gulf of Tonkin region off the coast of North Vietnam.

Nevertheless, The President of the United States went before Congress in August of 1964, pleaded his case for the authority for action, and was given a blank check in the form of the "Gulf of Tonkin Resolution" to do what he saw fit in Southeast Asia. He had stacked the deck and dealt himself the hand he wanted. Few politicians were about to be thought of as being soft on communism by openly criticizing the President of the United States for acting against the evils of that political ideology.

Just how long would it take a military giant with unlimited resources to bring a small backwards nation to total submission? Surely, a matter of months would be sufficient.

Our military involvement escalated to an eventual troop level of well beyond 575,000 U.S. servicemen. Along with the increase in troops and a direct role in the shooting war came the inevitable increase in casualties. It was a new and different war for the United States. An enemy who did not mass troops until the odds favored such engagements was hard to pin down. It became a war of body counts and no one seemed to know how many of the enemy had to be killed before victory was achieved.

The "conflict" dragged on from the first few casualties in the 1950s and early 1960s to a staggering number of about 500 deaths per week in the late 1960s before and after the *Tet Offensive* was launched all over South Vietnam by the communist.

It had been a war which attacked the American psyche. It came into the living rooms each night. It was *the television war*. The bodies were there in plain view. The sons and fathers who lay dead were visible. The wounded and dead, all bloodied and ragged, seared images into the minds of those who viewed them as they were dragged from battle and loaded onto the helicopters.

THE BUDDY PLAN

There were also horrible images of women, children, and old men who were massacred each day because they happened to be in the wrong place. American soldiers somehow had been tainted by the blood of the innocent.

Support later changed as the popularity of the war waned and people marched in the streets and on college campuses in protest of our involvement.

In 1973, the United States finally signed the Peace Accords with the North and South Vietnamese. This provided a formal end to the hostilities and the North Vietnamese agreed to release prisoners of war, some of whom they had held since the mid-1960s. Most of the POWs had been air crews captured when their planes were lost over North Vietnam.

In 1975, after the United States had withdrawn all military forces, with the exception of a handful of *protective forces* and CIA, the North Vietnamese Armies pushed across the DMZ, the 17th parallel, and suffered little resistance as the South Vietnamese Army collapsed in disarray.

The resignation of a President of the United States had left us in a politically weakened position in the world. The North Vietnamese leaders seized the moment, somehow knowing the United States would not provide necessary air power to stop the invasion of their now massed columns speeding southward toward Saigon.

Within months, Vietnam was reunited under the communist flag. The necessary re-education programs and the re-indoctrination programs were put in place to quell any possible resistance to the political plans of the new regime.

The United States normalized diplomatic relations with the Socialist Republic of Vietnam in 1995. Once again, all was well between the two nations.

The scars of the Vietnam countryside have been partially covered over and many of the old U.S. military bases have been converted to housing areas, schools, and play grounds for the people. Areas defoliated by the chemicals of the U.S. chemical companies were still barren twenty years after the areas were doused by U.S. aircraft. Birth defects are prevalent in those same areas.

U.S. soldiers who worked in the Agent Orange areas still suffer from a seeming myriad of unusual diseases. Many have died from cancers and other maladies directly traceable to this witches brew. Some have even passed defects along to children they fathered.

The new powers and their legal staffs who are still influenced by the old real moneyed plutocratic interests who initially sold the idea will fight to protect their cronies' fortunes until the last affected soldier is gone.

The war has faded away just as the soldiers who fought there have. The suffering and misery by both sides have been forgotten by the new generations. Each side will write its own history of the events. Each side will subject whatever bias they choose into the lines they write. Too many of the real truths, most of which will never be revealed, are hidden away in the memories of those who died in the battles or have otherwise passed on from this earth. Obviously, those truths will never be known.

THE BUDDY PLAN

"What was it all about _____? No - What was it really all about _____?"

"Naturally, the common people don't want war. But after all, it is the leaders of a country who determine the policy, and it's always a simple matter to drag people along whether it is a democracy or a fascist dictatorship, or a parliament, or a communist dictatorship. Voice or no voice, the people can always be brought to the bidding of the leaders. This is easy. **All you have to do is tell them they are being attacked and denounce the pacifists for lack of patriotism and for exposing the country to danger. It works the same in every country."**

--- Hermann Goering, Hitler's Reich Marshall, at the Nuremberg Trials after World War II.

(Comments made privately to Gustave Gilbert, a German-speaking Intelligence Officer and Psychologist who was granted free access by the Allies to all the prisoners held in the Nuremberg jail.)

Chapter Seven

OCS
(1967)
(The News about Jacky)

The Circumstances

In the 1960s, the U.S. Military, with the big troop buildup in Southeast Asia, saw a need for additional military officers. Like many times before in similar situations, they decided to reopen Officer Candidate Schools for the different occupational branches within the armed services. Advancement opportunities became available for thousands who wanted to apply.

Young men were taken from all walks of life and were given a challenge of leadership in the most extreme of circumstances. They responded extraordinarily well. With their commission as a military officer, many had reached a pinnacle in their lives never to be approached again. These officers served the needs of the army and when there was no longer a need, they were let go even though many wanted to remain. But the understanding has always been: "The needs of the service come first."

After finishing Advanced Individual Training in Fort Ord, California, I was assigned to Fort Sill, Oklahoma, for OCS training. It was and still is today The Artillery Training Center for the U. S. Army and other armies from around the world.

The severity of the plains' weather greeted me on my first visit there. We had flown into Dallas/Fort Worth to connect to a flight to Lawton, the home of Fort Sill. As we were waiting to board our smaller airliner, ably named Frontier Airlines, thunder storms were brewing over Texas and Oklahoma. Texas and Oklahoma thunderstorms were (and still are) considerably different from the ones which I had been accustomed to in South Carolina.

We boarded our flight and took off on a forty-passenger turboprop amidst formidable winds. It was a stoutly made aircraft and I'm pretty sure we had a cowboy at the controls, which was definitely to our advantage.

The first leg into our destination was fairly rough. As we were making our landing approach in Lawton, conditions were so severe that we were told we could not find an opening in the weather suitable enough to allow us an approach to the airport. As we flew around the area probing for a break, the lightning lit up the pitch dark swirling clouds which measured from horizon to horizon. These were exceptionally bad clouds even for the area. To say it was all eerie sitting and bouncing around in the thunder heads would definitely be an understatement.

The pilot finally decided we needed to head back to Dallas /Fort Worth. The weather had actually worsened there while we were on our flight northward, but it became a no option for our return flight. We had to land and we did. How our cowboy pilot got us on the ground in one piece is still a mystery to me. I hope they checked the tips of the wings after we landed for I am pretty sure they scraped more than once.

About one a. m., we were able to leave once again and this time we landed successfully and were soon headed to the U.S. Army Artillery Center. Any desire I might ever have had to ride a bucking bronco was satisfied that night.

Don L. McCorkle

What's it all about _____??????
(One of our favorite songs in 1967 asked this question)

OCS ran for twenty-six weeks. Like many of the training sessions in the military, the first few weeks are the most dehumanizing. As the training continues, the human side slips through the façade and you are treated more like their fellow man.

We were exceptionally fortunate to have had a realistic person as our battery commander. Maybe because of the fact he had been to West Point, he was more concerned that we received the best educational training we could. After all, it was artillery and it was paramount to know the technical math and other subjects necessary to launch a large projectile accurately from one point to another. Lives depended on our abilities.

We were assigned cube mates in OCS - there were three of us in a small area within the old WW II leftover barracks. The OCS area, Robinson Barracks, was named for a Congressional Medal of Honor winner in WW II: James E. Robinson, Jr., 1st Lieutenant, Field Artillery.

THE BUDDY PLAN

Entrance to Robinson Barracks as they looked in the mid-1960s.

One of my cube mates and I shared quite a bit in common. We were the same height, approximately the same weight, and had the same birth date including the same year. We even shared some of the same philosophical leanings.

Of course, some of his musical likes differed quite a bit from mine. I did learn to appreciate his Simon and Garfunkel albums, Elvis was fine, and maybe even some of his other choices were okay. Then again, I'm okay with a pretty wide range of music.

My other cube mate was a very nice individual who had originally gone to flight training but was later sent to OCS. His complete story is not known. He did successfully make it through the rigors of OCS.

One of my best friends was a candidate named Larry Goldman. He had been a swimmer at the University of Michigan. It was obvious as one looked at his physique that he had been an athlete of some type.

Topics of conversations lead to some interesting information. Larry was a draftee, but said he was proud to serve. He said it was in honor to his grandfather who had been a gatekeeper of one of the Jewish extermination camps in Europe during WW II.

Nazi death camps are still a blight on humanity. The complete denial of human conscience necessary for such cruelty is beyond understanding.

How could human beings have lost connections with the innate good that is ultimately visible within even the most hardened of criminals? Had Satan literally possessed them and controlled their every thought?

We all went about the rigors of training to become officers in the military. Many of us were there because we felt we might be better off serving our time as an officer rather than as an enlisted man. In fact, just as I was, there were several who had been drafted. Of course, there were some prior service and career minded individuals who saw this as an opportunity to advance their military careers.

We had a strict honor code and we had to help others about us if they were over-burdened. Our cube mates might become overwhelmed with additional duties. It was all planned by those in charge and it worked well. Some candidates were weeded out and others chose to disqualify themselves. All in all, the screening program for enrollment must have been pretty good because the number who left was small.

One of the punishments for too many demerits for small stuff not done or done incorrectly was a "Jark March" up Medicine Bluff Mountain on the weekend. "Jarking" was walking at a two steps per second march with rifle and light pack (enough water to sustain the fluids lost on the hot summer days). Two steps per second is twice the marching cadence.

THE BUDDY PLAN

The following is taken from the OCS website at Fort Sill: "When Candidates fall below the standards expected of them, demerits are imposed by Tactical Officers. In addition to being restricted to the OCS area during off-duty hours of the weekend, too many demerits will 'qualify' a candidate for participation in a weekend Jark March."

Named for Lt. Gen. Carl H. Jark, Retired, former Fourth Army Commander and the first director of OCS in 1941, the march is a four mile struggle up Medicine Bluff 4, a steep hill on Fort Sill's West Range.

One day the battery commander stood before our platoon and explained to us why one of our classmates would never graduate from our battery or any other battery. It seems the candidate had gone to a night club in Wichita Falls, Texas, and had later been involved in a shooting. Actually, he had been shot.

The candidate had brought dishonor to the cadet corps.

It was the same candidate who had shown us pictures of himself in front of a line of old WW II bombers on a dirt airstrip. He had told us a wild story about how he had been recruited by the U.S. Government as a young pilot and taught somewhere in Central America to fly the old planes.

They were supposed to have bombed some places on an island. They had sat on the runway with the engines running until they were told it was all called off. Rumors were that the orders had not come for the mission to take flight. The orders were supposed to have come directly from the White House.

We saw the pictures, but we paid his story little attention. The guy was older than most of us and did have pilot credentials to fly multi-engine aircraft. However, most brushed it off as some sort of made up fantasy.

It wasn't until many years later when I was teaching History and the topic was the Bays of Pigs invasion that I realized he was telling the truth. Books had begun to be published on the event. I was thoroughly amazed as I started reading about the details of the planning and what should have taken place. I already knew the story first hand.

Years after that, I was able to find out more about how the man had been connected to it all. Not only that, but his father or uncle had been a high ranking officer in the Army. Each and every detail he had told us matched perfectly with the information now being printed.

Time magazine ran a pretty extensive article on one of the requirements for OCS called "Escape and Evasion". Candidates were taken by truck out into the middle of a range on the post. The goal for the candidates was to avoid capture by a make-believe enemy force complete with vehicles, aircraft, and numerous other assets which tilted the odds totally in their favor. The capture rate was probably greater than ninety percent.

Quoting *Time Magazine:* "Under constant taunts from their captors, the artillerymen were forced to crawl, wallow in mud, hang by their legs from a horizontal bar, and sit for seemingly endless minutes with their legs wrapped painfully around a pole. The guards badgered them for information beyond the maximum - name, rank and serial number - sanctioned by the Geneva Treaty. A sympathetic 'Red Cross' representative tried to wheedle additional intelligence out of them, but most immediately spotted him as a phony."

It was apparent that the cadre who ran the encampment had done their homework. Many of the same techniques were used by the enemy in places where some of the soldiers would later go. I remember spending time down in a *spider hole* cramped with other candidates. It had a lasting effect.

The little camp and exercise caught the attention of the Soviet Government as well. They, in turn, used it as a propaganda opportunity.

A Soviet newspaper published an article on a special school at Fort Sill describing it as a *Camp of Murders*.

The article which appeared in *Trud*, a publication of the All-Union Central Council of Trade Unions in Moscow, says: "The class transforms young artillery officers into beasts - cruel unfeeling animals."

It further states: (in the captions beneath the photograph) "If the year 1943 were substituted for the year 1967, one might think that the picture was made by German SS troops in concentration camps. A gallows dominates the camp and future officers must dangle in the noose. He will have a rattle in his throat and twitch. True, he won't be allowed to die. He is only permitted to look death in the face."

Evidently, they did not know about the U.S. Special Forces training being conducted at Fort Bragg. Of course, it would not have had any propaganda value since they were non-conventional forces.

There were humorous times as well. Once during an inspection of the barracks, our TAC officer, making sure to be thorough, decided he would choose a laundry bag for inspection. It just happened to be the one on the end of my bed. I immediately knew there was trouble. I had stashed away some home-made cinnamon bread. Of course he found it and, for some reason, we were puzzled as to his next course of action.

He hesitated for a moment, and then addressed me, "Candidate, what is this... bread doing in your bag?"

As soon as he had he gotten the words out, he hung his head and began to walk out of the barracks. He had started to snicker and couldn't control himself.

Evidently, the loaf of bread had been such unusual contraband that he couldn't gather his thoughts about it without laughing. I'm not so sure I even got demerits for it, but it did set off considerable outbursts from candidates in the building once he left.

What are friends for if they cannot play wonderful little jokes on you? Even though such pranks may be life changing. Such was the case when an OCS candidate's buddies signed him up for airborne training.

"Dream sheets" were passed out during the last days of OCS. They are aptly called such because "dream assignments" are what they were all about. Of course, if the dream assignment you requested didn't serve the needs of the Army in some way, then it was indeed just a dream.

Soon-to-be Second Lieutenant Thomas Gross sat on the wrong end of a long table when the forms were passed out. Before the form was turned in, it had to be passed on by two of his buddies named Goldman and Dillingham. It seems they had decided that whatever plans Thomas Gross had in mind, it should no doubt include airborne training.

Going to airborne training might not have been so bad, unless you knew that Candidate Gross almost didn't graduate from OCS for a particular reason - his fear of heights.

One of the last rights-of-passage necessary for an OCS candidate to pin on his butter bars was to rappel down the face of Medicine Bluff. It is the same cliff where Geronimo allegedly jumped with his horse in his escape from the soldiers at Fort Sill. Once you have seen the site, it might be hard to believe anyone could have survived such a feat.

When we all had gathered as a class at the top of the hill to make the big step backwards on our way down, Candidate Gross balked and refused to make the leap. Was this finally something that would keep Candidate Gross from becoming Second Lieutenant Gross?

Thomas Gross was one who, when first looked upon, might make you wonder about his ability to become an officer in the military. He was skinny and had a noticeable curve to his frame. He looked as though he might drop over at any time.

However, his appearance was deceiving and he proved all first impressions completely and unequivocally wrong. He did it in high fashion. No one knew that Thomas Gross was a long distant runner. We were all embarrassed when he left us behind in our early morning conditioning runs. He out-shined us in the other physical exercises also.

Well, certainly someone from the hills of Kentucky would be lacking in the necessary mental skills to do the math required to be an artillery officer. We were wrong again. Candidate Gross was a mathematical whiz and none of the problems posed any threat to him whatsoever. It seems we had all underestimated Candidate Gross tremendously.

It was necessary that he go back with another class and perform the rappelling down the cliff feat in order to graduate. So now, his sudden desire to go to airborne training was not so unusual. He did go to airborne training and served with the 101st Airborne Division in Vietnam. No doubt he was an excellent soldier and officer.

The News about Jacky

July weather in Oklahoma was often unbearable. By late afternoon, we were usually exhausted. For those of us who were married, it didn't matter if we had to stand a while longer in the heat, as long as we could talk to our wives, if only for a short time. Besides, we did have a few small trees in the battery area that afforded some relief.

We had reached a point in our training cycle that allowed us visitations in the late afternoon and those of us who could were going to take full advantage of the privilege. We had to stand at parade rest, hands to ourselves, and maintain some military bearing.

Then, there was the terrible day in July when I stood by the car and listened to my wife Linda as she made an announcement which shocked my entire being. Had I not been so tired, I might have looked closer and would have seen the redness in her eyes and the uncharacteristic dread on her face when she first arrived.

"Don, Jacky stepped on a land mine," she stated in a solemn breaking voice.

In an instant, it felt as though I had just encountered an explosion myself. My body flushed completely and my knees weakened. I was silent as I tried to compose myself to react.

"He's not dead, he's alive," she stated before I could say anything.

There was a tremendous relief for the moment. **Little did I know, or did she, just how critically serious his wounds were.**

THE BUDDY PLAN

She knew Jacky well and had cried all day since hearing of the tragedy. We had all gone to the same small high school and shared wonderful outings. We had all marveled as he, in appearance, a most unlikely candidate, had performed his cagey tricks on the basketball court.

We remembered just how remarkable he was at adding flavor to a conversation with his dry, oftentimes, genius wit.

The rounded, freckled, devilish grinning face of my friend flashed to my consciousness. *With the news about Jacky, the war had become personal. It had become extraordinarily personal.*

OCS Training continued in the almost unbearable Oklahoma heat. Linda kept me posted with whatever news she was able to gather about Jacky. By August, he had made it back to the United States. *We still had no idea of how gravely Jacky had been wounded or about his struggles with death.*

Finally, in September, the day of graduation came. The young men could now join the ranks of officers in the U.S. Military. All felt we had earned the respect which we now would be given. Our new status carried with it a tremendous responsibility.

On the morning of graduation, the phone rang at my apartment that we shared with another couple. We had all overslept! My first responsibility as an officer - to get to graduation on time - was about to be fumbled. It was one of my classmates telling us to hurry. We did and all was well. We marched across the stage, received our certificates, and it was official.

One of our candidates was honored as the forty thousandth graduate of the Artillery School. He was presented a special plaque which he proudly displayed in a picture taken with his parents. Alligator Jack Johnson, as he came to be called, was from Florida.

I have three college degrees. I worked fairly hard for them. Well, at least they were time consuming and required quite a bit of effort. They took years and I did learn much. Anyone who completes the rigors of Officer Candidate School and goes on to serve will very likely have had an education which, in many respects, far exceeds that offered as a degree from a college or university.

My Cube mate Arty and his wife-to-be after she pinned on his bars. May he rest in peace. May God Bless him forever. We miss you.

Chapter Eight

Mothers Everywhere
(1967)

♦

Mother is the home from which we come.
She is ever mindful and remains attached to her
children in ways yet imagined.

♦

Back at Home

The long day had given way to night. It was hot and sticky as summers usually are in South Carolina. Windows in houses were open in spite of the heat. Whatever cooling there was came about because of the little bit of breeze that had mustered itself for whatever reason.

The goddess of night had breathed a haze that crept from the hollows and valleys and gently kissed the tips of the broom straw in the fields. Small animals wiped the sleepy day from their faces, peeked carefully with their bright glowing eyes, and quickly scurried from the safety of their hiding places to venture out for the night in search of food for yet another day's survival.

The lightning bugs turned their lanterns on and off producing an eerie iridescent beauty as they maneuvered about the now darkened sky.

Give pause and listen closely, very closely; Nature's heart beats in the rhythm of the night's sounds. Birds, crickets, and all things imaginable that can be heard make their unique contribution. It all blends together for the pleasure of the Great Maestro. The night is alive. It speaks to those who will but listen.

People all about have consumed their evening meals and a brief time of relaxation is in order before bedtime. All seems well... but a particular mother's heart knows different.

The umbilical cord of the womb is still mysteriously attached and she is sensitive to the warps in the Great Consciousness. It whispers, "All is not well... all is not well."

It is far beyond a mother's normal worry. The pangs are from her soul. She paces the floor and her uneasiness is noticed by her husband whose loving words offer little comfort. It is like nothing she has ever experienced before. She attempts to take away the feelings by doing small tasks. Nothing helps. She places her face in her hands and prays. It is a tearful plea to her Maker.

In Vietnam

Half the world away is no more than a second's time. Physics permits that. It is possible, very possible. Something is wrong, extraordinarily wrong. A mother knows. The connection is never broken.

Half a world away, the helicopters are lined up. Their blades beat the air as the pilots, usually youngsters, some who look as though they have shaved only once or twice, if that many times, read their gauges and make last minute checks. They

THE BUDDY PLAN

radio chatter back and forth to make sure all is ready for today's mission. The door gunners recheck their ammunition for their machine guns. They will give the pilots the okay that all the troops are loaded and the flight can lift off. The lead pilot makes the final calls. All is go.

Similar operations were daily occurrences during the course of the war. Helicopters were quite often the mode of transportation from the staging areas to the contact areas. The size and scope of each operation depended on what the intelligence reports indicated as to the expectations of enemy forces to be encountered.

The troops should have whatever support units necessary available to them. This could range from helicopter gunships to artillery and even airstrikes if such became warranted.

The soldiers had lined up to ensure each will get on the right machine and be deployed properly when they reached the destination. The last to load and the first off will be a young Specialist 4th class named Jacky Bayne and his dog Bruno, a beautifully colored blond and black German Shepherd.

He was half-jokingly told by the leader of today's mission, "If that dog falls out of the helicopter, then you had better be on the ground to catch it." To which Jacky gave a slight grin and replied, "Yes, sir."

Dogs were life savers. They were hated by the enemy because they could alert the GIs to impending dangers. Dogs like Bruno were specially trained along with their handlers to also "sniff out mines" or other booby traps. They saved lives, many lives. It was a dangerous job, one of the most dangerous jobs in the war.

These dogs truly were man's best friend... and we had put them here in this hellhole to do perilous work. They were loved, and loved dearly by the handlers. The depth of the bond was not measurable. Then again, anyone who has ever realized such a bond understands.

Bruno positions himself near Jacky's feet. Dogs have an innate awareness of height. Some overcome this fear relatively easy, others do not. Bruno knows his master will keep him safe on the flight. He remembers his master carrying him over a mile out of the jungle after he had suffered heat stress.

Jacky had volunteered to be a dog handler after he arrived in Vietnam. He loved dogs and besides, the extra pay helped him. Maybe he had forgotten the first rule his buddies and his father had told him about the Army, "Don't volunteer for anything."

Maybe he had not realized the extent of the increased danger to which he would subject himself. There was a bounty for him and his dog. He was a prized target for the enemy.

He had picked this particular dog because Bruno had in turn picked Jacky. For anyone who truly knows how to choose animals realizes that, "you never pick them, they pick you."

Jacky and Bruno

Off To the Fields of War

The flight was finally ready. The engines revved, collective pitch pulled, and the birds with their loads lifted slightly to stabilize the craft and they were ready to fly. The noses were tilted downward to gain speed and soon they headed away to the fields of war.

Even though the day's ventures have been planned, what it will actually bring is a great unknown. For the young faces who have mounted the birds, there is a meager hope for another day's existence after this day is over. The pulses begin to quicken as each stares around at the others. Anxiety is hidden by the looks of confidence each soldier now presents as a façade.

Each consoles himself to the fact that they have been well trained and armed. Each hopes that he has learned well. For some, it will be a new experience, while others have done this several times. Each time still has its perils beyond what is controllable.

Some soldiers may have their first chance at killing a fellow human being today. They have been sanctioned with such authority by the powers in charge on his side of the conflict. He has been taught that killing another human will be necessary for his own survival.

Former strangers from so many different places have been brought together under circumstances over which none have control. Whatever differences they might have had has become petty. Each knows that his very existence depends not only on what he brings to the situation, but what every other person brings to the mission as well.

Each has a name to his buddies and a number to the Army. He was processed into the service with his assigned number and under whatever circumstances, he will be processed out of service with his assigned number. But he is more than a buddy and a number. To many others, he is a warm loving individual who occupies a special place in their lives.

THE BUDDY PLAN

The ride is refreshing as the wind whips through the open doors. The land below is deceitfully peaceful. People in the small villages carved out of the jungle have awakened to another day of labor. They go about their business with little attention to the flights overhead. It has become the norm.

Soon, the landing zone will be in sight. Last minute thoughts and last minute checks are in order. Recheck everything! Door gunners prepare for the worst. They must protect the craft as much as possible if the landing zone turns hot as the flight takes on fire from hidden positions on the ground.

Just ahead is the clearing that will give the pilots room to touch down, let the men off, and hopefully lift away to return where needed.

Tensions mount, emotions tighten, and even the saliva disappears from the mouths of the soldiers as the pilots begin to pull pitch on the helicopter rotors. They slow and descend. The popping sound of the rotors is almost deafening. The fluttering bird is an easy target. There is an orderly panic as the men scramble to clear the wash of the blades. Each takes an assigned position. The experienced look out for those who are not experienced. All look out for one another.

The soldier with the dog will scout out ahead. Even though neither the soldier nor the dog has had a good night's rest, it was the orders of the day for them to be part of the mission. Perhaps it had been a lapse in judgment by the platoon leader or company commander. But soldiers often lacked sleep or proper rest. It was not unusual to push tired soldiers to their absolute limits.

The operation had begun. The routine was followed. Men were spread about... looking for any small movement, anything out of the ordinary.

The Sickening Sound
(partly dramatized)

Then, there was the sound, the terrible sound, the sickening thud of an explosion.

To the ground is a reflex action with rifles in firing positions.

"Was it a mortar?"
If it was, there would be more and all sorts of other explosions and small arms fire, and all hell would break loose.
Hearts are pounding as the adrenaline kicks in. Senses sharpen further still. Eyes and ears function as never before.
There was not a second thud.
No distinct pop, pop of enemy rifle fire.
No roars of machine guns.
It was a mine, someone had tripped a mine.
"Check it out, who was it?"
"What direction had it come from?"
"It's from the direction of the point man."
"It's the dog and dog handler."
"I don't see them anymore!"
"Get over there and see what happened."

Risking their own safety, a young medic and soldier were quick to scurry to the aid of the handler and his K-9 friend.
The scene was not good. The smell of the mud and powder was still in the air. The mud in Vietnam had a unique smell. Now, the smell mixed with burning flesh made the stomach ache.

THE BUDDY PLAN

"Sarge, you need to get over here."
"I think it's too late."

It was too late for the dog, he was destroyed. He had taken the full force of the blast. For some reason, the cleverly placed trip wire had eluded the detection of the dog and the handler.

The Vietnamese were ingeniously crafty people. They could make and hide all sorts of devices which could kill or wound an enemy. Quite often, these devices were nothing more than sharpened bamboo sticks which would wound an unsuspecting G I. Anything, big or small, meant a casualty the enemy had to attend.

"Check for a pulse on the handler."
"There might be a chance he's alive."
"He's pretty messed up and mangled."
"There's no pulse."
"Lieutenant, he's gone."
"Damn!"
"Get him out of there!"
"Don't leave any of him behind."
"Get a 'Dustoff' in here."

Or in this case, any chopper in the area might do. There is no need to rush.
The reality of the situation becomes more real. Grimness sets in. The enemy might still be near. The guard can't be let down.

"May God be with him!"
"Get him to place where you can load on the 'Dust-off.'"
"Load the dog too."

It would have been a breach of trust not to have taken care of the dog's remains as well. The dog also had his place on the chopper. The rule is: "No soldier is left behind." Bruno had earned that status.

Two of the soldiers carry the soldier's body to a spot in the clearing where the chopper can land and be loaded. Two more soldiers carry the remains of the beloved dog. Radio contact will be made and when the chopper is near - the smoke grenade will be popped to give the pilots a location.

The mission will continue. Contingencies have been made for dealing with casualties. It is an expected part of all operations.

Soon the chopper blades were beating full throttle back to the helipad at the medical unit. The *Medevacs* did a wonderful job in Vietnam. They were some of the bravest soldiers in the war. Oftentimes, when they went to pick up the unfortunate, the battles stilled raged. Too often, and illegally so, the big red or white cross of mercy on the side of the chopper was a perfect target for an enemy gunner.

One day, one of the Medevac crews from the base where I was first stationed had been gone for a long time. The word soon got around that they had been shot down less than a kilometer away from the base. The entire crew had been lost.

The helicopter with Jacky's and Bruno's remains would land at the nearest medical aid station. In the more developed areas, these were well equipped and well-staffed. There were medical personnel capable of stabilizing the wounded until, if necessary, the injured could be shipped to a more specialized unit in a safer area or out of country.

The doctors examined the casualties even in situations where there seemed to be no need. It was the general procedure. If there was any remote chance at all there was life left, the doctors would work on the soldiers until a consensus was reached that further efforts were futile. *The doctors were dedicated. Of this, I am absolutely sure. I've witnessed them work first hand.*

If the life could not be saved, the soldier was then moved to a unit located nearby whose job was to initially prepare the remains for transfer to a central location in country where the body would be prepared for shipment to the United States in a flag draped transfer case. From that point, the procedure turned into a ritual which was carried out in the most reverent manner.

Even with their best efforts, it was determined by the medical staff that Specialist Jacky Bayne was beyond hope. The next obvious step was to send the body to the graves registration unit. It was part of the S-1 division of the larger unit. They brought in the needed supplies and took care of the fallen. It was part of the organizational logic of the military.

In the processing room, depending on the number of casualties, each would wait his turn for the grim task which lay ahead. Young Specialist Bayne was no exception. He was placed with others who were the least fortunate.

But this day, there was uncanniness to the macabre atmosphere of the room. Bodies waiting to be embalmed always gave off sounds as the natural processes ran their course. Another young specialist on duty sensed something beyond normal.

"Look closely again at those awaiting you."

The young specialist, Bruce Logan, went in the direction of the unusual sound and then narrowed it down to Specialist Jacky Bayne. The twisted and mangled body, despite the look of almost certain death, caught the young embalmer's attention.

"Surely, this man is beyond help."

Regardless, he instinctively reached out to check for a pulse.

The would-be embalmer grabbed Jacky's arm as tightly as he possibly could.

Astonished, the amazed soldier realized there was indeed a faint heartbeat. He quickly checked another place. He could not believe what he was experiencing. Of all the bodies there, this would have been one of the ones least likely to be alive.

But the condition didn't matter. He quickly called a medic and got the soldier back to the medical unit. There, the life-saving procedures began once again. Bruce Logan would later say, "I had heard that he died again."

Exactly what happened from that time forward until Jacky is stabilized and sent to another hospital will probably forever remain a mystery. The records are sketchy at best and there is, by some logic, rationale to support the idea that Jacky Bayne was pronounced dead again and was sent back to be embalmed, at which time, the second time, an incision was made and he showed life once again and was rushed back to a medical unit where he continued to show signs of life.

What is known for sure is: Specialist Fourth Class Jacky Bayne spent a lengthy time assumed dead. There are no arguments to contradict that fact. His brain was deprived of oxygen for an extraordinarily long time. The circumstances surrounding the entirety of this situation are, by anyone's standards, not only bizarre, but must be categorized as truly miraculous.

"Can they ever get him out of here to a hospital where they have more equipment and more experts?"

"He will need all the help we can give him and for a long time."

The miracles would need to be many; no, it would need to one very long and very profound Divine Intervention into the situation if this young soldier is to continue to live.

The questions abound.

And, at the top of the list; if he does survive, "What would his life be like?"

The Telegram

Half the world away, the mother has drifted in and out of states of restlessness during the seemingly endless night. Each minute has been an hour. Each hour has been a day. The night has been like no other she has ever known. The hurting has been beyond any physical pain she had ever endured. It has been a cry from the depth of her very being.

The morning had finally dawned and she felt she had to start the day's chores. A thousand different thoughts tried to enter her mind. None were clear.

Soon... someone would tell her... She knew!

The flash of car lights in the morning dawn were the ominous warning. She watched intently as they came up the driveway, her heart raced further still. Would her chest explode?

She recognized the car. It was her son-in-law who worked at the funeral home in Fort Mill. By a quirk of fate, he had been informed by a telegraph operator about Jacky's wounding in Vietnam. He and the operator had agreed that he should deliver the news. At least the news would come from someone who knew the family. It would simply not be cruel impersonal typed words on a piece of paper.

Bunia Bayne hastily awakened her husband Eb. He, too, now realized his wife's concern had been real and not just a mother's worry. They both opened the door for Ernest Baker, the son-in-law.

Her eyes were filled with tears and although it did not seem possible, her heart ached even more.

Ernest had a telegraph. She saw it.

She cried out, "Read the telegraph, Ernest, read the telegraph!"

Ernest assured her that Jacky was not dead and with an embrace by him and her husband, he read the following:

"The Secretary of the Army regrets to inform you that your son, Specialist Jacky C. Bayne, has been wounded in Vietnam, 17 July 1967, while on combat operations. His wounds are the result of an explosive device. It has resulted in the amputation on his right leg below the knee and the fracture of his left leg. **His condition warrants concern, but there is no imminent danger to life.** Please be assured that he is presently receiving the best medical attention possible. We will keep you informed of his progress and any change in his condition which warrants immediate notification."

Bunia Bayne's name was on the form which had been filled out telling who to notify in case of injury or death. These are the routine forms filled out and filed away in a safe place back at headquarters.

"Wounded" meant there was still hope for her son. *He was still alive!*

Unknown to her are the extent of his injuries and his first bouts with death and the herculean struggle of the medical staffs to keep him alive. Unknown to anyone is the eventual fate of the young soldier.

Death kept a close watch over Jacky Bayne - waiting to claim its victim. The battle against it would need to be strong and on many fronts. Did the young soldier have anything left in his body to use for the fight? Only God knew the answer.

The struggle would also become a test of a mother's faith and her persistence, each of which would become another miracle.

When the chopper arrived at the medical unit, the beloved dog's remains were taken by two soldiers who were assigned the burial detail. They found a good spot in the special area, set aside for the service dogs, to place his remains. They placed a small marker as a head stone. Bruno would be respected as well he should. He was part of the unit.

"Should we say a prayer?"

"Yes, all of God's creatures deserve a prayer."

"He was someone's best friend."

After all, Bruno had saved Jacky's and his squad's lives weeks earlier when they came out of the jungle from a patrol. A young soldier on guard had been quick to recognize the light color on Bruno's chest. Only Americans had dogs such as Bruno. That recognition kept Americans from killing other Americans.

The patrol was quick to thank Bruno. Jacky, as if he needed another reason, hugged the dog and gave him some special treats.

"By all means, say a prayer."

"His handler and friend, amidst his tears, would have said a prayer for his friend."

> Chapters 9, 10, 11 are interesting and/or heartwarming but veer from the main story of Jacky Bayne. The reader can choose to skip these and continue Jacky's story in chapter 12, **The Coma**. Thanks. Don

Chapter Nine

Fort Sill
(1967-1968)

♦

The Native Americans called it the Soldier House at Medicine Bluff.
A small pyramid of rocks near one of the entrances to the post, along with Prayer Clothes in trees, mark the grave of the once proud Apache Warrior/Chief Geronimo.
Kiowa Chief Santanta and Comanche Chief Quanah Parker are among other Native American Chiefs whose graves are in other places about the post.
The last days of these magnificent warriors were spent there in captivity.
In their earthly death, their spirits were finally set free to roam the plains again amid the bitter winds of winter and scorching days of summer. They are freed from the White Menace who had claimed the land as his own and then relegated the Natives to less than human status.
Even in its harshness, the Natives saw the goodness and blessings of the Great Creator. They witnessed the beauty of the rising sun and the glorious moon and marveled as they gazed at the endless stars. They shared oneness with Creation there. Cruel were the winter snows and winds, the scorching summers with rolling pitch dark storms; but crueler still was the White Man who took it all away.

♦

Along with a few other officers who had just finished OCS and were awaiting further orders, I was assigned to a Littlejohn Missile Battalion. The assignment provided an excellent learning experience and the people I worked with there were cordial. In fact, my job was relatively easy. Of course, most of us knew what our next assignment would probably be because we were excess officers (we were beyond the unit's allowance for our ranks).

Specifically, I was assigned the duties of an assistant S-3 (operations) officer. It gave me a keen insight into the workings of units in the Army. I was at the battalion level and could see the focus from that perspective.

My wife and I and our dog Max would spend our free time taking in the sights around the area of Lawton and Fort Sill. It was an area rich in history and its own special beauty despite the extremes in weather which might take place in a single day as there was scant land features to slow the weather fronts from rolling across the flat lands.

Fort Sill made an excellent training facility for artillery. There were few hindrances to shooting even the longest range artillery weapons. There was plenty of room and not too much disturbance to the environment. People in Lawton had grown accustomed to the noise and even off target shells landing in places where they should not have landed. The post meant additional money to the local economy which makes all sorts of things better and the loud noise of the explosions almost inaudible.

THE BUDDY PLAN

Grandpa Jim

In the early summer of 1968, my wife's family decided to make the 1200 mile trip to visit us. Along with being a good vacation for them, it would also provide an excellent opportunity to see a part of the country they had never seen. Her father checked out the Plymouth to be sure it would make the long trip, decided it would, loaded up, and headed to Fort Sill.

Pinkney Spratt Harris would never buy a fancy car with all the bells and whistles. He had grown up during the depression and had done without many things. His early days were spent in a Civilian Conservation Corps camp as a cook and he had learned to be frugal out of necessity. He retained that mode of thought throughout his lifetime.

They decided to also bring Linda's grandfather. Maybe part of the reason for the visit was about him. His presence made the trip all the more special. Linda's grandfather had ventured to the plains as a young man. It was the early 1900s and the West still lacked the sophistication of even the state of South Carolina from which he had come. He was anxious to once again see the places of his youthful experiences.

We spent several days roaming the Oklahoma plains searching for sites that might look familiar to the now elderly man. As he looked out over the land, it seemed to those observing him that he felt a connection with what he saw - something which seems to have been lost by generations since.

The elderly man's senses glistened as we came across places which he told us he had roamed in his youth. I'm sure the memories were vivid, or at least as vivid as possible, as he gave pause to smile from within and without. The expressions on his face were delightful to us.

The occasional prodding of Grandpa Jim with, "What was it like when you were here as a young man?" usually got a reply of, "It didn't look too much different than it does now." Indeed, it seemed as though many of the places we came upon were locked in time.

Sometimes, to our amusement, he would spin a tale about what he had done at a particular place and some of the people with whom he had shared good times. "When I was here, they still traveled with horses and mules," and it would continue from there.

Many of the people we met were old enough to have been around a few years after the turn of the century and many of the buildings and settings looked even older. Like him, they found a deep pleasure in recollecting a short moment of days gone by with an old friend. I specifically remember stopping at a small post office which was literally in the middle of the proverbial nowhere and the elderly people talked at length about old times. I was not privy to the conversation, but it seemed as though they had been acquaintances in the earlier years.

Mr. Jimmy, as all the people of the Indian Land community called him, had been a steward of the land there much like the Native Americans had been. He had planted crops in the river bottoms near the Catawba River. Native Americans, long before him, had probably done the same. The methods used were different, but more than likely, the rows in the ground matched in many ways.

For hundreds of years before the White Man took these lands in Indian Land, the Native Americans had called the area home. The Native Americans of the area were part of the Cherokee Nation. Those who remained were remnants of those forced on the miserable trek into the wilderness to starve and die during the Jackson Presidency.

THE BUDDY PLAN

Mr. Jimmy's olive skin and his full head of black flowing hair, now graying with age, made him look as though he belonged to one of the tribes that had dwelt on the plains at one time. Imaginings of him on a painted horse or in a Native American setting with tribal dress was not beyond reason. He would have fit well sitting in a tribal leaders meeting. He would have been at home.

When we had finished our journey about the plains near Lawton, we all felt he had closed a chapter in Mr. Jimmy's life, a very important chapter.

Sergeant Thompson

My battalion was on a required yearly field training exercise. The full moon gave off enough light to clearly identify soldiers moving in the cold windy Oklahoma night. Personally, I wasn't very thrilled to be there at all. It was hard to leave the comfort of a warm home and go out and play soldier.

An older NCO (Non Commissioned Officer) running around our encampment, as though he was much younger than he was, caught my attention. I had to stop for a moment and admire his enthusiasm. It was hard to believe that he was showing such energy. I even envied him. Surely he would soon be getting out of the Army and going home safe to his loved ones. Maybe he was playing the game of army for the last time in his career.

His appearance reminded me of my father. No doubt this man should be somewhere in a rocking chair with his grandchildren on his lap. He had probably made it through Korea and maybe even WW II. No doubt he had paid far more than whatever his dues were.

As for me, there was an uncertainty as to whether or not I might be so fortunate. I had gotten some dreaded orders from the Department of the Army that I would "arrive in country wearing short sleeves," and that meant Vietnam. It was mid-1968 and I had thought the war might have been over by then. Was I ever wrong!!!

About a week later, for some reason, I guess just out of curiosity, I asked some others in our personnel section about this NCO I had seen out in the field. Our unit got people on temporary assignment who were either going to another duty station or were being processed out of the service. Surely, this man was on his way out of the Army.

To my surprise, I was totally wrong. Well, maybe I was partially correct. He had retired, but had gone to the trouble of contacting his U.S. Representative in order to petition the Army to let him back on active duty. This action was totally baffling to me.

Intrigued, I made time to talk to this man. "Sergeant Thompson, why would you decide to come back into the Army? You had it made," I matter-of-factly asked and stated. Believe me, I was serious about what I was saying. At that time, there would have been no way I would have volunteered to come back into the military.

I had set up myself quite well to be floored by the answer he was about to give.

He looked directly in my eyes and said, "Lieutenant, I'm an old man, but if I can come back in here and take the place of just one young boy, then I will be happy to do that."

His answer stung me deeply and I could feel myself getting smaller by the moment. I was quite a bit taller than him, but at that time, it was hard for me to look up high enough to see his rank.

I guess I could say that was one of the *defining moments* in my service life. Shortly thereafter, I began to feel a change in my attitude. If this man could make such a statement and believe it with all of his heart

THE BUDDY PLAN

and soul, then I needed to do some reassessing of my own. I did.

The day came when all of the officers in the battalion were assigned to write Efficiency Reports on the NCOs. It's a believe it or not, but I was given Sergeant Thompson's name along with some others, of course. It was obvious that I was going to praise him as much I possibly could. I would not say anything that was not true. I could write a glowing report without any exaggeration. I did.

Several weeks later, and not too long before I was about to leave the unit, I was standing in the S-2's (Intelligence) Office talking to the officer in charge when someone walked up slowly behind me. I turned to glance and it was Sergeant Thompson.

He looked directly at me and stated in a solemn and penetrating voice, "Lieutenant, I want to thank you for what you said on my ER. I don't think I have ever had someone say such good things about me, and I just want to thank you."

The fatherly look from the weathered face and the sincerity beaming from his eyes caught me off guard. I immediately felt a lump in my throat and by the time he was done, all I could respond with was, "You're very welcome."

I wanted to say more but I couldn't and still control the moment. I'm sorry until this day that I didn't, but with all my heart, I believe he knew. He could see it in my face, I sincerely hope.

There was never another chance to talk to him. In the haste to finish up there and go on the usual 30 day leave before I went for my tour, such an opportunity never occurred.

Hopefully, Sergeant Thompson got his wish and went to Vietnam and returned safely to live out his life with friends and relatives. Just maybe, he sat in a rocking chair somewhere with a grandchild on a knee, maybe one on each knee.

As for the "thank you," - no Sergeant Thompson - let me thank you. That would be the least I could do.

"Sergeant Thompson, Thank you. Thank you for your service and for your selfless act of courage."

I wish I had found out more about you.

Colonel Wilhelm Löser

We rented one half of a small duplex just off the main entrance to Fort Sill. Next door to us lived an NCO from West Virginia who had chosen to make the military a career. He had served in Vietnam and also in Europe. Just as many Americans before him had done, he, too, had met and married a German girl.

Pete and Hannah Ballard were cordial. He was a big robust individual and she was shorter with dark hair and very pretty. In the spring of 1968, her parents from Germany came to spend some time with them at Fort Sill.

Pete and Hannah invited us over one evening to meet her father and mother. They were a delightful older couple. During the course of our conversations, her father asked about attending church services. We told him it would our pleasure for them to go with us to the small chapel on post where we attended services each Sunday. They accepted our offer and we had the good fortune of their presence on more than one occasion. Even though their use of the English language was very limited, we were able to communicate using Hannah as an interpreter or by using simple phrases.

Hannah's father had been a full Colonel in the German Reich Army during World War II.

THE BUDDY PLAN

His years of difficulty in the military and his advancing age had taken a toll on him and by the time we met him in 1968, he had a noticeable curve to his frame as well as other obvious damage to his body.

Like some other German military personnel, he had been specifically sent to the Russian front during the war because he had questioned a decision by one of his superiors. He had survived the extreme conditions there, but had not escaped completely unscathed. He had been wounded in his right elbow which created serious problems with his right hand as far as normal use was concerned.

Through determination and self-therapy, he had learned to compensate by using his left hand and had become so proficient with the transition that he now was able to paint simple landscapes. They were therapeutic for him and interesting to the viewer. His use of color was very pleasing. I suppose there is a little irony in the fact that his supreme commander, Herr Hitler, had failed as an artist but had found his calling with his evil tongue.

Colonel Löser's paintings displayed a sense of serenity. Why should they not? After all the tumultuous disaster he had been witness to during the years of the war and afterwards, what would his inner being have sought?

Having majored in History, I was obviously interested in this man's first hand opinion on WW II and his personal view of Hitler. During the course of our conversations, we asked if he had ever seen Hitler in person.

To our surprise, the good colonel conveyed to my wife Linda and I how he had indeed witnessed the "golden tongue beast" give one of his infamous speeches at some of the propagandist Hitler rallies.

We quizzed him as to what the man who had been given blind allegiance by millions had to say that was so effective in creating a cultish following. I was expecting Colonel Löser to respond with some awe inspiring words that the evil leader had mastered.

He said matter-of-factly, "People would stand and listen for hours at the harangue. People would walk away mesmerized and never really understand Hitler had said nothing. He had said nothing of substance at all!" Colonel Löser was adamant.

The mindless masses had stood there mesmerized by the harangue put forth by the golden tongued beast in human form. They were beguiled by the rants and raves as he spewed his hatred. Over twenty years later, Colonel Löser was still baffled as to how such a man could have controlled a nation.

His answer shocked me. How could such be the case? The information had come from a man who had stood at a Hitler rally with his family in a crowd and listened to the evil man. Obviously, it appeared to me, Colonel Löser had been and was still a man of conscience who got caught up in the politically turbulent times and had no escape other than the role which was cast upon him.

How the masses supported such an evil conspiracy against other people remains a great mystery. Perhaps such is the power of pure evil - if you let it be that way.

It was not so much different from those today spewing hatred at the expense of the unsuspecting and unsophisticated listeners who fail to be the least bit analytically skeptical. No one seems to see the real danger of it all.

Colonel Löser took pride in his works of art. I complimented him on them. Before he left to return to Germany, he presented me with one of his serene landscapes.

THE BUDDY PLAN

Each time I look at the small painting, I wonder what became of him and his wife. It also reminds me of all sorts of other things about people and human nature. The tranquility of the painting is an irony to all the circumstances which led to it. For without each, there would be no painting with such a fantastic history hanging on the wall.

Lessons from that era ought to be learned by all and never forgotten, but they will not be learned.

Landscape by Colonel Wilhelm Löser.

Camp Eagle
(The Hand Grenade Debacle)

The battalion of which I was a part was chosen to be the service battalion for ROTC Summer Camp in the summer of 1968. Working with college people should have been a pleasurable job. Unfortunately, the

ROTC leaders felt we should be at their every beck and call.

Supplying live ammunition for use in their training exercises was part of our obligation. We took their orders and delivered the supplies they needed from the main post ammo dump some 14 miles away.

Camp Eagle was the headquarters we used near the ROTC training sites. I had been chosen as ammo officer. This was probably the hardest work I had ever done in the military.

July Fourth was supposed to be a day of rest after weeks of seemingly endless hustle and totally exhausting activity necessary to keep the ROTC people happy. The much anticipated break was not to be.

The phone call came early in the morning; it was the S-3 and I was to report to Camp Eagle. One of the ammo handlers had decided to be bravado and take some hand grenades and brandish them at a local night spot in downtown Lawton. The police were called in and the Army authorities were notified and it was all traced back to the local unit and then to my small outfit.

The battalion commander was gracious in handling the situation. All of us thought we were in serious trouble, but there seemed to be understanding by the people in the chain of command higher than our battalion. We were very fortunate and perhaps blessed more than we ever thought and were thankful that every hand grenade was recovered and none of the really bad things which could have gone wrong did go wrong. Whew!

Personal note and I knew better-

We handled all sorts of live ammunition and explosives. I stopped to have a blast myself one day by setting off a couple of left over sticks of explosives. Two range NCOs heard the blast, investigated, and were very nice in explaining to me why I shouldn't have done something such as that, but they let it go. Looking back, it could have been serious. Whew, again!

Linda and I left in the summer of 1968 with the memories we had made there. Even though the circumstances were trying, the friends and good times had become and would remain some of the most memorable we would ever have the opportunity to share. They, like the people, were real and genuine.

Mount Scott

View from the Summit of Mount Scott

Perhaps no chapter on Fort Sill could ever be complete without a mention of Mount Scott. Probably every soldier who has ever been stationed at Fort Sill has visited that mountain since the time of the first road leading to the top of it was completed.

The Wichita Mountains are geologically old. They are thought to be among the earliest formations on earth. At one time, they were as high as the highest peaks presently on earth. Today, the highest summits among them are around 3,000 feet. Time and other forces of Nature have had their effect, just as they do on all things of this planet.

The ancient formations of boulders look as though they are of a distant time on a foreign planet. Near Mount Scott, people have constructed *The Holy City of the Wichitas* which closely resembles the actual places where Christ walked and died on this earth. Located in the Wichita Mountains Wildlife Refuge, this 66-acre area looks much like Israel during Biblical times, and is the site of the nation's longest running Easter Passion play, *The Prince of Peace*.

My brother Dean and our families spent a considerable bit of time there during their visit in the spring of 1968. On their way out to Oklahoma, they, too, were greeted by some of the harsh Oklahoma storms.

Those who stand atop Mount Scott are afforded a fantastic vista of the Oklahoma plains below. Once hunted nearly to extinction for the pure pleasure of sport by the White Man, the now replenished herds of Buffalo roam peacefully in the tranquil meadows below. Prairie Dog sentinels stand watch over their colonies and warn other members when danger approaches so they might scurry deep into their burrows to be safe from harm. Deer roam in large numbers along with a variety of other animals that enjoy the freedom of the openness.

Missing among all the wonders of Nature are the proud Native Americans who once called the land home and shared the spirits of all that existed in their paradise. There is emptiness to the unique beauty as you look for miles and miles until the haze fades the distance views.

The winds are ever persistent as they swirl about the ancient boulders. Perhaps within the swirling winds are the spirits of the proud Natives who once lived there and saw the goodness and blessings of the Great Creator. They witnessed the beauty of the rising sun and the glorious moon and marveled as they gazed at the endless stars. They shared oneness with Creation there. Cruel were the winter snows and winds, the scorching summers with rolling pitch dark storms; but crueler still was the White Man who took it all away.

Yes, within all the beauty, there is a particular emptiness.

Chapter Ten

Tour of Duty
(1968-1969)
(1LT. Gene Lucas – A great Human Being)

♦

"Un Jour, j'irai la bas [pour] te dire bonjour, Vietnam
Mai mot, toi di ve tham chao da't nu'o'c Viet Nam."
One day, I will go there to say hello Vietnam.

♦

I will see the beauty of your sunsets amid the grimness of the impending dangers yet to be awakened before the dawn.

♦

If you are going to San Francisco, good luck on your trip over, your adventure there, and your return home... hopefully...

♦

The Trip

As the time came closer for my venture to Southeast Asia, sobering thoughts about all the possibilities that lay ahead entered my mind. I strongly believed then and still do today that the dream I had in which I saw myself back home at a time after my trip overseas was indeed true and lent comfort to my anxious state of mind.

Summer turned to fall and the time for me to go see what everything was about in Southeast Asia drew nigh. My thirty days leave was spent in Indian Land, SC, hoping that the days might last forever, but such was not the case. Eventually, like others before me, I bid a tearful farewell to my pregnant wife standing at the airport, boarded an Eastern Airline flight, and was on my way to join my comrades.

THE BUDDY PLAN

At Fort Sill, there had been a conversation among the many young wives with whom we were acquaintances. The topic centered on the question of whether or not wives would choose to have a child while their husbands were overseas. The discussion had two legitimate points: (1) should the woman have a child so if something happened to the father, she would not be left alone - she would have the child to remember her husband, and (2) some wives wanted to not have a child because something might happen to the father which might prove problematic if the young wife might want to remarry. I saw validity made in both points.

The first leg of the long trip to Vietnam was a stop in Oakland, California. The processing station there took care of matching soldier assignments and flights overseas. After missing two manifests, the first because of an already full flight and the second due to misplaced orders, I was on an aircraft bound to Southeast Asia.

My original assignment to a unit operating out of Nha Trang was changed to a unit in the delta region of the country. As it turned out, the new unit was an air defense outfit attached to the Ninth Infantry Division. Because there were no enemy aircraft operating in South Vietnam, air defense artillery was adapted to a ground support role.

Most American servicemen who served in Southeast Asia usually arrived by chartered airliner. Many of the airlines which provided the flights are no longer in existence. The trip was especially tiring along with the added element of anxiousness about things to come. "The serviceman will arrive in country wearing," and the orders went on to describe the uniform and some other particulars.

Well out over the ocean, our pilot came over the intercom with the announcement, "The noise you will hear in a few moments will be the landing gear and flaps dragging. We need to burn off a little extra fuel before we land."

Of course that stirred all sorts of feelings. On final approach, we were told how to exit the plane and prepare to use the bunkers on either side of the runway in case there was an attack of some sort.

There was no attack, except for the friendly harassment by the troops ready to catch our plane to go the other direction to the homeland. Thank God they had made it safely through their experience, even though there was plenty of envy to go around.

Vietnam was a paradise in turmoil. The people had become the pawns caught between two political ideologies. Sides had been chosen and the gentle, polite, hardworking people had no choice. They suffered because of the actions of either side.

The Delta Region where many rivers and canals intersect. It was the source of travel and livelihood for the people there.

The fields, the source of their livelihood, were often turned into battle grounds. Small quaint villages were disrupted or destroyed because one side or the other thought it might be friendly to the other side. The

THE BUDDY PLAN

villagers had no choice, they were powerless. They were victims twice.

Perhaps to say that the war itself was a war of victims might be an accurate statement. But then, aren't all wars just that - wars of victims? The powerless get caught up in the politics of the power clubs.

Wasn't the mission just? Weren't the Americans there to save the people from the brutal grip of the evils of communism? Weren't the people worth saving and being liberated from a totalitarian state of control? The case had been made time and time again, had it not?

Or was it some ploy to divert attention from the real motive? Wasn't the real motive to put the brakes on a political ideology different from ours? Was the Military Industrial Complex too influential in the decisions made? Would it have been different if Kennedy had not been assassinated? Kennedy and Johnson, as U. S. Senators, had been against our involvement in Vietnam, but as U.S. Presidents they had gotten us bogged down in a war few Americans understood.

The old frontal wars in which we could march with superior forces over an enemy didn't apply here. It was all different. It was a war of occupying an area today and the control of it tomorrow might be lost once the forces had gone. It was a big war of small fierce battles.

It was still a war of heroes, as are all wars. The worst in men, who could not solve problems, real or imagined, by any other means, brings out the best in the good men who are sent to do their dastardly deeds.

"Was it anything new?"
"The answer is no."
Even in all the seeming madness, there was goodness. There was the beauty of country side and the decorated buildings of worship. Intricate designs

and details had taken much time and skill by the exceptional craftsmen among them.

One of the real dangers in Vietnam in my area of operations was a two-lane recently paved road called Highway Four. It linked the delta region with Saigon. As you got farther south from Saigon, the possibility of being sniped at or hit by a rocket propelled grenade increased significantly.

On the lighter side, the greater danger by far was the traffic itself. The Vietnamese are geniuses when it comes to making vehicles run. It was not unusual to see old American cars which had been converted to diesels.

Whatever genius they used with making vehicles run was sort of lost when they made a perfectly good two lane road into a multi-lane road. I was fortunate to have had an experienced jeep driver who got us safely to and back from our destinations. He had learned to dodge oncoming overloaded buses quite well. We never even hit one of the people hanging on the side of the large vehicles.

My driver was also well noted for his driving skills on the backroads. He wasted no time going to and from our gun positions at some of our remote firebases. Of course I understood the reason for his haste and hung on as best as I could while he dodged holes in the unpaved roads. During a discussion years after we returned home, a friend stationed at one of the bases informed me of the exceptional dangers of a particular road. Now he tells me.

The name Eiffel on the abutments of steel bridges told of the former occupation by the French. The French also left other evidence of their occupation, just as the Americans and others would do.

The French had left children born to Vietnamese mothers. Americans had later done the same. In some situations, the children were accepted; unfortunately,

THE BUDDY PLAN

in others, the children were not so well received. It was another sin and shame of the war - a child left to wonder.

I was fortunate enough to escape unscathed, at least physically, from my tour in Vietnam. It was far beyond any life learning experience I had ever known. We were at the out processing station and were making the last minute preparations to board a chartered airliner much like the one which had taken us there when I looked about and saw other fresh soldiers coming into the terminal from a recently landed plane. Many of those ready to board with me were jeering at the new arrivals, just as they themselves had been greeted. I had no heart to participate. I understood the odds against all of the new arrivals leaving in the same manner in which the very fortunate ones with me were now leaving.

The conflict still raged in areas. Thoughts for many years that the war might be over before I had gotten there were nothing more than a fantasy due to the total misunderstanding of the situation. Seems as though I had underestimated the situation - just as so many of those responsible for our involvement had done. *I had an excuse, maybe they should have done better in their assessments.*

We boarded the plane and shortly thereafter taxied to takeoff position. The engines revved, the wheels were rolling, and soon the big bird rotated and we lifted into the air. There was a "deafening silence" in the cabin until we reached a safe altitude; then, there was a deafening roar of applause, shouts, and whatever other noise which might be made. The cabin fell eerily silent once again, unless of course, you could hear the silent prayers that pierced the skin of the big bird and winged their way upward. No one stared at anyone else; each sat as though he/she was removed from the world for the moment, until all the thanks had been given – there was not a sound except for the beautiful roar of the engines.

Without any verbal commands, it had all been done as if we were responding to orders. None were needed.

For most on the plane, we had made it past a great obstacle in our lives; the war was over for us, or was it?

The flight became routine, except maybe for the refueling stop in Guam. We were able to leave the plane briefly while it refueled and readied for the remainder of the trip. After re-boarding, the pilot taxied the big bird to the end of the 15,000 foot airstrip. Three miles of runway was necessary for the huge B-52s stationed there which carried a full load of bombs used in bombing raids over North and South Vietnam. Even though we were told not to photograph the loaded bombers, many did anyway.

As for our flight, we started our roll and we rolled and rolled and we were still on the ground. I looked out one of the right side windows and saw the one thousand foot marker. About the same time, I felt the plane lift slightly from the ground. Anxious thoughts of impending disaster had rushed into my mind, but the plane slowly rose, dipped slightly, and then rose again as it went beyond the cliffs at the end of the runway.

Now, it was a long routine and, thankfully, boring flight.

Wars cause great miseries for the people who are affected. When they are over, no one understands what they were about. The brave lads and lassies who went to Vietnam are now relegated to their place in history.

The brown people who were to be freed by the Americans have gone through an even stranger transformation. They were "conquered" by the communists only to be freed to work for the corporatists who have enslaved them again with wages less than the good American GIs paid for laundry and clean boots.

The dominos did not fall and brave American boys were sent to Asia to do the job that Asian boys should have done for themselves. The light at the end of the tunnel was never reached and the world still spins about with humanity still subjugated by those who have the political and economic means to disrupt the lives of those unable to fend for themselves - which includes most of the inhabitants of the world.

Lieutenant Gene Lucas
(For the love of his fellow beings – a great human)

Lieutenant Gene Lucas was the executive officer of the battery to which I was assigned in Vietnam. Luke, as we called him, was from Clinton, SC. He was an excellent officer who cared a great deal about his men and provided whatever they needed to make their situations as pleasant as possible.

Aside from his concern for his men, he had great compassion for others as well. My fondest memory of him occurred one day while we were at battalion headquarters to check some paper work at the personnel section.

As I returned to the area where I thought he might be, I saw him talking to the battalion chaplain. Luke had his back to me and failed to notice I was close enough to hear the conversation.

"Did they get money?" he asked the chaplain.

"Yes, they did," was the chaplain's reply.

My approach interrupted that particular conversation and a new one was begun about other topics.

Later in a private conversation, the chaplain told

me about the meaning of what I had overheard. Luke had a hundred and thirty-five dollars taken from his check each month and given to a local orphanage. I am pretty sure that only he and the chaplain knew about it. Such a sum was an exceptionally generous donation from a Lieutenant's pay.

I had the good fortune many years after returning from Southeast Asia to reestablish contact with Luke. He informed me of all the things that had happened after I had left. He retired from a career in the military and now lived in Pennsylvania.

Just as he had done in Vietnam, he was still performing his extraordinary acts of loving kindness. *He had adopted three nieces to care for.*

One of the reasons I really wanted to talk to him again was to thank him for his contributions to the orphanages. I finally got the courage to tell him.

"Luke, I know about the money you gave to the orphanages in Vietnam," I said in a somewhat subdued voice.

On the other end of the phone was a long pause of silence. I'm pretty sure he didn't know how he should respond.

"You do," finally came an answer in a seemingly uncomfortable voice.

I quickly changed the subject and quizzed him about some of the others with whom we had served. The conversation continued as a celebration of times of past glories.

We kept in contact by e-mails. One day I received the following e-mail from Luke:

"Most of you are unaware that I had two stents put into the arteries of my heart approximately 4 weeks ago. Tomorrow I will undergo the knife again to remove a portion of my carotid artery, which will be cleaned out and returned. It is 85% blocked."

"In the event that it doesn't work out, I want you to know that each of you had a significant effect on my life and helped me through the many briar patches that we all encounter as we mature and work in this life."

"I wish the best for each of you and thank you for the relationship we had and the many things that we did."

"I tried to explain to the Dr. that they had everything wrong. The problem with my heart is it was broken many times by you girls and that I had to glue it with super glue and it had started to deteriorate. All they would have to do is re-glue the heart and I would be fine. It didn't work on the Dr."

"Anyhow, again thank you for relationships we had and I love each of u\you."

"Take CARE"

"Love,"

Gene

There was an ominous tone in the message. He had not told us all we might have needed to know. Unfortunately, the uneasiness surrounding the message had a reason. Several days later I received an e-mail from Bill Stender, a former battery commander, who Luke thought had been an outstanding man and commanding officer. It read:

"To all of Gene's friends,"

"I talked to Gene's wife a short while ago, and I am sad to report that Gene passed away two days ago. I did not get any information about the arrangements, etc, since it just didn't seem appropriate on the phone."

"It is a sad day, indeed."

"God Bless Gene Lucas and May he rest in peace."

Bill

Indeed, it was a sad day. Lt. Colonel Gene Lucas, Retired, deserves a place with the best of people who have ever walked this earth.

I had ridden through Clinton, SC, while attending Newberry College. I had gone right by the old Duster sitting out front of the National Guard center there. It appeared to be nothing more than an old antiquated machine from WW II, but it was the same type of "old machine" we used in Vietnam. This was the same unit Luke had served in before he had been one of the patriotic ones who had gone to the trouble of contacting the powers that be in order to be placed on active duty rather than continue his military stint in the reserve forces. I'm still pretty sure I would never have done that. He also must have extended his tour in Vietnam, because he was there when I arrived and was there when I left.

Not far at all from the old National Guard Armory on another street nearby in the 1950s was a large curved sign over the entrance to a group of granite buildings. Foot high painted letters spelled out Thornwell Home for Children.

Among the youngsters who lived and played there during that time was a young boy who, I suppose, often wondered, among other things, what his future might behold. Perhaps he even dreamed of becoming an officer in the military. If he did, his dream was fulfilled. Lt. Col. Gene Lucas, as he was later known, never forgot the compassion he was shown in his time of need. He repaid several times over whatever debt he might have felt he owed. He became an outstanding leader of men in difficult times and also a great man with deep rooted concern for others. He will be sorely missed.

Rest in Peace my dear friend.

THE BUDDY PLAN

Well, maybe I should tell at least one war story. You may see it as you wish.

My wife Linda felt as though she had to leave church one Sunday morning because of the extreme anxiety she was feeling. She relayed that story to me on more than one occasion.

For years I never gave her a response. Then finally one night, I did. She had a reason for such a feeling. Seems that a foolish Lieutenant was standing in full view on a perimeter bunker that night (12 hours difference) and someone had him in view in a sniper scope. The rounds missed. One story is enough.

Chapter Eleven

Cry For the Children

♦

The children of the past, the present, and those who are yet to be, cry out to the universe, please care that I should live, that I should be.

♦

Tan An

My first assignment in Vietnam was at Tan An Airstrip as an assistant platoon leader. Our prime weapons were 40 mm anti-aircraft *pom-pom* cannons adapted to a post WW II tank chassis. They were fine weapons despite an antiquated appearance. We could defend perimeters, installations, structures, and do all sorts of other jobs to include convoy escort, mine sweeps, and even an occasional direct support for Infantry.

Tan An Airstrip was a fairly good size base located near the city of Tan An in the delta region of Vietnam. A hodgepodge of units or portions thereof called the installation home for operations. Facilities included a runway, a helicopter assault staging area, and a base for helicopter gunships whose protection probably played a significant role in our presence there.

A medical unit, M A S H, was located there as well. The S-1 stationed at the end of the runway took care of the most unfortunate who had to be prepared for a very sad trip home.

I felt exceptionally fortunate to have this duty assignment. The platoon leader and I shared a small building for our headquarters.

There would be no forward observer duty, which was a very likely assignment for a newly commissioned artillery officer. Forward observers were prime targets in a military operation because of their role in directing artillery fire onto the enemy.

By no means was I home free, but compared to others, it wasn't a bad assignment.

The Shell Factory

The 40mm ammunition we shot was made at the old shell factories of WWII. When I was much younger, in the 1950s and early 60s, at times, my family rode from our small community to Charlotte, NC. Along the way, situated several hundred yards off the main road were the dilapidated remnants of a huge abandoned building along with some smaller ones.

The old rusty metal side panels hung in disarray in places and whatever glass remained was either totally broken or partly missing. In its hay-day, it must have been magnificent with the shiny panels glistening in the sun while people bustled in and out during shift changes. It now stood shamefully disregarded as vines and brush grew all about - a casualty of peace after World War II, thank goodness.

Surprisingly, well, maybe not, most of the plant's employees were women. They actually did the largest share of the work putting the shells together. Men did some of the more strenuous jobs.

When the workers were laid off at the end of WWII, each was given a souvenir shell, among other things.

At times, my father-in-law would tell us about working there during the war. He was responsible for insuring the detonation fuses were placed properly. "We had a hand-press and it actually pressed the detonation fuse on the end of the warhead," he explained.

More than once, as we sat on his porch, he told us about the operations at the plant and what had happened at the end of the war. As he spoke, the words came out slower as the emotions grew in his presentation and soon he simply had to stop.

He turned away to gather his composure and then someone quickly asked a question to change his immediate thoughts.

No doubt the recollection of those times also triggered thoughts of the loss of his brother, Robert, during the war. Perhaps, in a short moment, the good times they had as youngsters raced through the mind. Then too, the lack of any closure to the whole situation brought on the strong emotions. His brother had been lost in an air raid over Germany. Like so many in WW II and other wars, his brother's remains had never been found.

The closing of the factory was a mixed bag for the workers; they had gone from being unemployed before the war to working long hours to do their share to win the war and now back to being unemployed.

The camaraderie must have been great. All were working for the very existence of a nation which offered the best hope to wrestle the soul of the world from the truly evil. Each realized that however small their part might seem, it was important to the overall effort.

Apparently, the remaining shells they produced and were not sent away to the war had been safely packed, sixteen to a coated metal container complete with a water proof sealed lid, and shipped off to an ammunition depot for storage. The Navy and the Korean conflict had consumed their share, but still, there had to be an abundant stockpile from which to draw to send to our type of units in Vietnam.

When we used our share of the shells, we knew by the markings on the steel cases where they had come from. It all seemed to be a rather eerie coincidence.

THE BUDDY PLAN

The Walk into the Jungle

A good might's rest at my platoon headquarters had left me feeling perky, even in the morning heat. After breakfast, I was headed to one of our gun positions on the perimeter and came upon what appeared to be a local man excitedly talking and making hand gestures to our camp commander who listened intently as if to absorb every word without any argument. It was obvious the exchange was not an angry confrontation. There did, however, appear to be a great sense of urgency on the part of the local man. The Major (base commander) glanced away for a moment and noticed me staring at what was going on.

He summoned me over. Evidently, he thought I could be of assistance. I gladly obliged.

How much he had clearly understood from the conversation with the local man was not certain, but he asked me if I would walk with them through the jungle to a small village maybe within a hundred meters distance. The camp commander mentioned something about a mortar impacting, or that was my thought at the moment.

I was thinking I was going into the village to do an analysis of a mortar impact. For me, that was a piece of cake. With proper analysis, one could determine the direction of the mortar and other information about it.

I remembered the technique from my training at Fort Sill and actually looked forward to the excursion. The area was secure enough that neither of us took a weapon. In hindsight, going without a weapon may not have been a good idea. It was a brisk walk through the jungle.

Sometimes, you let yourself get set up to be bowled over by your own thoughts or actions. Here I was all bright and shiny with a fresh coat of paint and with no idea in my mind that I was about to get blind-sided, and it wasn't going to be by some enemy's weapon. However, it would be psychologically worse, something to always be remembered, something of my own making.

Palm limbs had to be brushed back as we walked along the narrow, well-worn, dirt pathway. Some of the villagers worked at the base, so it was well-traveled. Other villagers visited the base for medical care which was offered at times.

In my smugness I thought how I would go there, show my expertise, and be recognized as a fairly sharp young Lieutenant. Looking back now (with a proper analysis of me), *cocky smart a*** would definitely be the better term.

About half way there, the faint cry of a woman caught my attention. I was a little curious but not overly concerned. As we drew closer, the cry became more pronounced and I became somewhat more concerned. It was becoming more obvious now that it was a painful wailing. I wasn't quite sure what was going on, but, nonetheless, my thoughts still centered about me.

We stopped at one of the mud huts on the edge of the village. As we did, the local man once again turned to the camp commander and started jabbering excitedly and pointing to the top of one of the mud and palm roofed "hooches", as we called them. It looked as though something had blown a sizable portion of the roof away.

I assumed a mortar had fallen short and had done the damage. Since the hole was on the side of the roof away from the base, it looked as though, if it was in fact a mortar, it was headed toward the base and not away from it. Also, I didn't remember any mortars ever being shot from the base. Probably the man was one of the village leaders and had been sent to tell of the damage.

It was policy to compensate the locals with a few

dollars or something in kind when we did damage to some of their property. For the moment, such a conclusion sufficed even though evidence contradicted the damage being done by us. It would still be better just to give them a few dollars and not argue.

"It's Only a Mud Hut with a Palm Roof!"

And why were people so concerned over a bunch of palm leaves being blown off a roof? Just how much trouble would it be to fix something that simple? And certainly, the woman I kept hearing in the background didn't need to be that emotional. It could all be fixed relatively easy.

I still had no idea about the real topic of the conversation between the camp commander and the local man who began to appear considerably more concerned than I thought he ought to be about a bamboo roof being damaged.

The woman's wailing was incessant now. She was still several yards away and hidden by some sort of barrier, exactly what, I can't remember. I do remember I couldn't see her initially and she was hidden well enough that the sound was not right in my ear. I also remember, unfortunately quite vividly, how I wanted to find her and tell her, "It's only a damn bamboo hut and it can be fixed with a small amount of effort."

It is no coincidence that you always remember the really stupid things you think, say, or do. To this day - and every day - it creeps into my consciousness. My real arrogant stupidity will haunt me... forever.

My attention was still focused on the task at hand. The camp commander was still listening intently to the jabbering of the local man. My curiosity about what was going on grew. Maybe the camp commander was being very courteous and didn't want to upset the man.

The woman had not stopped her screaming and wailing yet and finally the moment came when I felt I had to walk a few yards and see what in the h*** was wrong with her.

One second after I made that decision, there was a strong uncanny desire not to follow up on it. It was then that something extraordinarily strange occurred.

If was if I had felt the heat of an explosion. My body was flushed and no longer was I in control. I would do whatever I was instructed to do.

The voice said to me, "You will go look."
"Man, I really don't think so."
"Yes, you will go look."
"I really don't want to go."
I absolutely did not want to go.

Without knowing what was awaiting me, I felt the dread... I didn't want to go, but it was beyond my control. The battle was lost.

I slowly ventured far enough to see the woman.

The pure agony she was experiencing was beyond belief. The pain was visible not just in her body, but it was literally, in the true sense of the word, visible in the air about her. It was also captured in her swollen tearful face and in every movement she exhibited as she paced uncontrollably back and forth.

It was as though her heart had been torn from her chest and she did not know what to do.

My eyes shifted from her and ....

"Now, take a good look. Do you see?"

At Fort Sill during OCS, one of the first Artillery weapons we learned to use was the 105 mm howitzer. It was used widely in Vietnam as well. As part of our training, we had to serve on all of the positions of the gun crew.

One position on the gun crew was that of ammo handler. He had to physically lift the ammo crates from the hauler and take them to the gun pits where he broke open the boxes. A tool was provided to snap the metal bands which had been placed on each box for transport. After the bands were broken, turning a small metal latch permitted the box to be opened.

Inside were two round fiber containers. Each contained a 105mm artillery shell and charge to propel the round to the target. The early shells had a brass casing. In Vietnam, the locals made beautiful vases and such out of the brass. They used most of the stuff the Americans and others discarded.

The boxes were about eight inches deep and a little over a foot wide and maybe 3 feet long with rope handles on both ends. They were big enough to make an excellent storage utility. Of course, in OCS, we had to put all of the casings back in the box and load them back in the truck after we had fired the rounds.

In Vietnam, the boxes were prized by the locals for all sorts of reasons. Usually, the GIs gave them to the people unless there was a need. There were so many of the boxes that they were fairly commonplace among the civilian population.

The Vietnamese people were small in stature. The young children were small boned with delicate features and usually very beautiful golden olive skin. Their eyes.... their eyes.... they always sparkled. How they could have such a glow in them while living in such wretched conditions, I don't know. The toothy smiles along with the always bright eyed looks could melt icicles in a witch's heart. They were easy people to love.

They identified well with the GIs. More often than not, when the soldiers and vehicles were just outside the base camp, the young children would gather around "GI number one".

The young soldiers loved the small children and gave them food and whatever else they could spare. For this, the soldiers got more than they could ever buy - the warm tender laughter and smiles of small children.

"Do you understand the mother's cry now?"

It was the universal cry of motherhood. It came from the soul. It was the hurt of all the mothers of the world, those before her, those to come after her. No one listens. If they did and understood, there would be no more wars. There would no more useless killing and hatred.

The Vietnamese who lived in the jungle usually had a makeshift table of sort on the front of their hooches. Food and other articles were usually placed there after the day's harvest and the food was readied to be prepared for the next meal.

Today, the food and wash pans were missing. In their place, neatly arranged side by side on this table, as if to display... and it was for that purpose... were two of the 105mm ammo boxes. They had been sent overseas with two artillery shells in each one. Their intended purpose had been served. They had been discarded and somehow found their way into the village.

Fate now saw a different use for them. How ironic the new use.

The small beautiful rounded face was at peace with the world. The bright eyes closed forever. The toothy smile was replaced with sealed lips.

THE BUDDY PLAN

A bright yellow dress, something so unusual for them, adorned her small delicate silent body. It was a body that should have been laughing and playing with all the other children.

Beside her in another 105 mm box was the body of a still younger child. It was her sister.

My body flushed again. I sank to a depth lower than before. The sensation went from head to foot. I was frozen for the moment. No words.

Could anything have been said to explain the feelings I now experienced?

I wanted to comfort the mother. I wanted to make it all go away. I could do nothing.

If the mother saw me, maybe she saw the look. Maybe she knew how truly sorry I was.

May God have a special mercy for all the mothers of all the wars who saw their small children become the victims of the asinine stupidity that wars bring. Innocent lives taken for causes that no one ever seems to understand.

It's all blank until we started back to the camp.

The trek back to camp was long and slow. I could smell the dirt. It was pretty easy as low as I was.

The mother's wailing was soon out of ear shot, but it didn't stop. Numbness set in. The images were burned into my memory forever as well they should be.

Maybe a mortar which had been intended for the camp had fallen short. That would explain what had happened. I don't remember if we had been shelled the night before or not. There are some other explanations. None of them will ever do.

They were victims who would never know anything about the world. They would never have a chance to experience a life to any degree of fullness. They were the children of all the wars.

We should all have a place alone to ourselves so no one can notice; some things hurt more than others can know.
May God have a special place for the mother and her children.
These scenes don't make the television screens. We have no stomach for it. How many times has it been repeated throughout history? How many times more will it occur?

Children who are never given the chance to know the world are never known about. Even as rotten as some of the circumstances under which they live might be, they each deserve a chance to make the best of it all. Who knows what they might have become or what they might have contributed? The only thing for sure is that, now we will never know.

"Vietnamese Mother, I can never tell you how sorry I am. You and your children will be remembered. Each day you will be remembered. May God comfort you and all the other mothers until your last earthly thoughts are gone."

The voices are stilled and silenced and never to be heard. They've gone quietly from this world. What does it matter? They are of another world so far away. It is so far away from our shiny world of material things that occupy our senses until we lose connections with anything except that which is important to us - our own selfish little world of lost compassion.

Chapter Twelve

The Coma
(July, August 1967)

◆

"To sleep, perchance to dream – ay, there's the rub;
For in that sleep of death what dreams may come,
When we have shuffled off this mortal coil,
Must give us pause – there's the respect
That makes calamity of so long life."
But perhaps, not to the extent or in the manner
Shakespeare writes.

◆

The Questions Have No Answers?

The lifeless body had been taken to the morgue twice, but an Angel of Life had decided that death was not to be. The attending corpsmen were alerted each time and they took instructions well. Each noticed the tiniest glimmer of hope still there. What minute ember of life had dared defy the Angel of Death and refused to be extinguished?

But then again, what would it all be worth? How many countless hours of pain and suffering lie ahead even if the ember of the miracles continues to glow? *What kind of life would there be?*

The extensive injury to the body was evidenced by the missing right leg, the broken bones, and shrapnel entry wounds which covered most of what remained of his lower body and stomach. The shock from the blast had rendered Jacky unconscious. *The initial blessing of freeing him from suffering the awful pain might now become an everlasting curse.*

The wonderful mechanism of a human body with all the miraculous codes running in the background which make all the movements and thought processes possible along with all the other happenings which are taken for granted were now compromised.

The codes running in a single body share a connection to all the other codes running in Nature to allow our consciousness to exist in an orderly sensible manner which gives us our human experience. Was Jacky disconnected from it all?

One of the awful things that simpleton minds create to reduce all the wonderful things happening to their lowest level or stop them all together had done its dastardly deed. It's almost as if evil had prevailed this time as it has so often before. Too often, it was and is on a much grander scale.

Was it possible there was an active mind in turmoil with itself inside an unresponsive body? What an absolutely horrendous thought!

Or could it be... his mind was a void? Had the deprivation of oxygen to the brain been so prolonged that it was beyond all miracles that he might recover any cognitive processes at all? Indeed, what kind of life did remain in this hapless body?

These were not just questions for medical professionals; they were obvious to anyone who had but a little knowledge. Jacky lay in a fetal position. His muscles had contracted from the injuries to the nervous system. Had his mind taken him back to the security of his birth? Was this an omen of a situation which was to be permanent?

There seemed to be a *million questions, maybe more*... none with answers at the moment... perhaps no time soon... maybe never. The historical references on such injuries were clearly not in Jacky's favor.

Questions and comments from me the others who care deeply about you.

Jacky, if your mind is working and you are forever trapped away from us... we pray that your thoughts are pleasant... we sincerely hope. We would love to talk to you again.

"Jacky, are you back sitting under one of the magnificent Oak trees in the school yard at Indian Land talking with friends, making your famous wise cracks while the warm breezes blow the laughter all about? Are the smiles of unspoken thoughts witnessed and enjoyed by everyone?"

"Are you grinning as you always did when you made the 'smart remarks' and then sheepishly looked around to see the reaction of your peers? You have a special knack for that, don't you?"

"Indian Land seemed to be a small slice of Heaven, didn't it? It wasn't Iowa either, was it?"

Indian Land School was a small rural school where each student knew the others. The teachers were friendly and knew the students regardless of whether or not the students were in their classes. I first learned about sex education there from a mutual buddy (Jacky got to know him later) who asked me questions about which I had no clue. He knew an awful lot for a first grader.

Mr. P. H. Neal's true status as a giant of a man was belied by his smaller physical stature. He was the principal. He was strict in discipline, but he was fair and compassionate in all of his dealings with students. As a visitor at the school in the summertime, more than likely you would see him on a ladder in his painting clothes sprucing up the school building. He scraped together money for repairs and often did the work himself.

"You liked Mr. Neal a great deal, didn't you Jacky? Well, do you remember the wooden paddle he had hanging on his wall in his little office where he also sold pencils to those who didn't or couldn't make it to the store to buy one?"

"Now the big question, and tell the truth, did he ever use the paddle on you? You were a little mischievous, well, maybe more than a little, weren't you? But I doubt you ever reached the point of needing such correction."

"There were the days we played baseball in high school. I was a grade ahead. You always seemed to have on baggy britches. Maybe you wanted the opponents to think they should hit the ball to you or slack off as they pitched to you?"

"They would have all been fooled, would they not? You would have thrown them out. You were magic at your position in the outfield. You were quick and agile and could throw the ball farther with accuracy than anyone would ever believe until they had been caught in the trap."

"You could make the play with ease. You could

outwit the fox."

"And you would have hit the ball where they least expected it to be hit."

"You, the red (actually your brown hair looked red in the sun) headed freckled face boy who would make remarks to the opponent as they batted and then grin from ear to ear once they stared back at you. Laughter ruled the day."

Are all the memories of the splendor lost forever?

"Your baggy britches, red from the old dusty clay infield had been swapped for the baggy britches of a soldier. You were pleasantly surprising and deceptive in any uniform. In the military garb, you didn't gather the teams together after the game and shake hands and then go to the local grill to get a hamburger and fries. Or the most favorite thing of all, we stopped at the local Dairy Queen in Lancaster late in the afternoon on the way back from a baseball game in Heath Springs, Kershaw, or Flat Creek - places known only to the people in the county in our time."

"If you were real friendly to the young lady running the ice cream stand, you might even get a little extra ice cream in your cone or even a little extra chocolate on your sundae."

"Even as shy or bashful as you were, I'll bet you would flirt a little for some extra ice cream."

"Those were the days, along with you - one of the ones who had made a big contribution to the enjoyment of it all. The kids all fit so well together. One's weakness was the others' strength. The days of summer were splendor, pure, and perhaps not as simple as they seemed."

"The days of summer gave way to autumn and winter and we found ourselves in the old tiled floored gym with the antiquated dressing rooms barely big enough to change in. It didn't matter. It only made us feel closer together."

"We could go get the key from Mr. Neal and shoot

basketball on Saturday. We usually had enough for a good pickup game."

"You were an unlikely candidate for a basketball player. You didn't look as tall as you are. You were scrappy and the magic in your movements fooled many opponents and led to points scored for the good guys. I will not swear that you could jump, but you did rebound on occasion. We did have taller players. I was one of them. I, along with others, could jump."

"The desperation shot from half court stripped the net in the state playoffs. You had not made the shot, but you had made the pass to the person who had made the shot. The crowd roared. You and Paul K. Neal had gotten the ball to half court. Thanks Jacky for passing it to me."

Jacky with the basketball team in 1962. He is the second number 4.

"Did you realize there was another red-haired guy there that day? He was sitting high in the stands in the old Carolina field house watching us play. He had

THE BUDDY PLAN

taken his smaller team in 1957 and beaten a much bigger team for the Collegiate National Championship. It was Frank McGuire, Jacky. The famous red-head had watched us play."

"There was the year before, we had gone to the Marine Base on Parris Island to play in a tournament. Coach Potts had commandeered the money somehow from limited funds. It was a long, long trip on the school bus."

"We signed on to go with Fort Mill on their activity bus. It would go no more than thirty five miles per hour. They were somewhat of a rival in basketball. They were a bigger school, so we might or might not play them in football."

"Your nephew Bucky was a basketball whiz there. But we beat them anyway. I guess that gave you a chance to hold him hostage to all sorts of ribbing, not that you might ever do that."

"The bus broke down on the way to Parris Island, but it was fixed shortly thereafter and we made it. It was only a small bump in the road."

"Coach Potts had unshakable confidence in us. Imagine that, the smallest school there in numbers and he thought we had a chance of winning the whole tournament. Of course we had talent and some size and as much desire and determination as the Marines who trained there. That was back in 1961."

"Coach Potts gave us a curfew and made us act as though we were part of the training there. He made us almost march into the gym proudly displaying our little bags with Warriors on the side each time we played. It was as though we were in the military."

"I guess we showed him. I guess we showed them all. I guess we were the pride of the Marines who watched us in the final game beat a much bigger school for the championship."

"Even our buddies from Fort Mill were proud of us as we all rode happily back home. We all shared in the glory of the moment."

"The Marine hospitality had been grand and the food was good. Maybe breakfast was a little early, but we made it. That was our first chance to sleep in military style bunk beds. By the way, did you sleep in a top bunk, or was that simply a silly question?"

"I think I know the answer."

"Remember the time in Basic training when we met the guys from all over the country - well, the east coast at least. You made friends easily. There were many who worked hard. It was called cooperation."

"Do you remember tank hill, the awful tank hill? They had it all planned, didn't they, the platoon sergeants? When we were coming back to the barracks from one of our daily outings, they had to push us just a little more. We just had to go up that blasted hill to take our last bit of energy, didn't we?"

"What about the kid who dropped the hand grenade, the real hand grenade, and the platoon sergeant grabbed it and threw it and all was well. Wonder if that guy ever make it out of basic?"

"Of course, there was a particular recruit who had to be given a bath with a scrub brush to help him cooperate. But we were not in on that, were we?"

"What had happened when you went away to Fort Knox? We never got back together to talk about any of the stuff that happened after basic. You went your way to Kentucky and I went to California."

"Was your time at Fort Knox as interesting as it was at Fort Jackson? Did you have to sleep out in the cold again? We slept out again, but the weather was only brisk. I met a guy from New York who was my bunkmate. We were a little slack, but we made it okay. I wished we had talked before you went overseas."

"Do you remember the plane ride into Vietnam? Do you remember stepping off the plane and the rush of warm air with all the humidity and the distinctive smell that caught your attention? What was your time like there before you were hurt?"

"Did we somehow think we would stay together after basic and serve out our time together? The Army has a strange way of doing things sometimes, don't they?"

"Are you thinking about being away from your unit? Hopefully you are not in a nightmare of being captured by the enemy.

"Or are you recalling all the times before I knew you?"

"I thought I heard someone say you played checkers. It was a common practice for men to sit around the old country stores and play games. All of them had boards and quite often the checkers themselves were bottle caps. The two colors on the board were differentiated by turning some of the bottle caps upside down."

"Your father ran a little country store and I can't imagine you not playing checkers. You had a particular demeanor to outwit someone and then get a thrill from it. As I said before, you could outwit the fox."

"Are you reliving the times you and your cousin Bucky were being mischievous? I can only imagine the two of you together."

"I never knew much about you until you came to Indian Land when you were in the 9th or 10th grade. I can't remember which."

Jacky, two last questions and I will let you rest..."Do you feel the presence of your mother as she watches over you and prays each moment she can? Do you know that others are thinking about you and praying for your recovery?"

Chapter Thirteen

The Medical Journey
(1967 - ????)

♦

The body was broken, yet the spirit chose to remain there.
It was for reasons beyond the understanding of the wise. There was indeed a purpose.

♦

The Beginning

The road for only a meager survival was to be long and precarious... if it was to be at all. The present problems had begun with the perils of the helicopter ride off into the fields of the war. Not long after the arrival there came the sickening thud of the explosion with its shockwave. Unless you've heard it in person, and under the circumstances which it occurs, you can't fully understand. It is of no use to attempt to describe. Those who face the danger are thankful if they are okay, but no one knows what comes after the initial explosions or if the next one will be for them.

Minds are frozen in fear of the moment, but it can only be for the shortest of moments.

The resulting horrible wounds which were created by the booby trap that respects no living thing befell the soldier. Next were the awful helpless feelings as his buddies attended their fallen comrade in arms. The initial sight of the mangled body cast no doubt... their comrade was surely dead or soon would be.

THE BUDDY PLAN

The first treatment of any wounded soldier is by the medic in the field. These specially trained soldiers are taught to care for those with whom they share the same dangers. They too can be targets and often are casualties of the battle.

In the absent of a combat medic, each soldier attempts to apply the emergency procedures taught in basic combat training. The first things are: (1) clear the airway so the soldier can breathe, (2) stop the bleeding by applying pressure in a situation and if an arm of leg is severely damaged, apply a tourniquet made from what each soldier carries (his belt), and (3) make the soldier as comfortable as possible.

In Vietnam, the next step was to summon a "Dustoff". Helicopters had first been used as far back as WW II. They were used frequently in Korea and extensively in Vietnam. In most cases, they were the only method possible to get the wounded from the remotest of regions where injuries had been sustained to a treatment facility.

Because of the bravery of the Dustoff units, wounded soldiers were extracted from an area as battles raged. Medivacs were, just as other assets to the enemy are, a target. Numerous crews were injured and many crews were lost.

A helicopter brought the damaged soldier back to the medical unit. Twice, he had been pronounced dead, but it was not to be. He still had life within him.

If he could be stabilized enough, he would be sent to a medical facility where he could receive a higher level of care. Surgeons must weigh all options carefully. Sometimes, moving the wounded can cause a greater problem than giving limited, albeit excellent, care at the present facility.

What Is to Be?

The clouds of uncertainty which now surrounded Jacky Bayne swirled with all different colors which no one except the most faithful could begin to understand and then there was both brightness and doubt in the cloud bands, but they were active, so hope was there.

There were only spasmodic reactions from the attempts to contact Jacky's mind by all who worked with the young soldier. At times, there was nothing at all. Other times, there were faint cries or attempts at sounds... or were they? Anything and all things happening still gave no definitive clues to the best trained eyes and ears of those who made assessments about the prognosis of the young soldier.

The tubes and bottles, along with all the other devices, hooked up to his body made the seemingly hopeless situation even more pronounced. It was part of the medical miracles at the time. He was an even bigger part of the miracle.

Whatever Angel stood watch over the young soldier must have been determined to have it her way. The tiniest glimmer of life would not go away and even began to glow minutely brighter.

Jacky made it to the next hospital and the ember, however faint, was still lit. He could get better care in the field hospital. The staff was more specialized and somewhat better equipped.

"Would he ever be able to make it to the next step from there?"

The next step was an evacuation hospital either in Japan or the Philippines. Either was a long, long way in distance and farther still in possibility because of the gravity of the injuries.

THE BUDDY PLAN

At hospitals farther removed from the combat zones, personnel and equipment would be upgraded. The logistics of supporting them is easier. There were some outstanding hospitals in the combat zone, but the offerings were still limited.

He did make it to the evacuation hospital in Japan. Still, he lay in a coma with muscles contracting as a result of the trauma to the brain. His body mass was deteriorating and the lack of functioning and movement of the muscles added further to the atrophy. However, there was hope, and maybe only hope. Still, no one knew what would eventually happen to the young soldier.

At the 249th Evacuation Hospital in Japan, he could receive the best medical attention available anywhere in the world, with maybe the exception of Walter Reed Hospital in Washington, D.C. Hope for all was that he and so many other seriously wounded could be transported to the United States. Consideration would also be given in an attempt to locate the wounded nearest their original home.

Were the doctors' charts conflicting with scribbles of "response to pain," "response to name," "no response to pain or any other stimulation?" Maybe it depended on the medical staff. Perhaps most of it simply depended on the expectations of those making the observation.

Had Jacky responded to the get well card from his mother when a hospital staff member read it? Then again, maybe he had not. Each movement or grimace had to be measured against a genuine response and the possibility that it was only a spontaneous reaction of a nerve.

If he could just make it to Walter Reed, it would be close enough for his parents and other loved ones to visit. There had to be turmoil in the minds of all who attended the young soldier and especially those who waited anxiously at home.

What would his family see if he did make it back?

How would they react?

Thus far, the medical staffs had performed magnificently.

Back to the States

Only the minds of those who were responsible know exactly why it was decided at the time, but it was determined that Specialist Bayne would indeed be sent to Walter Reed.

The telegraph was sent to his parents: "This is to advise you that your son, Specialist 4th Class, Jacky C. Bayne, will arrive at Walter Reed Hospital, Washington, D.C. on or about..." and it went on to tell what particulars the Army had chosen to tell. *He was coming home, and for the moment, that was all that mattered to his family and other loved ones.*

Jacky's parents had to prepare themselves for a journey. Their travel time, even by car, was measured in hours, but the distance in circumstances of Washington was impossible to measure. The journey to Washington, D.C. was the least of the journeys for which they would need to prepare. *They were yet to know about the true nature of their son's injuries or the ordeal which he had thus far endured... or what lay ahead for their son and them.*

THE BUDDY PLAN

Mercy Flights

Among the many uses of the C-141 *Starlifter* aircraft of the U.S. Air Force in the 1960s was that of a medical evacuation and transport. It could be specially equipped with all the necessary apparatus to care for the wounded on the long trip from the pacific to the United States. Sometimes, it might carry as many as a hundred wounded, depending on the particular mission configuration.

They collected the wounded and made a place for them on the huge silver bird which would wing them back to the United States. It had brought the tools of conflict to Vietnam. It carried back the cost of the use of the tools of war. It almost always carried, on its trips to Vietnam, the *green boxes* neatly stacked first on the aircraft. The boxes, complete with flags would make another trip home, maybe on the same type of aircraft. There was an irony to the reverence in which the boxes were handled in either direction.

The flight was long and arduous for all concerned. The preparations took time and skills of the upmost. The flight itself would take a minimum of nine hours under the best conditions. If there were weather fronts or storms, then it would be longer. The big bird with the precious cargo of wounded had to seek the least turbulent route possible.

Altitude was limited to no more than 28,000 feet because of those on board who might have chest injuries or otherwise be affected by pressure. Nothing was overlooked in preparation for the flight. The pilots were the best, as were the flight crews.

The medical crews were tops and the flight nurses - what can be said of angels? Their mere presence to GIs who had not cast their eyes on American girls for a time was enough to lift the spirits of the wounded who could notice them.

No matter how many flights each of the personnel had experienced, each one was special, as was each new patient who got the best care and attention humanly possible.

There were so many. In the peak years of the Vietnam War, there were as many as ten thousand wounded a month flown on these big metal birds. The numbers were staggering. It wasn't just about numbers. Each bay or stretcher that was ever occupied had a real person who suffered the wounds of war and who would forever be changed. For some, parts were missing and others were even less fortunate.

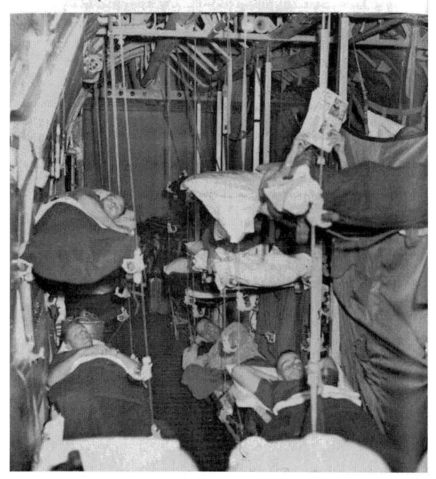

FLYING HOSPITAL: A C-141 flying home with its load of wounded will go far off course to avoid rough air. It cannot be flown above 28,000 feet, for men with chest wounds suffer at higher altitudes, even in the pressurized cabin. *U.S. Air Force photo.*

They flew the *Big Bear Route* as it was called at the time. That particular route took the aircraft over Alaska and down the Pacific coast. The flight was long and strenuous even on a healthy body, let alone those who were injured.

Among the suffering young soldiers on one particular manifest was a specialist 4th class named

Jacky Bayne. The fact that he was even aboard a flight for the wounded and not another aircraft configured for those even less fortunate was beyond amazing.

Elmendorf, We Have an Emergency

(ATC and Pilot Conversation Dramatized)

The cold air streamed over the exterior of the aircraft as the wonderful flight nurses and other medical staff watched over those inside the silver tube. Outside, the night stars glistened overhead. The lights were dimmed inside in hopes that the young bodies might have some respite from pain.

Flight nurses and the other nurses were the unsung heroines of this war, just as they have been in all the other wars. One dedicated flight nurse was alarmed as she checked the vital signs of one of the young soldiers. He as fast slipping away.

His kidneys were not functioning. This was very critical. The toxins could build up in his weakened body and he would surely die. Perhaps this time, Specialist Bayne would not beat the odds.

"Elmendorf tower, Mercy Flight two three seven heavy, over," the young captain calmly spoke into the aircraft microphone.

"Mercy Flight two three seven heavy, this is Elmendorf," the ATC replied.

"Elmendorf, we have a medical emergency situation on board; we'd like some ground assistance."

"Mercy flight, we will see what we can do."

"Elmendorf, can you patch my medical personnel through to a hospital unit?"

"Mercy flight, can do."

"Elmendorf, we are about three five zero miles out, could you give us a straight heading into a runway?"

THE BUDDY PLAN

"Mercy flight, can do, we'll clear a runway for you and have medical assistance to greet you."

"Elmendorf, thank you much."

With that conversation, the series of events necessary to get the young wounded soldier his critically needed medical attention was underway. There would be a complete medical team on the ready when the aircraft stopped its taxi. The young patient would get the best medical care that could be offered.

While such a situation was somewhat unusual, it happened occasionally and the medical response teams knew exactly what to do.

If he survived this, he could catch another flight from Elmendorf to Walter Reed, but to everyone's surprise, the procedure was finished quicker than thought and he was returned to the same flight. Unless I have forgotten what GIs are all about, those who were able and knew what was happening would have given him a hero's welcome back aboard the craft. Unfortunately, Jacky was still in a deep coma and knew nothing of the stop or the cheering.

The aircraft taxied to the runway, began its roll, and soon the big metal bird was airborne. The next stop was Travis Air Force Base near San Francisco/Oakland. It had become an exceptionally busy base since the buildup in Vietnam in the 1960s. While there, the plane would be prepared for the final leg of its journey. The wounded soldiers from the area or that region of the nation would be transported to the closest military medical facility to handle their wounds.

Washington, D.C., in August can be as hot as SC. The only air stirring at times is the same old politics. The *light at the end of the tunnel* was finally visible and the Vietnam debacle had an end in sight, or so they very erroneously thought. The next year would bring about the big surprise of the TET Offensive and the war would continue to rage and the casualties would continue to mount.

The TET Offensive brought a shock to the American psyche. They now saw what a formidable enemy America faced. They saw a spike in American casualties, something for which no one was prepared.

The political credibility of those managing the war was lost and the demonstrations against the war continued and the public's support of U.S. involvement was waning. The nation was becoming even more politically divided over the issue. It was front page coverage in the major papers each day and the headlines each night on the newscasts.

The politics were strange to the mothers and fathers and loved ones of those who fought. How anyone could not support the troops was beyond the understanding of those who were patriots. In fact, the demonstrations were misplaced when they targeted the troops and called them names. As always, the soldiers were the ones acting in good faith. They were, as always, the heroes who go away to war. They were not the politicians who determine the involvement in conflicts. Many soldiers had become victims twice.

On this day in Washington, D.C., anxious loved ones awaited the aircraft which they had been told carried their wounded heroes. Many wondered why the flight was late. Among the anxious were Bunia and Eb Bayne and Ernest Baker who had driven them from Indian Land, near Fort Mill, SC.

A phone call to the U.S. Representative from the Congressional District representing the Baynes revealed that the plane was late because of an unscheduled stop. Little did the awaiting Baynes know, *the life-saving stop had been for the sake of their son.*

Their Congressman arranged for them to lodge while awaiting the plane. He had also arranged for them to have transportation to the hospital.

Washington, as the Baynes soon discovered, was an entirely different world contrasted to the slow pace at their home.

Congressman Tom Gettys had served in WW II (1942-1946) in the U.S. Navy in the Pacific. He had also grown up in a small town and had come to the big city. He had been a teacher, a high school principal, and had held many other positions in which people care for other people, so he was very understanding.

The Arrival

"The Homecoming"

The excruciatingly long day was over. Midnight had stolen upon the already emotionally exhausted loved ones who had gathered to welcome home their soldiers. He or she would be returning from the fields of war half a world away. The true condition of their being was uncertain. The telegrams had given some detail of the wounds, but how accurate and truly forthcoming had the brief words been?

The bright lights of the ambulances streaming into the area pierced the night as each driver made his/her way to an offloading area where the patients could be taken to a ward or room. Hearts of those awaiting sight of their loved one used the last reserve of adrenalin to pound even more.

Bandages on each soldier hid away the physical wounds. To be painfully honest, none of the wounds of war are good – some are just not as bad as the others. Some of the wounds are everlastingly cruel. The range of wounds this night would include the most horrendous.

On each stretcher being brought into the hospital were part of the real costs of any war which are exacted on those whose lives were now forever changed. The minds of the wounded which were functioning were racing - still trying to comprehend the madness and horror that had caused them to be in the situation they now found themselves. Some of their last images had been that of a buddy beside them who they knew was even less fortunate than they were.

On each stretcher, there was a story. For most, their particular story would never be heard except to the consciousness of the individual who had lived it. It would forever be hidden away in the deepest crevasses of their minds until, in a moment of weakness, it would creep painfully again to the surface.

The awful sounds and flashes that will never go away were seared into their memories along with the other madness and confusion of it all. Many things would never be reconciled - the missing body parts – the last helicopter ride, some among the least fortunate that might have been packed aboard the helicopter to get them back to a place where some sanity still existed.

It would be the beginning of the healing process for some, and for many, the healing process would take an extraordinarily long time. None would ever fully recover to the soundness of mind and body they once enjoyed.

Somewhere among all the stretchers was the son that Eb and Bunia Bayne were anxious to greet. They had prepared themselves as best they could. *Neither could have been prepared for what they were about to witness.*

They had no idea that the injuries were as severe as they were. They had not been properly informed. Why had someone not told them the true extent of the injuries and the real condition in which their son now existed? How many other similar situations were there on this manifest?

THE BUDDY PLAN

One of the medics who knew who Eb and Bunia were looking for approached them, pointed and said in a solemn tone, "That's Bayne on that stretcher."

At the moment they saw him, they stood together. Each needed to provide strength to the other. They had to be strong for the young soldier regardless of the range of thoughts that now ravaged their minds.

Bunia Bayne looked at her son. She did not see the bright, smiling, boyish grin she last remembered when he left to go to war and she so longingly desired to see again. What she saw was what she saw - a son she had been sent to reclaim and return him home regardless of his condition. No mortal being was going to stand in her way or prevent her from fulfilling her mission.

Jacky's father later told someone that, "It was... the awfulest sight I have ever seen."

When Jacky reached Walter Reed Hospital, he weighed a mere seventy pounds. He was only a shadow of the individual who Bunia and Eb Bayne had last seen walking to board an aircraft for his trip to the unknown. He lay motionless and silent on the stretcher except for a rare muscle contraction. The medical view of him was still extremely guarded. The expectation of the first medical personnel to attend him at Walter Reed Hospital was that he simply was someone who had been lost to the war. Would there be any progress in his medical status... the odds were greatly against it.

He would need constant care and more than likely would never recover even the most elementary functions of the body or mind.

"He will be in Ward 35," a young medic told Bunia. "We will need some time to prepare his room."

They had time to put together what they had seen. There was time to panic, to break down, or do all sorts of other things they could have done. But they didn't.

They were given counsel "to cry" and perhaps it might make them feel better, but they didn't.

They would not break down and Bunia Bayne told the medical staff right away that she would be there to take care of her son. And that is what she set out to do.

Soon, the helpless looking body was in a room and hooked up to all the modern life support devices available at the time. **Beside Jacky's bed stood a mother who would remain with him, in prayer, throughout his ordeal.**

Somewhere in Jacky's unconscious mind was the God given desire - the greatness which is in every living creature - that said, "I must live." How the tiny brain cells contain such thoughts is another one of the great mysteries, well beyond the comprehension of the wisest of the wise.

> **Special Note**: Although the focus in this chapter is about Jacky Bayne, my thoughts and prayers are also about all the wounded and their loved ones who were present that night and all the others who have been wounded in war and those who were/are affected. Without doubt, Eb and Bunia Bayne felt the same as I do.

Chapter Fourteen

A Mother's Faith
(1967-1974)

◆

She stood steadfast as threatening storms might surely take her away. But her heart would worry not about herself until her offspring was safe.

◆

"For a Mother's heart and a Mother's faith
And a Mother's steadfast love
Were fashioned by the Angels
And sent from God above..."
(Author Unknown)

◆

Her Mission

She had gone to Washington, D.C., with a singular mission. That mission was to bring her son home where she knew he belonged. From the core of her being, she was determined. What she had not known was the extent of her son's injuries. No one had ever told her how badly he had been hurt. Then again, maybe she had known more than she thought. Had she not been told the night she paced the floor at home and felt the pain come from her soul.

Nonetheless, she saw beyond the broken body and realized his spirit was still there. It was trapped away in an abysmal dungeon, but she knew her prayers could make the body better and release all the wonderful things she had once seen in her son. She realized this on a level that others about her could not understand. She somehow knew what others did not know. She believed beyond what even the most faithful believed.

Jacky's mother had assumed her position by his bedside and looked at him with the loving kindness a mother reserves for newborns as she marvels at the new creation. She gently touched him and spoke words ever so lovingly with hope that he might respond. She kept a truly Angelic presence.

It was late into the night when she left his bedside. Early each morning, she found her way back to the same place. She was in continual prayer, openly and silently.

In the part of the country we were from, most people were committed to strong religious beliefs. It was a deeply ingrained part of life. People attended church on Sunday and believed in the words they read in the Good Book. They found strength in difficult times in their faith as had the generations among them who had survived the Great Depression and endured the sacrifices of World War II. They were still connected to Nature and gave thanks for each new day and the many blessings they were provided therein.

Their faith grew each time they exercised it. The kindness, generosity, and genuine concern for others were an extension of and a witness for that which each felt they had been given.

But now, this mother felt that this was the greatest test she might ever face; it would require every ounce of faith she knew she might ever be able to muster. There was a cry from her soul that God might grant this special miracle to her and her gravely wounded son.

She found strength in connections to a consciousness from which we have strayed. We have become spiritually blinded from staring into the bright lights of man's doings. We have learned nothing from the poor moths and other seemingly sacrificial creatures sent as object lessons. We still, in our madness, move in a seemingly meaningless endless circle of our own self-made obsessions.

Still, her presence became somewhat of an annoyance to the medical staff charged with giving her son the continuous attention he needed. More than likely, the staff had seen similar cases before and were somewhat numbed from experience... not in a bad way... they cared greatly for each patient.

The Assessment

The doctors at Walter Reed Hospital had seen the worst of the worst wounds that soldiers suffer. These physicians had more years of experience in this type of medicine than any other teams anywhere on the face of the earth.

They knew the workings of the systems of the body. In this particular case, they had enough information from the reports that had followed Jacky to help reach a conclusion. They also had a body which lay contracted with a mind trapped in a coma, a coma from which there was most likely no escape.

The neurologists knew how the fantastic systems had to work almost perfectly if the wondrous mind of a human was to be able send signals throughout the body to make it work and to connect to the outside consciousness we all share.

This body could not have gone through the trauma of the explosion without extraordinary damage. It had been too long deprived of the lifeblood that gave the nourishment necessary to keep all the neural synapses of the brain firing in order.

Had all but the most elementary functions of the brain been compromised beyond hope? The very learned and experienced staff thought so.

The complexity of it all is simply beyond the comprehension except of the very knowledgeable. Even to the most knowledgeable, there were still the unexplained "whys".

For certain, too much damage had occurred and circumstances were simply too overwhelmingly negative to have any other outlook than that of gloom. The known trauma to the body and the manner in which it now displayed itself was another indication that the motor control mechanisms of the brain were damaged severely.

Some believed they already had seen an extraordinary miracle in the fact that the young soldier was alive and had any brain function at all. To expect more went beyond miracles.

It was an honest, straightforwardly honest, assessment by the medical staff that Jacky Bayne would probably not get better. He might remain for years just as he was now. To add to the dismal prognosis, some malady, seemingly insignificant to others, might be too difficult for his fragile body to survive. The medical staff gathered to work out what to say and how to say it.

"How could they explain it all to the mother?"

They not only had medical concerns, but there was the possibility for political repercussions as well. They bore a heavier burden than most thought. If it got out into the media that everything possible was not being done to make survival possible, then it would be bad news for the military. The military was already getting undue criticism. If there was blame, it should be directed at the politicians. But the politicians, as always, have the ability to scapegoat a situation.

THE BUDDY PLAN

The doctors were very careful in handling the situation from all perspectives. He was still a medical miracle and would be a tremendous learning experience regardless of what they already knew. Nevertheless, they still had to give an honest assessment to the family of this soldier and every other soldier who was a patient in the hospital.

They would call Jacky's family together and give them what they thought was the best information and advice they might offer.

The Face to Face Meeting

It was set. The meeting room was prepared and the medical staff was gathered around the table. All agreed about what was to be said. An orderly had been sent to tell Bunia Bayne that: "The doctors wanted to talk to her."

She acknowledged the request and later was welcomed into a medical staff room with the courtesy which would be extended to a dignitary. She sat down - anxiously awaiting what the team of doctors might tell her.

"Mrs. Bayne," the lead ranking officer began with his hands placed on top of Jacky's medical files, "We have reviewed the case of your son and regretfully, we have concluded... "The prognosis for your son is not good. It is our considered opinion that your son's condition will not improve. We believe he will, for the remainder of his life, need constant care. We are equipped to provide that care."

"Furthermore, we feel that is in your best interest and your family's best interest to return home and continue with your normal life. We will keep you informed on a regular basis as to any change in his condition that might warrant your attention."

"Mrs. Bayne, do you understand?"

"Yes, sir, I understand," she politely replied. "You are telling me my son will never get any better. May I say something to you? I believe there is a greater power than you. I believe He will help my son get better. I believe my son has come back home for a reason."

The medical staff was taken aback by the unexpected reply. No one knew what to say further. The room fell silent.

With a polite nod, Bunia stood and left the room to once again take her position by her son's side and continue her prayerful vigil.

Shortly thereafter, an orderly came into Jacky's room with a lounge chair comfortable enough to rest and to sleep on if necessary. Bunia Bayne had won her argument. She, a mere unlearned country woman armed with her faith, had faced the very learned and experienced medical staff and had come away the victor. She always felt she was in the majority when she made her beliefs known. All indications are, she was. But it was only a minor victory, the real battle was still before her and it seemed there was no end in sight.

The Tear

The days had grown into a month since Jacky had left the field of battle in Vietnam. Bunia was still as relentless as she had been the first day. Her small frame with the true Irish determination would unwaveringly stay the course until there was a conclusion.

One day as she stood over the helpless body, she grasped his rigid hand which had contracted from the damage to the spinal cord. She pleaded with the comatose figure before her, "Jacky, show me a sign you are living, just show me a sign you are alive."

At the moment she finished her plea, a small tear formed in one of his eyes and trickled down his cheek and... shortly thereafter, another tear formed as his eyelids looked as though they had tried to respond. Her heart raced. She choked back her own tears. Were her prayers being answered? "Son, you are going to be okay," she said softly, containing herself as she wiped away tears flowing down her face.

She summoned the duty nurse. "Nurse!" she exclaimed. "There were some tears from his eyes and he tried to open them."

Not sure whether this was a wish or if something significant had actually happened, the nurse approached the bed, gently lifted an eyelid, saw something she clearly had not expected, looked excited and left the room.

Bunia Bayne had seen a sign; the nurse had seen something, too, but even to the faithful, what did it mean? To the medical professionals, it meant all sorts of things. *Some of them could be good. Some of them could be disturbing.*

Would he progress further? Or did it tell the horror of an active mind locked away in an unresponsive body with no hope of escape? Only God knew for sure.

Even in the midst of the new excitement, the reality was that whatever lay ahead was full of more difficulty.

Several days had gone by and there was nothing new and no more signs of tears or anything which gave further hope. *Had it been only an anomaly never to be witnessed again? Was that it?* When Eb Bayne was told, he was visibly shaken and through his tears thanked God that some hope had been visible, but now, all wondered what actually lay ahead. Bunia prayed even harder than she had before.

"I Can Eat Now"

It had been almost a week since Jacky had shown the tears. Bunia still stood watch looking as she always had for any sign of hope. The duty nurse was going about her routine of cleaning the feeding tubes and Bunia, perhaps wishing more than asking a practical question, quizzed the nurse about whether the tubes might ever be removed from her son.

The nurse, a spiritual lady lovingly called Mrs. Sarah, casually replied, "As soon as he is able to eat by himself, ma'am, the tubes will be removed." Maybe the nurse's answer was one designed simply to appease Bunia. She had painfully dealt with patients who had never recovered.

As Ms. Sarah was finishing her routine, total shock filled the room.

THE BUDDY PLAN

"I can eat now," came the muttered labored sound from the frail body. It was a coherent sound! Words! Distinctive words! But for the lack of physical ability, they would have been clear... maybe? He had heard and he had responded!

To Bunia, the miracle she had prayed so intensely for was unfolding! Her son would get better - just as she had known all along.

To the nurse and the medical staff, it was far, far beyond what they had ever expected. *Maybe, just maybe, they had all been wrong.*

Soon, all the medical staff and so many others would know about the miraculous sounds. Medical staff made haste to the room. What they were saying outside the room after they left was unknown. But the atmosphere in the room by all who entered seemed charged to a different level of hope... and amazed disbelief.

Jacky had awakened from the abysmal sleep. It was a small step in his healing process, but it was the gigantic first step that had to take place before anything else could happen. *The brain had not lost abilities that some felt were surely gone forever.*

Through the fog of the re-awakening, the groggy thoughts, "What is my mama doing in Vietnam? She has never flown in a plane. I have been captured and they are playing a trick on me to get me to talk. If I could only get my eyes open." He was all confused. His last clear memory was a look at his dog as they scouted out ahead in the jungles twelve thousand miles away.

Finally, Jacky's eyes opened. "It's really my mama."

"Where am I?" The speech was barely understandable, but to Bunia, it was beyond fantastic!

"You're in the hospital, son," she replied.

Again the speech was groggy and slurred, "Which hospital, Charlotte or Columbia?"

"Son, you're in Walter Reed," she said, not stopping to think he might not know where that was.

"How long have I been here?" He again questioned in labored speech.

Bunia lovingly replied to the whispered speech, "It's a long story."

The wonderful inquisitive mind was working. The speech was lacking clarity, but it was all there. The thoughts were beyond amazingly coherent, but the physical injuries would not let the words come out clearly.

To Bunia, it was all still wonderful!! It was beyond wonderful!!

She had reconnected to a son so many thought was lost forever in an abysmal world of silence. She felt the real presence of the Angels who had watched over the young soldier. The tears rolled down her face. She pulled the glasses from her eyes and wiped away the tears, again and again.

The feeding tubes could be removed soon. Bunia could feed her son. She fed him some applesauce with the loving care and patience a mother gives as she feeds a newborn. It took almost an hour to eat a small bowl of it. But it didn't matter. In each spoonful, she saw further hope.

The word spread. The once hopeless soldier was the talk of the hospital. The good news would not stop there. Others would know. It was soon to be big news outside the hospital. *The Dead Soldier Was Recovering.* The story would be told to the world, literally - a *story that Bunia and Eb Bayne had known nothing about.*

Eb Bayne did not know what had just happened. He had gone back to South Carolina to tend to the family store. He must be told. When the excitement of the moment was finally over and Eb could be contacted, a phone call back to South Carolina would be placed.

"Son, do you feel like talking to someone on the phone?" Bunia asked Jacky.

"Yes," Jacky uttered.

"Hello," Eb said politely as he picked up the receiver back in Fort Mill.

Bunia was on the other end of the line. "Eb, there is someone here who wants to talk to you!" she said excitedly.

Eb was confused and shocked. He had no idea what was taking place. He thought the worst - *his son was dead and they were going to tell him. His heart pounded. He prepared himself.*

His shock deepened as the voice on the other end of the line asked, "Daddy, when are you coming back up here?"

The phone was *deafly silent* for a long moment. Eb Bayne was trying to compose himself. He wanted to speak. The words would not flow.

"Daddy, when are you coming back up here?" Jacky repeated.

Then the reply came through in a tearful voice, "I'll be up there first thing tomorrow; I'll catch the first plane out."

Bunia took the phone from Jacky and finished the conversation. She explained to Eb how all the present miracles had come about and the two tearfully lost the words to provide further conversation.

As soon as Eb Bayne could catch a flight out of Charlotte, NC, he was on his way to Walter Reed. Regardless of the hot August weather, he had donned the black suit his church members had given him.

When Jacky first saw his father, he quipped, "Daddy, you look like a Baptist preacher with that suit on."

As Eb had promised, he found his way back to Washington and so did others who could now witness more than a helpless body lying hopelessly in a bed. Jacky would later recall that even though he was fully unconscious at the time, he felt the presence of his mother and Mrs. Sarah as they worked and watched over him.

Eb came back into Jacky's room one day after a short absence and Jacky said, "Daddy, I'm so mad I can't stand it."

Eb, not knowing what to think, quizzed, "Why is that son?"

"These men came around asking these boys if they wanted to re-up and they didn't ask me," Jacky jokingly answered.

Eb, not to be outdone, "Well son, would you have gone back?"

Jacky, "No, but I wanted them to ask me."

The wonderful sense of humor once again brought sunshine into the room and to the lives of his loved ones who heard the conversation.

One of Jacky's foremost concerns was Bruno. He finally had the courage to ask about his friend and companion. Eb Bayne, as kindly as possible, told him what had happened to Bruno. Jacky's eyes filled with tears, but he graciously accepted the loss.

Nephew Bucky Baker, Ernest Baker's son, paid a visit to Jacky in Washington. One day as he stood near Jacky's bed while Jacky was attempting to communicate, Bucky shook his head as if to acknowledge he understood. Suddenly, all were startled as an apparently frustrated Jacky shouted clearly, "Aw, you don't know nothing boy."

It was a good indication that Jacky was more aware of the goings on than anyone suspected. Jacky did progress to a point where some of the medical staff thought speech therapy might help him communicate better. There is the recollection about one pretty blonde speech therapist. To quote Jacky: "She had so much going for her, except the fact she was from Pennsylvania." For a Southern boy, it is just a little more difficult to understand a Yankee girl. But as usual, the memories of her were pleasant.

No One Had Ever Bothered to Tell Them

Bunia and Eb Bayne had never known the full extent of Jacky's ordeal until Bunia sat down one day in the hospital corridor at Walter Reed. Jacky was now recovering, talking, and receiving limited therapy. His mother now had a chance to go about the hospital and other places for at least short times.

One day, as the staff was working with Jacky, Bunia stepped away from his room and found a soothing place on a bench. Finally, she was coming to the realization that she need not be with her son every moment.

As she sat resting, there seemed to be a constant parade of people moving about who would pause for the slightest moment, stare at her, and then proceed about their business. She had been around the people before and never had this feeling of "being watched". She was becoming uneasy as she glanced around. Perhaps she just looked out of place, she thought. Maybe reading the left behind newspaper might help alleviate some of her uncomfortable feelings. She had not taken time previously to know what was going on outside her own confined world.

As she picked up the paper, the headline, **Dead South Carolina G I will Recover**, shocked her to the depths of her being. She read on with amazement about her son in ward 35 of Walter Reed Hospital.

She had never known that Jacky had been pronounced dead. What the story didn't tell is that he was probably given up for dead on two occasions rather than one as the paper had mentioned. She had not known any of the details which she was now reading in the newspaper.

The story had been published. It had circled the world, but no one had bothered to tell the Baynes. There was talk and people in the hospital looked at Bunia and Eb and made remarks, "Those are his parents." It was a fantastic story and deservedly so, but no one had bothered to tell them. Then again, they were living another miraculous part of it.

As the medical staff made their rounds, Jacky could hear the mumblings and see strange faces looking in on him. Of the mumblings about a soldier being pronounced dead he had overheard, he asked his mother, "Are they talking about me?"

Her reply was, "Yes, son, they are talking about you, but you aren't dead."

Once, in a state of confused thinking, Jacky was adamant about returning to Vietnam. "I have to get back to my men."

The sergeant near him assured him he did not have to return.

"But you don't understand, my men are depending on me and Bruno," Jacky replied with elevated concern.

Finally, after a Colonel confirmed to Jacky that he had completed his mission in Vietnam, Jacky told his father he didn't need to return to Vietnam.

Shortly before Jacky was released to go to the VA Hospital in Columbia, the head nurse, Major Mead, came on the intercom and announced "That she loved all the bums she had been working with, but she was going back to Vietnam." Before she left, she paid Jacky a visit and as she was leaving jokingly demanded that he salute her. Jacky tried to do his best, but his arm would barely move.

"I tried to salute, but I couldn't. I saw a tear roll down her cheek," he later recalled.

The Fan Mail

Soon after Jacky's story appeared in newspapers and magazines all across the United States and around the world, mail started pouring in by the bags, literally. The young shy soldier's story had touched the hearts of people young and old and of all circumstances.

One of the letters wishing him well came from personnel at Elmendorf Air Force base in Anchorage, Alaska. No doubt it was from those who had attended a young soldier from a medical emergency landing on a Mercy Flight from Japan. Perhaps, many there had serious doubts as to his survival even though they had saved his life on that fateful occasion. I can only imagine the relief each felt to know the young patient had survived and each felt blessed to have been a part of a truly amazing story.

There were letters from mothers who had sons in service. There were letters and get-well wishes from grandmothers. And yes, there were letters from the infatuated young girls from all around the globe.

Much to Jacky's chagrin, he was unable to write and could not talk much at a time to allow someone to write for him. As much as he would have loved to have answered each and every letter, it was not possible.

My mother told me that not only had Jacky received letters but Bunia Bayne had received special requests for her prayers. I can certainly understand why.

The Trip to Columbia

Once again, a medical staff decided that Jacky was well enough to travel. He would be going to the Veterans Hospital in Columbia, SC.

This time when Bunia Bayne was asked to sit down with the medical staff, it was under much more pleasant circumstances. Jacky would be discharged from the Army and receive a full pension. Best of all, he would be within an hour and a half drive from his home in Indian Land.

Bunia Bayne would also be able to accompany her son on his flight to his new destination. She was nervous and excited for two reasons now. One, Jacky would be nearer home and two, she had never flown before. But under the circumstances, she would gladly board the aircraft.

Extraordinarily Important

Footnote:
As Bunia Bayne sat and read the news of her son's story, there had to be many obviously glaring questions, none of which might ever receive a satisfactory answer.

Question number one: Why had the Baynes never been told about the extent of their son's injuries and about his "death?"

Other questions: How had this story finally gotten into the media? Somewhere along the way in the paper trail (the medical records), the information had to be reviewed by someone with medical knowledge and in a thorough manner who made a conscious decision to make this information available to the public. Otherwise, it could have and more than likely would have remained hidden away in Jacky's medical files without any public outlet. No one would ever have been any wiser about the details of his ordeal. Who was the person or persons who had given this information to the press? Were there consequences for their decision? Surely, someone in the higher commands could determine who had given the information. Obviously, someone was given a tip and chose to pursue the matter; for without that tip, the world would have been robbed of the story about the miracles of Specialist Jacky Bayne.

There is a sincere thanks to that person or those persons and to the late James K. Batten.

James K. Batten, who was given credit for the initial story, died in 1995 after rising in the ranks to Chairman of the Knight-Ridder newspaper group. He, in turn, had given credit to Bob Dennis for the original tip.

I personally talked to Bob Dennis. He could not remember all the details as to how he had gotten the tip. At the time, he was working for the Rock Hill bureau of the Charlotte Observer. The story was handed over to James K. Batten.

Chapter Fifteen

The Medical Journey Continues
(1967 – 1974)

♦

The journey had already been long and unrelentingly physically painful for Jacky. For those who cared deeply about him, it had been and continued to be emotionally draining, but it must be endured, if not, all would be lost; that cannot be.

♦

In November of 1967, Bunia Bayne boarded an aircraft for the first time in her life. Her son's stretcher had been secured on the "Nightingale Flight" and she and the medical attendants found their seats nearby and readied for takeoff.

Clearance was received from the tower personnel; the aircraft rolled down the runway at Andrews Air Force base and was soon climbing into the crisp clear blue sky. From a distance above, the city below looked deceptively peaceful. It was anything but peaceful and the years to come would see even further political division.

Bunia Bayne would continue her vigil by her son's side as she had done for seemingly endless hours in Walter Reed Hospital in Washington while awaiting the miracle she knew would occur.

She and her family could leave behind the traffic and turmoil of a city foreign to them and head for a place closer to home. It was the beginning of another journey and at the same time, the continuation of a long and painful one ahead with origins in the fields of a faraway country. No one knew for sure where it might eventually lead. The path thus far had led to successes that no one, except the ever faithful mother, had ever imagined.

What she could never leave behind were the horrors of her first view, late that particular night, of her gravely injured son as he lay helpless and seemingly hopeless on his stretcher with tubes and bandages abounding. Nor would she ever forget the sea of other wounded and maimed she saw the same night as they were unloaded from the ambulances. Her heart went out to all of those she had seen as well as a very special concern for those who loved them. The night had seemed so surreal, but the real images were deeply etched into her memory.

She certainly could never forget the conversation with the medical staff when she was told her son might live to be fifty, but he would never communicate with the world again. She felt deeply within her being they were wrong and she was right. She and her faith had prevailed.

What would glow on in her being were the facts of the miracles she truly believed would happen and she then witnessed. The happiness of the day when her son awakened from the abysmal coma and spoke to her just as she had hoped and constantly prayed he would always do - this would remain and comfort her until her last days on earth.

In less than a couple of hours, the plane would touch down in Columbia, just fifty miles away from her home in Indian Land. It was also the city of Fort Jackson, the place where Jacky had entered the Army just over a year earlier.

It was close enough for family and friends to visit on a regular basis. It was close enough that maybe, just maybe, Jacky might be well enough someday to go home. How far away such a milestone was – no one knew.

There was no doubt that people who were aware of the initial miracles of Jacky's survival might now believe he had clear sailing for the remainder of his life. **He was far from a stable recovery that would guarantee him a significant lifespan. There were all sorts of seemingly harmless maladies (to the normal person) which might set his progress back or stop it all together. He was still extraordinarily deep in the forest as far as recovery was concerned.**

The Veterans Hospital, Columbia, SC

A story which ran in one of Jacky's home state newspapers best describes the situation with him after he reached the VA Hospital in Columbia: "John L. 'Buck' Smith, Administrative Assistant to the Chief of Staff, says, "I wouldn't have bet you two cents on his recovery when he was admitted. He had suffered massive neurological damage, no doubt from a lack of oxygen during those hours he was unconscious. We had absolutely no idea what to expect."

Despite the pessimistic assessment, Jacky was getting better - just as Bunia Bayne had predicted. However, how much progress he might make at this hospital was still anyone's guess. He had begun to eat better, but he was still a frail specimen who weighed only eighty pounds and lay on his left side.

He was gradually beginning to become fully aware of the world in which he now existed. He had escaped the hellish dungeon of the coma. *He could not escape the new reality that he had to fight a body so badly damaged that it would not respond to any of his commands. It would do nothing of the sort regardless of his best efforts.*

Tremendously difficult times were ahead. His body seemed to be in rebellion. The nerves and muscles wanted to act without any consent from Jacky. There would be long hours of therapy and operations and more therapy - a seemingly endless cycle.

Some beyond miraculous happenings had allowed his mind to survive intact. The wonderful memory and personality had not been squashed by the awful explosion. The grin and quick wit were recovering at an unbelievable rate and to a level that caused doctors to marvel more than they already had. He became the subject of medical conversations and writings shared among medical professionals.

Although the motor nerves were damaged beyond total repair, there were some therapies which might help to some degree, how much ever that might be.

Even with all of the problems Jacky faced, he wanted desperately to go home this first Christmas after his injury. There is little doubt that Bunia and Eb Bayne prayed for this to happen as well. It would be a magnificent celebration. No, not in gifts and presents wrapped under a tree; it would be a magnificent celebration of the second greatest gift they could imagine, the return of their son from the hostile fields of a foreign country.

The following is excerpted from a story by the Associated Press on December 23rd, 1967: **"Dead Soldier Has The Flu"** - COLUMBIA, S.C. (AP) "Jacky Bayne, the young soldier pronounced dead in Vietnam but revived by an embalmer, hopes to spend Christmas day with his parents away from Columbia Veterans Hospital. His doctors will permit the one-day leave 'if his slight temperature comes down.' Bayne has an infection and mild case of the flu.

Hospital officials say Bayne is making steady progress, talks well for short periods but still had not been told everything about that July day. Bayne also hasn't yet been formally awarded a Bronze Star he earned for 'meritorious service' in Vietnam."

With the determination he had shown to survive, Jacky made it home for Christmas. He spent the day at his sister's house along with the families and they had a joyous time. He did go back to Columbia to spend the night, but it was at the home away from home which his parents were renting to be close to their son. He was confined to a stretcher for the event, but there was the familiarity of the home out of the confinement of a hospital setting. This lifted the spirits of the entire family.

After the delightful Christmas, the reality of the situation once again had to be faced. In February 1968, an article in the *Florence Morning News* describes his medical condition: **"Soldier Fights Brain Damage"** - *Columbia, SC (AP)* — "Jacky Bayne, who eluded death in Vietnam, is now fighting a different enemy—brain damage.

Doctors at the Veterans Administration Hospital in Columbia describe Jacky's condition as cerebral encephalopathy, a general term for brain damage.

In Jacky's case, the malady had affected his memory and his coordination, leaving him with pronounced tremors.

The Fort Mill soldier was brought to the hospital in November from Walter Reed Army hospital where he was sent from Vietnam... Army Records do not show how long he was deprived of oxygen, but doctors say it was long enough to cause damage to the brainstem where the brain connects with the spinal cord.

Dr. Harry Zankel, chief of physical medicine and rehabilitation at the VA hospital, says in extended periods of unconsciousness, the body tends to draw up in a fetal position, muscles contracted.

When Jacky sleeps, his arms are crossed over his chest, his hands are drawn down and his left leg is drawn up. His right leg was amputated above the knee.

Doctors have set up a daily routine for Jacky to get back on his feet, literally.

Jacky gets corrective therapy exercises from F.E. Huskey.

'He does what he can,' Huskey said, 'and we assist him the rest of the way. We work with him to get him to go through all the range of motions in all planes to strengthen and stretch his muscles.'"

Jacky's struggles continued, but he made more progress. Another article in a South Carolina paper in July 1968, noted this progress: **"S.C. G I Is Recovering After Death"** - Columbia (AP) – "Jacky Bayne, the soldier who came back from the dead, is slowly regaining his health at the Veterans Hospital in Columbia and would like to attend college someday, perhaps the University of South Carolina."

He still spends most of his time in a wheelchair. One of his legs was badly injured when a land mine exploded. 'However, his improvement has been phenomenal,' says Buck Smith, administrative assistant to the hospital chief of staff.

The 23 year old expects to return soon to his parents' home at Fort Mill to stay. Smith agrees he will do so. Already, Bayne has been making trips home on some weekends.

Nervous tremors that plagued him when he first came to the Veterans Hospital Nov. 4, 1967, no longer are evident and he has regained much of his weight from a low of 70 pounds during his ordeal."

All of this was good news indeed and Jacky had even reached the point that he could become feisty on occasion. Once while he was receiving therapy, the big therapist, according to Jacky, was being too rough.

"What is wrong, soldier?" the therapist asked as he saw Jacky beginning to cry.

Jacky was quick to respond, "I'm so mad at you I would hit you if I could lift my arm."

The therapist looked at Jacky and laughed.

Not to be outdone, Jacky laughed back at him.

From that time forward, the two became the best of friends.

Was it planned by the therapist and those who taught them to handle their patients in a somewhat "rough" manner? Was it planned to keep them from feeling sorry for themselves? It had worked quite well in this situation.

Jacky Loses His "Best Friend"

In 1968, those who knew Eb Bayne began to notice a significant change in his outgoing personality. The man who had passed on a superb sense of humor to his son, which had benefitted everyone during Jacky's struggle, was now, for some reason, less and less jovial himself. He was not as outgoing as he had always been before. Had the stress of the ordeal caught up with him or was there something else more seriously wrong?

Stress might have been the answer, but Eb's frequent doctor visits indicated something more serious. Eb and Bunia were not broadcasting Eb's malady. They feared, and rightfully so, that worrying about his father's condition might seriously affect Jacky's progress.

There was little doubt the secret about Eb's condition could not be kept for too long. They would find a satisfactory time to tell Jacky, just not yet.

In 1970, Eb was admitted to the same hospital where Jacky was still a patient. It was a strange set of events. The man who had been a pillar of strength to his wife during these particularly difficult times now himself lay deathly ill. He was now an old man well beyond his years.

Jacky's father qualified for medical care at a Veteran's hospital because he had served in WW I, as had his brothers. Jacky was a late-in-life child of Eb and Bunia Bayne.

Eb and Bunia had lost a young son when the child was about two years old. Eb had lost his first wife while his daughters by her were still youths. Bunia helped to raise the two young girls. He had since lost one of his daughters.

The two people who meant most to Bunia were now in the same hospital. One was making remarkable progress. She realized the other would not recover at all. Again, she would need to reach deep into her being to gather more strength... she would.

Jacky was rolled in a wheelchair to another section of the hospital to his father's room. It might seem a cruel twist of fate, but then again, was it not a blessing that Jacky was able to see his father up close and be with him and each feel the other's presence? Jacky could share some of his best friend's last earthly moments.

As pain ravaged his body, Eb sensed his own time was near. He asked that others simply go away and let him die in peace. He had escaped the first war he knew unscathed, but this one, of which he was only a bystander, might have help exact a toll on him.

The witty and gentle man who had experienced a painful life in many respects, passed from this earth on February 5th, 1970. He could now know peace.

Jacky was mobile enough to attend his father's funeral in Fort Mill. One of the few times I have ever seen Jacky without a smile was at his father's funeral. It was strange. As he looked out the back window of the long car, I caught a lengthy glimpse. The puzzled distraught look from his face seemed to be one of despair. The image still haunts. It is still clear. He looked as though he had just said goodbye to his best friend... he had.

As a young boy, Jacky had been taken to school by his father and his father's store was his afternoon retreat. An elderly family friend shared the task of keeping an eye on Jacky. They sat and played checkers there and the friendship grew. It would be easy to imagine Jacky learning to be a competitive checker player. Such was his nature.

Jacky fondly remembered the days when his father watched him play little league baseball. Evidently, his father helped him to develop a strong love for the game. Jacky was an excellent baseball player in high school. He still loves to watch baseball on television.

There is little doubt that he will always remember one of his father's "last at bats for him." Eb's persistence prevented doctors at the VA Hospital from removing Jacky's troublesome remaining leg.

Jacky's father's death was very hard to accept. He was concerned about the effect on his mother as well. Even the medical progress he had so miraculously made appeared to be at a standstill because of his father's passing. Somehow, some way, he would overcome this as well.

November 4, 1970

Jacky was officially discharged from the Veterans Hospital in Columbia. Of course he would be back for treatment when necessary and he could come back for everyday care if the need be. Medically, he had improved to a point that he could now decide his times spent in the hospital.

The VA granted him $12,500 toward the purchase of a special house adapted to accommodate a wheelchair. He would receive $1,143 a month from the VA as compensation. "I don't lack for much of anything," he admitted.

Jacky had endured operations to correct serious problems. He also had kidney stones removed and had weathered a whole host of other treatments and physical therapies.

He would go home, for the most part, to the care of his mother or aides who were paid for by the Veterans Administration. Bunia Bayne was an older lady now and she began to have health problems of her own. She was simply not able to give Jacky the care he needed.

Henry Stegall, his wife Minnie, and others were of as much assistance as they possibly could be. As Bunia's health finally deteriorated to a point she could no longer care for him, Jacky went back to the Veterans Hospital.

Was there more to all of this than anyone at the moment could realize?

Friends and Visitors

Among the many whom Jacky had befriended while at the hospital was the chef at the VA Hospital. The chef asked Jacky what he wanted for his twenty-third birthday, also in July.

"I have heard of something called a Baked Alaska, but I don't know what it is. I'd like to have one of them," Jacky told the chef.

"Tell you what I'll do, I'll make you one of them," he replied.

Jacky responded, "Well, can you make me two?" This was a typical response from Jacky, forever cunningly playful.

Jacky celebrated his twenty-third birthday with the sugary dessert and a wide grin on his freckled face. He was happy.

Because of such treats, and the fact that his parents had brought him fast food on occasion, he was beginning to gain weight. He still had some more to gain to be back to normal, but his appetite was getting better along with all the other progress he was making. The doctors did eventually advise Bunia that it might be better if they watched his diet.

Lieutenant Ian Jones

When Jacky reached Vietnam and decided to be a dog handler, he chose one of the dogs that had been part of the unit which had been formed at Fort Benning, GA, and then shipped to Vietnam. The original commander of the unit was 1LT. Ian Jones.

Lieutenant Jones was now in Columbia. When he discovered Jacky was nearby, he decided to pay him a visit. One day, much to Jacky's surprise, Lieutenant Jones appeared in front of him. He had, like any good platoon leader would do, come to see one of his men who had been injured. As was expected, it brought a delightful heartfelt grin to Jacky's face.

Like Jacky, Ian Jones was a huge baseball fan - so the conversation was lively about baseball teams. Jacky has historically been a Dodger fan and except for the fact that Lieutenant Jones was a die-hard Yankee fan, the conversation would have been cordial. Actually, Jacky liked many of the Yankee players. For some reason, he didn't pull for the team. That was especially true if they were playing the Dodgers.

Jacky missed viewing his first World Series in a long time in 1967, but it was for a good reason.

General William Westmoreland

Not often is a soldier visited by the commanding general, but such was the case when General Westmoreland heard about Jacky at the Veterans Hospital. There is little doubt that he also paid the other soldiers there a visit as well. General Westmoreland was a home grown South Carolinian.

He was born in Spartanburg County, South Carolina, and attended the United States Army Military Academy at West Point and graduated first in his class in 1936. He had distinguished himself as a combat leader in WW II.

He was given command of U.S. forces in Southeast Asia in 1964. The war there escalated under his command but he was optimistic about an eventual U.S. victory. The TET Offensive by the communist brought problems for the general who had to shoulder the blame for underestimating the strength and abilities of the communist forces in South Vietnam. They had, without warning, launched a series of attacks all over South Vietnam. American casualties soared into the hundreds each week as the fighting raged.

Television brought it all into the living rooms of the American public each night as they sat for an evening meal. Support for the war was waning and student protests mounted.

General Westmoreland was replaced as commander of U.S. forces. The timing of the move was suspicious.

The famed Army general eventually came back to his beloved state of South Carolina. His thoughts of entering politics were dampened by his connection to the Vietnam War.

He confided in Jacky that he could have actually won the war had he not been so constrained politically. He had believed, and still believed as any general might, that his strategies would have brought success in Vietnam.

A man who was concerned about the loss of Bruno gave Jacky a dog that looked eerily similar to Jacky's Vietnam companion. A former dog handler like himself, who had also been wounded in Vietnam, also paid a visit. Although the former dog handler was confined to a wheelchair, he traveled about the country visiting and speaking.

There were many others; all were very special to Jacky.

Footnote:
If reporters were going to speak to any of the veterans, the staff preferred that it was Jacky. He was once asked to give up a weekend pass (to go home) so he might entertain questions from reporters. The staff knew he would also say good things about them. Such was Jacky's true nature.

Chapter Sixteen

Jacky Meets Another Angel
(1950s - 1970s)

♦

May an Angel care for your every need
And comfort you with kindness at soul's depth.

♦

Neither Angel had ever met the other... or had they met in ways not known to the conscious mind?

♦

Patsy Lane

In Lancaster, South Carolina, in the 1950s, a young five year old girl named Patsy Lane experienced the realities of having an emotionally troubled father. Although he posed no threat to any particular member of the family, his problems bore consequences for the entire family.

Her father, a veteran of World War II, now found himself unable to cope with the memories of what had happened to him and his comrades. At times, he was unable to keep the painful horrors suppressed. When they surfaced, the resulting behavior made it necessary for him to seek professional help. He actually reached the point of *clinical paranoia.*

Joe Lane, Patsy's father, had been one of only five survivors of a troop ship which had been attacked and sunk by the Japanese in the Pacific Ocean. The absolute horrors of the initial tragedy and then the seemingly hopeless struggle to cheat certain death a second time as they floated helplessly in the unbelievably dangerous waters had to be forever stamped deeply into their psyches – so much so that horrific flashes of the events would frequently battle their conscious minds in an attempt to control their everyday thoughts and behavior. Their minds would never escape the constant extraordinary turmoil created by their horrendous experiences.

Young Patsy could not understand why the blinds were always pulled in her father's room as well as most of the home. She could not understand why her father never left the house at times. The young mind had neither the knowledge nor capacity to comprehend the reasons for her father's behavior. But she did assuredly know one thing - she was the proverbial "apple of her father's eye." She would remain that treasure until his passing and she would reciprocate unconditionally with her love.

Her father was able to work for a time at a small restaurant near Fort Lawn, SC. He cooked there and occasionally the family would drive the short distance to share a meal with him. Her mother worked at the local textile plant, as did many from the area. Lancaster was primarily a textile town and a large percentage of the population was employed in the mills.

By the age of fourteen, Patsy was the sole driver in the family. She had taken on a new responsibility. Most teenagers who get their driver's license see such an achievement as a new found freedom, but Patsy's situation called for it to be an obligation. Indeed, it was.

Her father Joe and those about him realized that his condition had not improved and most likely would not get better without professional help. He was finally admitted to a veterans hospital closest to Lancaster that provided the type of care Joe Lane needed. He was evaluated by the VA in Columbia and sent to another VA hospital in Augusta, GA.

THE BUDDY PLAN

Her mother felt that Patsy's father's condition was not so severe to warrant the strict confined treatment offered in Augusta. She once again petitioned the doctors at the VA Hospital in Columbia for him to be approved for treatment in a less restrictive environment. His situation was reviewed and he was sent to Salisbury, NC, which was over seventy-five miles away.

To compound the problem, Patsy, who was only fourteen at the time her father first started treatment in Salisbury in 1963, was not supposed to operate a motor vehicle in North Carolina. However, all turned out well because she was never stopped by a highway patrolman.

While her father was in treatment, Patsy, her mother, and older brother would go to Salisbury each weekend to visit him. Sometimes her father would welcome them and at other times he might turn them away. Not upset in any manner, Patsy's mother would simply say, "That's okay. We will be back next week and we'll see you then." Regardless, if Joe changed his mind, Patsy's mother remained steadfast in her decision and she and the children would head back to South Carolina.

There were times when Joe just might decide to go home without anyone's permission. He would plan an *escape* from the hospital, make his way to the main roadway and hitchhike home. The hospital would call several hours after they discovered him missing. Geneva Lane, his wife, would tell the hospital officials she was aware of his *escape* because he was safety stowed away in his room. He usually managed to get home about thirty minutes before the notification.

Joe was a good man. He was ornery at times, but he liked people and was good to those who treated him with respect. In his earlier years, there had been "some trying episodes."

He had been discharged from the Army after WW II.

Somehow, he had found a way to reenlist and was sent to Europe as part of the post-war occupational forces where he was assigned duties as a cook and performed exceptionally well.

But all was not to stay well with the assignment. Joe and some of his buddies decided to celebrate one weekend. During their celebration, they became mischievous - well, a lot more than just mischievous. They commandeered an idle streetcar and during their joyride, they managed to turn the streetcar over.

Each was arrested. In the case of Joe, when the Army records were checked during his disciplinary proceedings, it was determined that he should not have been in the Army at all. Rather than suffer an embarrassment, the Army decided to discharge him once again and send him home.

Geneva Lane had petitioned the VA Hospital in Columbia several times before Joe was finally accepted there for treatment. A particular doctor on the staff thought Joe could be treated in Columbia.

"Mrs. Lane, I will assure you that your husband should be treated in Columbia, and as soon as I am able, I will see that takes place," the doctor told her.

In the mid-1960s, the doctor who had promised Joe help was promoted to Chief of Staff and held firm to his promise.

Little did anyone know at the time how fateful a decision Joe's assignment to Columbia would turn out to be for Joe, his daughter, and a young Vietnam Veteran. Had all those circumstances not worked as they did, then a whole host of other circumstances would have been all-together different. But there were still other things which had to be written into the script to ensure all the elements necessary were present for what eventually would take place.

THE BUDDY PLAN

After high school, Patsy Lane went to work at The Celanese Corporation of America in Rock Hill. It was not a bad drive to and from work. Besides, the job paid well and provided medical benefits and was considered a prized gem for local workers.

Patsy's immediate supervisor was a man from Fort Mill named Henry Stegall. Henry had served in the Navy during World War II. He also had another role he played. In the late 1960s, he took on the role of a caregiver of sorts for a young wounded soldier, now veteran, named Jacky Bayne.

One day Henry Stegall approached Patsy and asked her if she knew Jacky Bayne. Henry had discovered that Patsy's father was a patient at the VA Hospital in Columbia and he wanted Patsy to pay Jacky a visit while she was there to see her father.

"No, sir, but my daddy does," she replied

Henry quizzed her again, "How does your daddy know Jacky?"

Patsy responded, "Every time he (Jacky) was on TV, my daddy called me and said 'come look at the boy from Vietnam.' I told daddy I'm not interested in that boy. I'm glad he's back and everything, but I'm not interested."

Henry was unrelenting in quizzing Patsy about visiting Jacky when he saw her at work each week. Each time he asked, Patsy gave the same resounding, "No!"

There was a somewhat strange turn of events one Sunday afternoon at the Veterans Hospital in Columbia. Patsy and her mother were visiting her father and while standing in the yard, Henry saw them and came by to speak. Patsy introduced the three.

Henry again asked her if she would go by and see Jacky. He had just brought him back to the hospital.

Joe Lane spoke up and said, "She will, I will make sure she does."

Even though Joe knew of Jacky quite well, he had never met him face to face.

Jacky Says Goodbye to One Angel

In the bitter sweetness of the now well-functioning mind, Jacky had gained the ability once again to realize fully the world about him. It had all changed so drastically. The once vibrant, witty, athletic, life-loving individual must now play another role. Gone were so many of the physical attributes which had allowed him do the things he so dearly loved.

The birth mother who had given him life once again and cared for his every need was now sick in a hospice fifty miles away from Columbia in Rock Hill and it was becoming evident that her condition would not improve.

The pain and anguish of the possibility of losing the one who had given the spiritual strength to the entire situation was almost overwhelming. Jacky would need to reach still deeper into his own inner being to rally what strengths he might have left.

Had his mother accomplished her final mission; her first mission being to have brought the young soldier to the earth in the first place? What was to happen now? The questions were beginning all over again; the uncertainty of a new seemingly impossible situation weighed heavily on his now miraculously functioning mind. As before his injuries, he could sense all the range of emotions that he had once felt.

Henry Stegall took Jacky to the hospice in Rock Hill to see his mother on occasion, but this time when Jacky went to see her, there was an ominous sign that she was fast slipping away.

From his wheelchair, Jacky reached out with his hand which had now grown strong enough to grasp his

THE BUDDY PLAN

mother's. He felt her loving fingers. They had shrunk and her hand was not the same as the one which had wiped his forehead and reached out to care for his every need as he lay helpless for months. The hand which had fed him as a child and had so joyously given his first bites of food after he had awakened from the dismal coma and the hand which had transferred the spiritual energy to hold on and to have the courage to awaken from a dreaded sleep was missing the warmth and strength it once possessed.

Jacky could sense the same loving spirit he had felt when his mother walked into his room at Walter Reed Hospital, even though he was not physically conscious to acknowledge her presence, slipping away.

Jacky, in a solemn tone, said, "Mama, I love you."

In a weakened voice, his mother struggled to ask, "Eb?"

Bunia Bayne then drifted away into her own labored sleep and there was no further conversation.

Jacky looked again at the loving face that had twice given him life and sadly turned away, tears pouring from his eyes, and agreed to be taken back to his home in Indian Land.

The short journey was solemn.

Jacky was pushed in his wheelchair into the house where he had planned to rest for the night and tomorrow determine what he needed to do about the new hurdles he would soon face. His mind was racing with thoughts of his mother.

In a few short moments after he had returned home, Jacky's aunt came into the house, approached him and in a tearful tone said, "Jacky, your mother has passed away."

He quietly acknowledged the words and hung his head in despair as he was handed a handkerchief to wipe away the tears.

It was as though fate had dealt another difficult hand and he must bear the brunt of it, this time alone. His parents were gone and he would now be in the care of friends, relatives, and orderlies. The friends and relatives must have their own lives. Perhaps the visits would grow less regular. Perhaps he would face the same forgotten loneliness that others in the hospitals and soldiers' homes faced.

Henry quietly consoled Jacky and told him that they needed to go back to the hospice and make all the arrangements for his mother.

The Angel in mother's form who had brought him through the seemingly impossible and lent spiritual strength to all those about her was now gone. The doctor told Jacky that he had done all he could possibly do for her and that her last moments were painless.

Jacky felt comfort in knowing that even though his mother had gone from her earthly home, she would soon have her place in Heaven alongside her beloved husband Eb.

Did Bunia Bayne somehow know that it would be okay if she finally rested? Did she somehow know that she could relinquish her earthly duties to someone who would be just as faithful and unrelenting in her devotion to her son as she had been?

THE BUDDY PLAN

The First Meeting

Four days before the death of his mother, as Jacky sat reading the sports columns in the newspaper as he often did, a young lady appeared in the doorway of his ward one Sunday morning. She was not wearing a nurse's uniform. Perhaps she had lost her way. Jacky had not seen her before.

He looked up from his paper as she asked, "Are you Jacky Bayne?"

The startled Jacky, with a slight grin on his face replied, "Yes, I am."

"I am Patsy Lane." She explained that she had come by to see him on the suggestion of Henry Stegall.

They made small talk. Patsy told him she had a father at the hospital and she and her family made the trip to Columbia each weekend. Jacky wanted to know more about her along with the answer to one special question.

"Are you married?" he blurted out. Where had the shyness gone?

Patsy replied that she was not. Her answer brought a smile to Jacky's face – an exceptionally large one.

They made more small talk and Patsy, before she left, promised Jacky she would keep in touch with him. She did.

Patsy soon found out about Jacky's mother. She had wanted to go see Jacky when his mother passed away. "Maybe that would not be right. Maybe people would talk." She didn't know for sure. After all, the two had just met. She did call and express her deep-felt sympathy. She was truly concerned for him. She wanted to attend the funeral, but she didn't. She had wanted to meet Jacky's mother, but she didn't, *or had she?*

She sent Jacky cards and they talked on the phone and the friendship blossomed.

Joe Lane finally decided he, too, wanted to meet Jacky Bayne face to face. He wanted to know more about this young man who was talking frequently with his beloved daughter. He had seen him on television and read much about him in the newspapers. They were in the same hospital but had never met. So one day, Joe asked one of the patients called Sarge, "Do you know Jacky Bayne? I want to meet him."

Sarge replied, "Of course I know Jack the Ripper." Sarge had assigned that name to Jacky for some unknown reason.

Sarge took it upon himself to find Jacky. It turned out that the three actually met in the hallway, whereupon Sarge stopped and stated to Jacky, "I want you to meet Mr. Joe Lane."

"Joe, this is Jack the Ripper," Sarge said.

Jacky looked up and told Joe, "I'm glad to meet you Mr. Lane."

Joe said, "You can call me Joe."

To which Jacky replied, "Yes, sir, Mr. Lane."

Each grinned and a friendship had begun.

One day as Jacky and Patsy talked, she broke the news. "My daddy will be going home soon."

But there was also the promise. "If you have to stay here for a long time, I'll come by on the weekends and spend some time with you."

Jacky told her, "I think I will be going home soon myself and I was thinking about coming to see you."

In fact, he soon would be able to be cared for at home.

As Patsy was readying to go, she reached out and took Jacky's hand and said, "Take care of yourself."

Fearing that an opportunity might be lost if he failed to act decisively, Jacky pulled her close and kissed her as though it was a forever last kiss.

THE BUDDY PLAN

Neither quite knew how to act. Patsy smiled and walked from the room. Jacky grinned and felt as though he had just kissed a girl for the first time.

Patsy was greeted by her mother in the yard of the hospital and her mother knew something had happened to change the course of future events in this relationship.

She looked at her daughter and matter-of-factly stated to her, "You got it bad."

Patsy, surprised that she was broadcasting her feelings, replied coyly, "Got what bad?"

Patsy's mother quickly responded, "You are falling for that man."

Patsy knew she might as well face the music and so she turned to her father who she had always trusted so well and asked, "Daddy, what do you think of this?"

In all of Joe's seemingly disconnections from reality at times, there were times when his conversations made perfectly good sense and were profound. None were more evident than at this time when he laid everything on the line for Patsy.

He cleared his throat and with a very serious tone began to speak, "Sweetheart, there's one thing I am going to tell you about this, and I don't think you are that kind, but I have heard some women say, 'If I had known this, I would never have gotten involved.' You know that man's situation. You know he is going to need help and he is going to need loving. I hate to tell you this, but Jacky is probably not going to get any better, but if you love him, go for it."

Patsy's greatest supporter had given his blessings, but he also had given his conditions to her.

"I don't want you to ever come into my house and say I can't handle this. I don't think you will. He needs a wife to take care of him. I will accept him and he will be a part of this family," he continued.

There is absolutely no doubt that Patsy had given all of this the depth of thought she knew it took. She was aware of the consequences of her decisions. Patsy Lane had long been a woman beyond her age. After all, this role in which she had been cast required a person as special as she was.

Joe's sobering words were right on target. He had accepted Jacky as much as Patsy and her mother had accepted him. Jacky and Joe had already developed a friendship that proved beneficial to both. Jacky would help Patsy's father exit his self-imposed exile from society.

Indeed, Jacky proved to be some of the best therapy Joe had received anywhere. They shared the horrors of what wars do to individuals. The bonds of comradeship were deeply established. Most importantly, they shared the love of a very wonderful person who gave special comfort to each in her own unique way.

Jacky was officially released again from the hospital in 1974. He could stay at home while attendants who worked shifts would provide care for him. He also had someone special who came by to see him and give additional care. Patsy stopped by his house each day on her way home from work.

The particular and very concerned Patsy was at times upset when she reached her home in Lancaster. She would cry because she felt Jacky was not receiving proper attention. She often saw him in the winter time when he might only have a short sleeve shirt on. In all fairness, sometimes that was all he required.

It was also during this time that Jacky needed surgery on his kidney to remove stones. The stones had become so problematic that it posed a serious problem, so much so that there was the real possibility of losing a kidney.

The kidney bled continuously. Finally after three days, the discharge from his kidney cleared and the critical time passed and he would not lose the organ.

Patsy had taken him to the hospital in Charlotte where the operation was to take place. She was by his side at this time (1975) giving Jacky the Angelic support he had been so accustomed to before his mother had passed away.

Special Footnote:

In 1983, Patsy's father suffered a massive heart attack. In spite of the best efforts of the emergency and hospital staff, he passed away. Patsy Lane lost the man who had adored her throughout her life. She had reciprocated that love as only a daughter can love a father.

Rest in peace Joe and thank you for your service.

Chapter Seventeen

"The Adoption"
(1967-1970s)
The Role and Story of Henry Stegall

♦

"I will extend my hand to you in our time of need. For we will both be better because of it."

♦

The Visit
April 1967
(Partly Dramatized)

"Gunny, I think we need to make a left turn on Holbrook just ahead."

"Affirmative, Sir."

"Then we have less than a mile and we'll make a right turn on Hamlin and we veer off that road to the left and that should take us there."

"There" was the end of the country road where a neatly kept yard adorned with flowers with a well maintained modest brick house sat. In the house lived the parents of Lindell Ray "Butch" Stegall and their two other children.

"I think this is it, Gunny," the captain solemnly stated to the sergeant as they doubled checked the address where they had arrived.

"I believe you are correct, sir," was the reply.

"Are you ready?"

"Yes, sir."

Of all the duty in the armed services, this was perhaps the worst of all. Combat may have been easier than what they were about to do. Like so many other duties in the Marines, someone is chosen to do it,

THE BUDDY PLAN

trained to do it exceptionally well, and then carry out that duty.

The two Marines exited their Marine Corps issued vehicle and walked in their military gait to the front porch. Each assumed a proper position. The knock on the door was short and firm.

Soon the door was answered by Henry Stegall. He looked squarely at the two Marines as they stood there in their green dress uniforms. Sensing what he was about to be told, he summoned his wife Minnie. They stood as one as the Marine Captain asked, "Are you Mr. and Mrs. Henry Stegall? Are you the parents of Lindell Ray Stegall?"

The utterance by Henry Stegall of, "Yes, we are" was wrapped in the shock of the moment.

"Mr. and Mrs. Stegall, we regret to inform you that your son has been killed in action in Vietnam. We extend the condolences of the President of the United States and the Commandant of the United States Marine Corps."

With those words, the worst dread for the family was realized.

The Enlistment

The year was 1966. The Vietnam War was gradually increasing in the number of casualties it was producing. The conflict had developed into a full-fledged shooting war with the U.S. combat role expanding daily. The United States was, at that same moment, preparing for an even bigger troop commitment. Eventually the buildup would be more than half a million men in the small country in Southeast Asia.

The Selective Service was reinstated and men of draft age and circumstance were being inducted into the armed services. Young Butch Stegall had no need to worry about being selected and sent away to war.

He was only seventeen years of age.

At age seventeen, the military would accept a young recruit if the parents agreed to the action. Butch Stegall wanted to join the Marine Corps. He wanted to be part of what was going on in Vietnam and made this clear to his parents. He was persistent, very persistent.

They finally gave in to his requests and soon he was off to the training station at Parris Island, South Carolina. He would be put through some of the most demanding basic combat training that military recruits anywhere suffer. He would return home in a few weeks proudly wearing a Marine uniform. There was little doubt Butch would make the rounds showing off that uniform. He had made the grade and had become one of a select group who called themselves Marines.

He had returned home a 17 year old man, but the leave would be short. Soon, he was off to complete more training which would further prepare him for his next assignment, more than likely a line unit in Vietnam. He had been assigned an MOS 0311. That was short for "Military Occupational Specialty" and the 0311 meant he was a rifleman.

Final Return Home

Unfortunately, from that assignment, Butch Stegall's next trip home would be altogether different. It would be in a flag-draped coffin. The Marine Corps took great pride in the details of ensuring their fallen were honored. They would help the Stegalls with all the details. They had but one request of them: "Because of the nature of the wounds, it would be best not to view the body." The local funeral director concurred and suggested the Stegalls accept the advice from the Marine Corps.

THE BUDDY PLAN

Henry Stegall told them with absolute certainty, "I have to see the body. I have to know my son is home." His insistence was enough to allow him his wishes. He later told others that, "It was the hardest thing I ever had to do." The only consolation was that Butch's body was intact enough for his face to be recognized. The view of the body had given Henry Stegall some closure, but only for the moment.

Each set of eyes at the gathering looked solemnly on as the somber-faced Marines approached the flag-draped coffin, took a position on either end, lifted the American Flag and began the ceremonious folding. Each movement was completed with pride, precision, and care. Each fold brought a short pause to honor the purpose for that particular fold (a purpose relative to each service branch's interpretation).

The final salutes were given, and one of the white gloved Marines kneeled, extended the exquisitely folded flag to the parents and stated, "On behalf of the President of the United States, the Commandant of the Marine Corps, and a grateful nation, please accept this flag as a symbol of our appreciation for your loved one's service to Country and Corps."

The lone bugler stood a distance away from the burial site as TAPS began. The first note pierced the otherwise silent air of the spring like day. Each note thereafter pierced into the depths of those who could not help but listen intently. No one in the crowd was spared from the heart ravaging emotions of the moment. Each note brought a new tear for some and a stream of tears for others.

As always, the Marines had given a stellar performance from the depth of their being. A fellow Marine had fallen. A part of the Corps was missing.

The minister gave his final message of comfort to the loved ones and concluded the service with his most thoughtful prayer. The crowd dwindled as attendees tried to console the family and walked away. Brokenhearted loved ones made their way home as well.

As the sun was disappearing on the horizon, the long evening shadows slowly crept over the newly covered grave. The lonesome night arrived for the young Marine. He was home. He was as peace with a world in which the violence that took his life in a faraway land still raged.

Perhaps many would pay their tribute over time. The vigil from loved ones would remain frequent, but the sharpness of his boyhood memories to those who had known him in his youth would grow dull over time.

The sun had set on young Butch Stegall's grave that first night as it has set each night since. His spirit would find a way to live on in this world through the deeds of his family. It would be under a strange set of circumstances yet to take place, but it happened, and the Angels who bore witness must have rejoiced in glorious tribute.

To Be a Marine

My first knowledge about the Marines came from Jack Ghent. *He was a Marine.* It sounds like a simple sentence unless you are familiar with Marines. A Marine is a Marine above all else. They have been conditioned to believe they are indestructible and will do, without question, whatever the missions demand.

I had also seen that Marines are human and are mortal as all men are. I had seen that in Jack Ghent.

Another experience I had with Marines was our high school basketball team's visit to Parris Island, the Marine recruitment and training facility, on the coast of South Carolina. I learned from that visit that Marines get up very early; they are extraordinarily

THE BUDDY PLAN

disciplined and they pull for the underdog in the fight. There is something all-American about that.

My other knowledge about them came from listening to a story told by a former high school student and friend named Eddie Hutto. If anyone had ever known Eddie, they would have known that he was definitely not Marine Corp material. Even though he was as thin as a rail, he wanted to be tough. He played football and stuck his nose in on every play. It was still hard to imagine him wearing a Marine uniform. Then again, "the Marine Corps Builds Men" was the slogan at the time when Eddie enlisted.

His first appearance back home after boot camp revealed only remnants of the former youngster we knew. He was still thin, but he was well-conditioned. He stood erect and had a particular demeanor about him that was all military. Strike what I just said and say, "It was all Marine."

Eddie told us about the time he had been assigned K P. It seems he could not resist the temptation of snacking on some freshly opened canned pears. The problem was that the grisly old Mess Sergeant caught him.

"I just had to have a bite of the pears," he stated to our group.

"About the time I got the first one in my mouth, the Mess Sergeant caught me."

"What you doing boy?"

"Eating a pear, Mess Sergeant, Sir," Eddie truthfully replied.

"Well, boy, you can have all the pears you want. As a matter of fact, you gonna eat the big can of 'em (one gallon)," the Mess Sergeant sternly told him.

"Then you gonna eat some more. You gonna eat till you don't want no more."

To all of this, Eddie's only rely was, "Yes, sir, Mess Sergeant."

So Eddie set about eating until he could absolutely eat no more. Then the real punishment took place.

"Come over here, boy."

"Stand up straight, boy."

The Mess Sergeant short punched him with his rock hardened fist in the stomach. What had gone down found its way back up.

Eddie related to us that the Mess Sergeant was then kind enough to allow him to lie in the corner and suffer for a while thereafter.

The obvious question from us was, "Eddie, did you want any more pears?"

Eddie was quick to answer, "Haven't wanted any pears since."

Then, there was the small picture with a short description in *The State Newspaper* about a Marine killed in Vietnam. He was from Beaufort. The portrait revealed an African American family who looked to be an older lady and a few friends with their backs to the camera. Why the photographer and editor had made the decision to print this particular small clip was obvious – the scene was emotionally moving.

The story behind it is not hard to imagine. Whether the young man was drafted or joined, it was similar to so many others. He probably never understood any of the politics of the war, didn't know where Vietnam was, and died amidst the confusion of battle in an unknown location.

Probably the proudest moment of his life occurred when he went back to his neighborhood to show off his uniform after basic training. He was somebody important for a while. He had become a Marine. He had accomplished something - perhaps a great deal for a poor African American youth.

THE BUDDY PLAN

Kids who go off to serve with the Marines soon find that there is a seriousness about it most people cannot imagine. Life and death is an everyday reality. It's written all over the pages of history. The Marine Corps is iconic with blood and sacrifice. Once people see the picture or the monument of the Marines raising the American flag at Iwo Jima, it remains forever in their minds as the epitome of bravery.

Whatever youngsters are out to prove, if they choose to do it via the Marine Corps and are successful, life will thereafter be viewed from an entirely different perspective.

July 1967 and Beyond

After Jacky was wounded in 1967 and later moved to the Veterans Hospital in Columbia, Henry Stegall decided there was a new role he must play. Perhaps it was Butch's death that drove it. To dismiss the role that played would not be easy. But there could be no doubt that most of it was simply the goodness of him and his wife Minnie.

There was the young lady (Patsy Lane) he knew from work who just happened to have a father in the same hospital where Jacky was now a patient. To Henry, all of this added up and he could help young Jacky in other ways as well.

Henry took a much greater role in caring for Jacky as Jacky's parents became less able to care for themselves, let alone Jacky. Henry would visit him and they would go places. Henry had assumed a fatherly responsibility. Minnie was quick to help Jacky with his finances. She had a banking background and it proved exceptionally beneficial to advising and actually doing all the necessary work to ensure his accounts were straight.

After Patsy went by to see Jacky in 1974 and the friendship began to blossom, Henry was quick to take him to see Patsy at her home in Lancaster. Of course, Henry got lots of pleasure himself. It just so happened that Geneva Lane, Patsy's mother, loved to cook and was very talented at the task. Henry loved to eat and voila, a match was made. More often than not, Henry and Jacky would leave the Lane's home with a supply of cooked morsels.

During Jacky and Patsy's courting time (between 1974 and 1977), they were taken to Hawaii by Henry and Minnie. They toured the islands and shared delightful times. Henry once went into one of the pineapple fields and harvested a pineapple, although urged not to do so by the others, just to see how good a fresh pineapple tasted. Perhaps it was also some of the boy still left in him.

When Patsy and Jacky were married in 1977, Henry saw a diminished role with Jacky. However, Henry still visited the couple quite often. Minnie, fearing that Henry's visits were troublesome, approached Patsy with concerns that the visits were a bother. Patsy very clearly made the point to Minnie that: *Under no circumstances were the visits a bother.* She emphasized the point more than once and was convincing enough that Minnie continued to take Henry there as often as he requested.

Henry oftentimes fell asleep on the couch and Jacky and Patsy would go about their daily routine as he dozed. They could never forget what Henry had done for Jacky. His peaceful slumber brought back the pleasant memories to Jacky and Patsy of the times when he had gone beyond the call of duty to take care of Jacky's needs.

It had also become known that Henry's visits to Jacky's home brought Henry pain. Minnie asked him "Why do you make such visits?" His reply was that "He could not stay away."

Was Henry Stegall trying to close out a chapter in his life for which there was not an ending that might give to him the total comfort he sought? No doubt that all of his caring for Jacky had come from the heart, but the heart also seeks comfort.

2002 Tragedy

The spring brought about the notion that the Stegalls, Henry and Minnie, would do some yard work. They loved to care for the yard and there were some underbrush and limbs, if removed, would make the area look much better. The day's tasks were set.

It was common practice to start a small fire when the brush was piled and ready for final disposal. Minnie and Henry had labored for several hours and Minnie decided it was time to ignite the pile of trash. A short time after lighting the brush, Minnie felt that the fire might be spreading into areas she did not want burned.

"Henry, I need to go get a rake to stop the fire; you stay where you are and I'll be right back," she explained to Henry as she left to go a short distance to the garage area to retrieve some tools to control the burn.

What should have been a routine situation soon turned to anything but that.

As Minnie came back into view of Henry, to her horror, he had, for whatever reason, attempted to manage the fire and had gotten so close that his clothing was now ablaze.

Minnie screamed as she ran to Henry to place him on the ground and put out the fire. When she finally extinguished the flames, she realized how badly he was injured. She called 9-1-1 and Henry was rushed to the local hospital in Rock Hill. His burns were so severe that he was transferred to the regional burn center in Augusta, GA.

Patsy and Jacky decided they must go to visit the family who had provided so abundantly for them.

Even though Minnie insisted that Jacky go to his bedside, other family members communicated to Jacky, though not verbally, but effectively, that it would be best not to go into Henry's room. They were there to lend the family support.

It seemed as though Henry's medical condition was improving and he would survive, but he developed complications unexpectedly and fell into a deep coma from which he never awakened.

No one can ever know what remained as the last clear thoughts as Henry's mind grew a little less sure of itself each day. Hopefully, he had found comfort by giving to Jacky and Patsy those things which he was never able to give to his own young son. He had two other children, but the void created by the tragic loss of Butch could never be filled.

This day, the bugler stood a distance from the gravesite as the lonesome notes pierced the air. Again, another flag had been exquisitely folded and presented to Minnie Stegall. This time it would be in honor of her beloved husband Henry. He had served in the Navy during WW II.

Perhaps the tears might be somewhat fewer. After all, he had lived a full life, but the circumstances under which he had left the earth were extraordinarily difficult to accept.

At the end of this day, the long shadows once again crept over a new grave in the cemetery. The final chapter was written in the life of Henry Stegall, but his spirit along with that of his son lives on in the lives of those who he had brought together and cared for so deeply.

THE BUDDY PLAN

In Memory of Butch Stegall

Engraved on Panel 17 E, line 097 among the 58,195 names of the Vietnam Memorial in Washington, DC.
    STEGALL Lindell Ray
    Date Of Event/Death: 03 APR 1967
    Date Of Birth: 22 JUL 1948
    Age At Death: 18
    Home City: Ft Mill
    Home State: SC
    Military Branch: Marine Corps
    Rank: PFC E2
    MOS: 0311
    Marital Status:
    Casualty Type: HOSTILE, DIED
    Air Ops/Reason: Ground Casualty   GUN, SMALL ARMS FIRE
    Country/Province: South Vietnam   QUANG NGAI

Footnote, A very special one:
    Henry Stegall did have some consolation with his search for closure with his son's death. Butch had lost his high school class ring in the vicinity of their home. He had evidently lost it doing odd jobs around the sizable yard. While searching one day, Henry's metal detector had a blip.
    He bent down and examined the grass and soil with care. He prodded the area meticulously. The probe struck something solid. It was the ring he had long sought. He paused briefly, looked to the Heavens, pulled away his glasses, and wiped away the tears.

Henry quietly walked into the house momentarily unable to bring forth any words and showed Minnie his discovery. They shared another tearful moment together.

Henry carefully cleaned each speck of dirt from the ring. He polished it and placed it alongside the picture of his son; the picture of a proud Marine in his dress uniform that stands out so prominently as you walk into the Stegall's living room. It belonged there.

Chapter Eighteen

The Wedding
(1977-2011 Recollection)

♦

For the union of the spirits has caused Him to remain...

♦

"You have an invitation, just show up."

♦

"Disabled veteran weds 10 years after his death" read the headlines in a local newspaper. The story, just like many about his "death", circled the globe in various news media.

LANCASTER, S.C. (UPI) – "Jacky Bayne was married Sunday, 10 years after Army doctors pronounced him dead from a land mine explosion in Vietnam.

Bayne, 32, nattily attired in white formalwear, smiled broadly after kissing his bride, Patsy Lane, upon completion of the 20-minute ceremony watched by 600 persons at Immanuel Baptist Church.

'Everyone was just elated,' said the Rev. Robert L. Tilley, who officiated. 'It was a very sweet, moving type of ceremony.'"

The best story of the wedding day is told thirty-four years after the fact as I sit in the couple's living room of their home on Barberville Road in upper Lancaster County, SC. The real count of people who attended the wedding was considerably larger than 600, more like 900.

Nervous?

I prepare myself to keep a straight face before I begin to quiz Jacky about their wedding. Actually, there is no way that this will happen and I know it, and he, too, knows it.

I look directly at Jacky, "Okay, I want you to tell me the truth, Jacky," I say to him as I glance at the picture on the shelf off to my right of a mustachioed long-haired young man dressed in a white tuxedo with a young lady in her full length wedding gown standing next to him as he sat in a wheelchair. Then I look directly back at him as he shows a somewhat quizzical look on his face, concerned about what I might ask.

"I'm going to ask you a question and I want you to think about it before you give me the answer."

"On which occasion were you more nervous, the first patrol you had to go out with Bruno and walk point man in Vietnam or the day when you stood there in your tuxedo and waited for your bride to walk down the aisle?"

To be honest, I had already heard Patsy tell about how nervous Jacky was on his wedding day.

To give this some perspective, probably the most dangerous job in Vietnam during the war was that of a point man with a dog. He walked out in front of the protection of the other troops and the fact that he had a dog with him made him an even more prized target. In fact, there was a considerable bounty placed by the enemy for the two.

Jacky looks over at me, smiles and attempts to keep a straight face as he states, "I wasn't scared in Vietnam but one time. That was the day I got there and it lasted for 6 months until I was hurt," then he grins and laughs.

"Okay," I half-giggling ask, "One more time, when were you more nervous?"

THE BUDDY PLAN

Knowing that I would continue to prod until I got an answer, Jacky smiles his wonderful ear to ear grin, blushes a noticeable shade of red and answers, "I think I was more nervous on my wedding day."

A few feet away, Patsy interrupts and says, "You should have seen him," as she demonstrates by grabbing her shirt and pulling it in and out from her chest to simulate the action of Jacky's heart pounding out of control.

"He was so nervous, you could see his tuxedo moving," she further added as she laughed.

All the while Jacky is still grinning and blushing as he cuts his eyes up at me concerned about what I might be thinking.

I look back at him and grin and think of how anxious he must have been at his wedding and jokingly say, "You must have really been nervous."

Again he cuts his eyes at me and laughingly says, "I was really nervous. My best man said, 'you don't have to hang on to me so tight, I won't let you fall' and I told him I wasn't worried about falling, I was so nervous I might pass out."

Each of the three of us chuckle and gaze at one another waiting to see what would be said next.

"Was Henry Stegall your best man?" I asked, assuming that he might likely have been since he had cared for Jacky so long.

"No, Kelly Harvell, one of my cousins, was my best man. He had been a long time buddy. I needed someone strong enough to help me stand at my wedding," he replied to me.

Jacky had been determined to stand for the ceremony despite his injuries, and so with the help of his best man and an artificial leg, he did. Compared to all the other hardships he had determinedly overcome, this was a small feat. In reality, most other people in a similar situation would never have attempted it.

Because no one had expected Jacky to stand, there had been a special note in the wedding program "not to stand" when Patsy entered the church. It was ignored when Jacky, to everyone's surprise, stood up as he awaited his beloved soon-to-be bride.

By Invitation Only?

"And why was I not invited to your wedding?" I asked jokingly, knowing I was about to get a response that would escalate to "verbal quipping". (benignly so)

Without a lost moment, he quickly responded, "You were, it was printed in the church bulletin."

Patsy and I both laughed as I reminded him, "I don't go to your church. At the time of your wedding, I was going to a church thirty miles away."

Not to be outdone, he laughingly replied, "Well everyone was invited."

Patsy laughs and says, "Let me tell you what Jacky did. We would be in the parking lot at a mall or somewhere and someone would approach and say, 'Jacky, I heard you are getting married, I surely would like to attend, but I don't have an invitation.' Well, Jacky would tell them, 'well I'm going to give you an invitation,' and you know those people took him up on it."

Patsy continues, "We had about 900 people at our wedding."

Me: "Are you serious? And I didn't even have an invitation. Did you not ask for an R S V P on your invitations?"

Jacky: "No. that's for important people and the only big shot I invited was Strom Thurmond, and he said he couldn't make it. He did send me a silver tray for a wedding gift."

Strom Thurmond had helped before the wedding and would help tremendously when Ron Dunn came onto the scene.

The aides who had helped Jacky so faithfully when he was at home after his mother had become ill and later after her death were curious as to whether or not they were invited to the wedding. Maybe this had been an oversight by Jacky and Patsy during the planning or someone forgot to tell them. But all was made well when Joe Lane told them that Jacky and Patsy would be deeply offended if they did not attend the wedding and stay for the reception as well.

Jacky told me on one occasion that he had gone to see one of his care givers for her 100th birthday. His voice sparkled when he reminded me that she still recognized him.

The wedding had truly been a marriage of the hearts. It is a moment that sparkles in his voice each time he makes mention of it. His pride escapes from his otherwise shy demeanor when he shows the wedding pictures. If Patsy is nearby, and you look at her closely, you will see the twinkle still, after all the years, in her eyes.

The Proposal

The friendship had grown and developed over the course of time. Patsy had become Jacky's best friend and made sure he was cared for properly.

They had also been on outings and had traveled extensively with Henry and Minnie Stegall. The obvious next step was in order. Jacky felt he needed to proceed with that step. His nephew, Bucky Baker, agreed to take him to pick out a ring. Jacky had it all planned. He would give the ring to her at the party he was having at his house just before Christmas in 1976.

During the festivities, Jacky presented Patsy with her other Christmas gift, a very elegant gold bracelet. Having gotten the bracelet, she would think that was the extent of her Christmas surprises. It was the first part of Jacky's plan. He now had to complete phase two.

A while after the presentation of the bracelet, he very matter-of-factly asked, "Patsy, will you take me into the bedroom?"

The actual account as described by the two goes as follows:

Patsy says, "I had never been in his bedroom with him, and he said, 'take me to my bedroom.' I was puzzled, but I said, sure. I thought he had gotten too warm. He had on a sweater, one of these turtleneck sweaters, and when we got in there, he said 'close the door.' We had a whole house full of guests and I was concerned about leaving them alone."

I interrupt and jokingly ask, "Why did you want to get away from the other people to ask her to marry you?"

Jacky looks at me and grins, "I didn't want them talking. I wanted to do it in private so if she said no, I wouldn't be embarrassed."

Patsy continues, "He then went to his drawer and came back, and bless his heart, and he took my hand and held it and said, 'will you marry me?' And I said, yes, I will."

"He said, 'Put your hand out,' and I put my hand out. Jacky tried to put the ring on my finger and I said, 'Honey, it's too small' and when I said that, his jaw dropped. You should have seen the look on his face."

"He said, 'well, I did the best I could do,' and I said no, honey, I'm not talking about the size of the diamond, I'm talking about the size of the band. I can't get the ring on my finger."

"Then he cheered up and said, oohh, I can do something about that."

I ask him, of course half laughing, "Jacky, did you not bother to check out the ring size?"

He replies, "I thought I did. Her fingers were bigger back then."

I quickly reminded him, in a joking way, knowing Patsy was listening, "You might need to be more careful in your choice of words."

Patsy looks on and grins.

The Engagement Period

All was made well. The setting was put into a gold band which Patsy preferred and, of course, this time, the size was correct for her finger.

Patsy told Jacky that she would love him and care for him, but he had to realize that her family would always be first in her heart, in a different way of course, and she would care for them as well if they needed her. Jacky agreed to this. He certainly understood the importance of family.

Now it was official, the two would wed.

When Joe Lane, Patsy's father, found out about the engagement, he told Patsy he wanted to talk to Jacky. So the meeting took place and Joe gave Jacky his blessings with some special instructions to him. "You know you are getting a good woman and if you don't take good care of her, you'll have to answer to me." Joe was showing his approval in a strange way as he usually did. He and Jacky had become the best of friends.

Jacky assured his future father-in-law that he would take good care of Patsy.

Jacky was good for Joe. He had brought Joe out of the shell in which he had hidden himself away. They would later go on trips to the mountains together and Jacky could reason with him on other matters when Joe needed someone to calm his mood.

As Jacky and Patsy began to talk of actual nuptial details, they decided the wedding was going to be a simple event without fanfare. Yes, that is what would be best for all. There would be a trip to the courthouse with a few friends, a short ceremony, and a private honeymoon.

Patsy explains to me, "We had agreed that Jacky and I would go to the courthouse with just a couple of our closest friends and family, have a quiet ceremony, and let it go at that."

The simplest plans don't always stay simple.

Jacky's sister, Ellen, got wind of the original plans and things changed drastically from that point forward. The wedding had to be held in a church along with an invitation list, people dressed up, and a reception afterwards.

Ellen contacted Patsy's mother and the ball was rolling to have a considerably larger wedding - maybe a couple hundred guests - in fact. Things didn't work out that way either.

By the time the planning was completed, the total might be as many as several hundred. Well, maybe... again. There was still a "problem". If it had not been for Patsy's father who insisted, "I know how those people are; you need to have food for at least seven hundred people," there would have been an even greater problem in attempting to feed all the people who finally decided to show up for the ceremony and reception.

Jacky and Patsy look through a scrap book prior to the wedding.

The Wedding

The wedding was all planned and August 28, 1977, the day for exchanging vows, had dawned. Later that day, Immanuel Baptist Church in Lancaster would be literally filled with well-wishers for the short ceremony. It was witnessed by members of the congregation who wished to attend and others who had been invited by formal invitation and a slew of reporters.

As per Joe's insistence, seven hundred people could be fed. There was still a problem - more than seven hundred people were present, many more than seven hundred were there. Barring a tense bride or groom suddenly developing cold feet, the ceremony was set to proceed.

The clock had reached three in the afternoon. The groom was positioned in the front of the church in his white tuxedo. When he had gone for the fitting, he had jokingly requested from the store manager that he be given trousers with one leg shorter than the other. The manager appeared to find no humor in the request.

Jacky had donned an artificial leg so he could stand to greet his bride. The church was filled with nine hundred or more. Within the audience, the numerous reporters had all the normal questions and many more. Some even wanted the details of the honeymoon plans. The people with such knowledge cooperated with Jacky's and Patsy's requests and the secrets were kept.

The attendees, despite having been told not to stand when the bride came down the aisle, stood anyway because Jacky was standing as the beaming bride entered.

The white gown was full with a long train and hid well her nervousness. Patsy joined the party at the altar and stood beside her father. She later confided a conversation she had with him.

"I don't think I can go through with this," she whispered to her father as they rounded the corner and saw the huge number of people.

"It's too late to back out now, you're getting a good man," he said, trying to reassure her.

"No daddy, that's not it at all, it's just that I'm so nervous," she responded.

The excitement of the moment and the almost uncontrolled anxiety gave way to the sincere desire of the two to confirm their love for one another in the bonds of matrimony. The brief ceremony in which the preacher told those in attendance, "It was a match made in Heaven," was correct. Each had found the other in a set of circumstances which could have only been orchestrated by powers beyond mortal man. The ceremony concluded with the Lord's Prayer.

The now mustachioed Jacky finally sat in his wheelchair and was wheeled out by his best man Kelly Harvell. Patsy followed closely by. White was evidenced all about the audience as handkerchiefs wiped away tears. Emotions soon changed to smiles and happy grins.

The reception had been planned for more than seven hundred people. That was supposed to have been enough to feed all who might attend. When the celebration was over, there was a small chunk of wedding cake and a very small amount of punch left.

"If they had not saved that, we would not have had anything to eat on our wedding night," Patsy is quick to interject.

If there was a sad note to the wedding, it would have to be that of the special people who did not live to see their son at his happiest moment in his new life. Then again, maybe they had their own special perch to witness it better than anyone in the regular audience.

I look once again at the wedding picture and question Jacky about the mustache.

The question sparks an unexpected discussion between the three of us.

"Well, I grew it thinking Patsy would like it," he grinningly states.

"I thought he liked it and I wasn't going to say anything about it," Patsy counters, "but I was really happy when he finally decided to shave it off."

I had to add, "So you thought she liked your mustache. Did you ever think to ask her?" I wanted to get him started, but he didn't take the bait. Instead, we decided to talk about the honeymoon.

The Honeymoon

The honeymoon was off to a rather amusing start.

Reporters wanted to know the details of the plans, but the family and friends were united in protecting the privacy of the newlyweds. It was going to be a simple trip to Gatlinburg to enjoy the fresh air and take in the sights of the mountains. There would be a stop for the night in Spartanburg some fifty miles or so away.

The wedding had been at three o'clock in the afternoon. What was to be a routine trip to Spartanburg, perhaps an hour or two away, took hours.

"We got lost on the way. I had never been anywhere driving at night," Patsy laughingly explains. "It was late when we got to Spartanburg and I couldn't find my way to the motel."

In all fairness, Spartanburg is an unusually confusing city in which to drive. It is a maze of one-way streets with "not so good" directional signs. One can become lost to confusion in a short time.

"I could see the motel we wanted to go to, but I couldn't get there," she explains. "So I finally see a policeman and ask him how to get to the motel. I told him we were just married and couldn't get to the motel for the night. He laughed and gave us the directions and we finally got there."

I explain to her that I had driven in Spartanburg and it was indeed a very difficult town in which to drive.

"Maybe the policemen had heard similar stories," I joked.

"Well, we got to the motel and I told Jacky I would put him to bed and then I would go find something to eat because we had not had anything but the piece of cake and some punch," she explains to me.

All the while Patsy is explaining this, Jacky sits in his chair and peeks an occasional grin and I look back and can't help but laugh.

"Well... I put him to bed, and I go find something to drink and eat and when I get back, the door would not open. Now, it was a nice motel - it was over a hundred dollars a night," Patsy says to clarify that they were not in a dumpy place where such might be expected.

THE BUDDY PLAN

"We were in a very nice motel."

"I said to myself, now don't get rattled, maybe you're just nervous. But I still couldn't get the door open," Patsy continues. "I finally found a guard and asked if he could help me get in the room."

"The guard told me to get my husband to let me in the room. He asked if my husband was too lazy to get out of bed and unlock the door. I told him the circumstances as to why Jacky could not let me in. When I told him, he said 'I'm really sorry, Ma'am,'" Patsy continues with the plight of the first night.

Jacky laughingly interjects, "He thought I was drunk."

Jacky was aware of what was going on and eventually responded during the commotion, "Patsy, if you cannot get in the door, I have the gun, and I'll shoot it open." This was out of character for Jacky unless you realize that everything he says is always tempered with humor.

Patsy had given her handgun to Jacky when she left to get food. Patsy, in order to ensure the safety of the two, had years before learned to shoot a handgun and had qualified for her Concealed Weapons Permit. I would be certain that she might issue only one warning if she felt the two of them were ever in danger.

"No, no, Jacky, just be patient, we got it under control," she was quick to respond.

"Well, the guard finally had to use a screwdriver to get us in. The next morning, I went to the office and told them they needed to get that fixed," Patsy said, and again she explained it was an expensive motel.

"We didn't have any problems getting to Gatlinburg. The only problem we had was that there were very few places for us to go to because they were not very handicap friendly. So when I got back home, I wrote them a letter and when we went back to Gatlinburg several years later, they had all sorts of places we could go to."

I, of course, congratulated her on being a consumer advocate and she was quick to reply that someone needed to do it and she didn't mind.

Actually, it was just her nature and there is no doubt her concerns were for others as well as Jacky.

The Anniversary

The 28th day of August marks their anniversary.

Jacky states, "When I met Patsy, it was in Columbia, so each year for our anniversary, we go to Columbia. We don't go to the VA Hospital, we go to a motel near there."

Patsy adds, "We've done that every year since we were married except for the year my mother got sick. We stay down there right beside the Veteran's Home."

Me: "Let me make a suggestion," knowing full well at the time it would get an immediate and pronounced response from both of them. "Why don't you go to Spartanburg?"

Jacky immediately responds, "We ain't going to do that now."

Patsy in the background laughingly replies, "Uh, we're not going to do that. I knew that was coming, you'd better hush."

Jacky repeats, "No, we ain't going to Spartanburg."

Of course, I couldn't stop there. "Go to Spartanburg, get a room, take your pistol and shoot the door down."

Jacky quips back, "Noooo, we're too old for that now."

Patsy repeats the same in the background.

Jacky: "I might end up being a widower," as he giggles, "I can't shoot that good no way."

Patsy: "We are just going to Columbia so we can stay all night, and come back the next day."

Me: "That will be good."

Jacky: "When Patsy's mother was living, I bought Patsy an Anniversary Ring. I wanted her mother to see it. I told her mother not to tell Patsy."

Of course, I could not pass up the opportunity. "Now let me ask you this, when you bought the anniversary ring, was it the right size? Was it the right color?"

Patsy: "Yeah, it was the right size; he's come a long way."

Jacky: "I knew this time. I know a little better now."

Me: "You're wising up a little bit, aren't you?"

Patsy: "Yeah, he does real good now."

Me: "You didn't think I paid that much attention, did you?" I was making reference to an earlier conversation.

Jacky: "I got her a ring and took it the hospital where Patsy's mother was so she could see it. Patsy didn't know I had gotten one."

Jacky had grown very close to Patsy's mother until she passed away in 2005.

Me: "So you had planned all of this with her mother?"

Jacky and Patsy: "Unhuh."

Jacky and Patsy discuss whether it was their 25th or their 29th anniversary.

I ask Jacky, "Don't you remember when you got married?"

He turns his head to look at me and grins as Patsy tells him how many years it has been since the wedding.

Jacky was still as witty as he had ever been. Never to be outdone, the one line quipping, at which he still excels, went back and forth. The sheer joy of the witty remarks, each countering whatever I might say, and each with the humor no one might ever imagine brought laughter to the heart.

"I was once married to a young lady with long brown hair. Now I'm married to an old lady with short white hair," he jokingly says.

I just look at them and laugh. I thought about questioning his remark, but I didn't. To all of this, Patsy displays her soft caring grin so suiting of the Angel she is.

Chapter Nineteen

Lieutenant Ron Dunn, USMC (1980)

♦

And yet you might never have known them at all, but for the curious circumstances which introduced them to you and the roles you were chosen to play.

♦

The First Meeting

From the first moment Bunia Bayne had discovered the shocking truth about her son's wounds in Vietnam from a newspaper left on a bench where she sat at Walter Reed Hospital in Washington, D.C., she had wondered about the person who had been sent to save her son from death. There was no doubt whatsoever in her mind that this had been an act of Divine Intervention. She often spoke of this man unknown to her and how she would love to someday meet him and personally express her heartfelt thanks for the wonderful deed he had done.

In her mind, he deserved a medal of some sort. Whatever the medal might be, she did not know, but she felt he definitely should receive one. Whatever material token he might have received would have paled in comparison to the look he would have seen in a mother's eyes. There were others; the doctors and nurses who had provided the care, but still, had it not been for this initial act that made all the rest possible, nothing would have mattered. Bunia Bayne would have loved to have met each and every one face to face who had any part in Jacky being alive and graciously thanked them all.

The occasion was not to be. Bunia Bayne passed away in 1974 and no one had any idea how to locate this mystery man and thank him for the miracle his actions had allowed to unfold. It had become almost a certainty that his identity would never be revealed. Thoughts of ever finding him were filed away and maybe the best thing was to let such thoughts fade away completely.

His discovery would, even with the most knowledgeable individual(s) pursuing it, require a herculean effort. For beginners, there was the confusion of that fateful day twelve thousand miles away from civilization as we know it. Jacky certainly had no recollection of it. With the disbanding of the units serving there, who might remember exactly what had taken place? The soldiers had gone their own separate ways. Whatever records were kept would have been conveniently filed away with tons of other records gathering dust in a room of "who knows where".

It had happened in the fog of a war that would soon be forgotten along with most of the soldiers who had served in it, except for the names on the "The Black Marble Wall" in Washington, D.C.

The headlines and the stories were over for Jacky as well. He had settled into the day to day routine, if there was anything routine about his life, and whiled away his time reading newspapers, books, and watching television. Patsy still worked at the plant near Rock Hill where she had been encouraged by her supervisor and friend Henry Stegall to visit Jacky in the Veterans Hospital in Columbia. It all seemed that everything would settle into the hum drum of everyday life, maybe?

THE BUDDY PLAN

One day as Jacky, now in his thirties, sat at home, the phone rang.

Jacky wheeled his way to the phone and answered, "Hello," as was his customary greeting.

"Have I reached the residence of Mr. Jacky Bayne," asked the professional business mannered voice.

"Yes you have," was the response from a somewhat curious Jacky.

"Mr. Bayne, Jacky, if I might call you that?" the voice continued.

Jacky, of course, who would find it quite amusing that anyone might refer to him as Mr., responded, "You certainly may."

On the other end of the line was an insurance professional from Durham, NC. The intent of the call was far removed from offering Jacky an insurance policy.

Ron Dunn, former Marine and Vietnam Veteran, had read the stories about Jacky and his mother. He had taken an exceptional interest in them before he had gone to Vietnam and still had a very keen interest after his return.

He was yet to realize that he, himself, had an extraordinarily important role to play as well in this story.

When Ron was released from the military in December, 1969, he and his wife went to New Jersey. While there, using the G. I. Bill, he received an M.B.A. in insurance.

In 1979, he moved to Durham, NC, where he became the Director of Field Training for an insurance company. It was in 1980 that he discovered just how close Jacky and he lived from each other.

He contacted Ray Corn, an insurance agency manager in Rock Hill, and Ray told him he knew Jacky and Patsy quite well. In fact, Ray's wife worked with

Patsy. So Ron decided he would take a trip to Rock Hill and pay a visit to Jacky while he was there. Perhaps, he might even take them out to lunch and discuss some things of interest.

What Ron did not know was, none of this was going to happen until the ever protective and somewhat skeptical Patsy Bayne did a background check on this man who would later become the "wonderful stranger" from the proverbial "out of nowhere". Or was he a stranger? After all, didn't he have a mission to fulfill, even though he was initially unaware of it?

To make sure Ron was okay, Patsy Bayne called Ray Corn, only fifteen miles away, with whom Ron Dunn was supposed to meet for business. Ray gave Ron a glowing report. Patsy Bayne knew Ray and was satisfied that this man passed muster and all would be well for him to meet with Jacky.

The Promise Made

Ron Dunn came to see Jacky and the two of them talked. Jacky showed him around the area. They visited Jacky's parents' graves. It had been a very rewarding afternoon, but there was an even bigger, much bigger, reward yet to be.

As Ron was preparing to leave, he asked, "Jacky, is there anything I can do for you?"

Jacky responded, "Well, there were some people who had said they would help me find the man who saved my life in Vietnam. But no one has finished that job. My Mama always wanted to know who he was, but she died before we found out."

Ron Dunn looked straight into Jacky's eyes and promised to take on the challenge. Maybe in the excitement of the moment, he had overstated his capabilities or perhaps anyone's capabilities. Would Jacky ever hear from him again? *But he had promised. A Marine had promised.*

THE BUDDY PLAN

In the early 1980s, nothing such as the Internet with all the quick references and links to things all over the world existed. Research and locating people had to be done the old fashion way with letters and phone calls. There were no "instant replies". There were also the bureaucratic entanglements of the government Ron would have to confront if he were to find the mystery man. Even with the best efforts of someone with his determination and intellect, there would need to be some factors beyond his control to work in his favor, very dramatically in his favor, if he were to succeed.

Where does anyone start? Just how determined was this former Marine? Maybe Jacky had never met a Marine with the skills and determination of Ron Dunn. Regardless of what Jacky's favorite sergeant, Platoon Sergeant Carlton B. Talley, had said in basic training about the Marines, this Marine could think.

Ron Dunn knew that the military was very responsive when politicians became involved. South Carolina had the powerful, long-serving Senator Strom Thurmond. Ron Dunn knew that his chances of being more successful would be better if he let all the people in the military he wrote know that Strom Thurmond had given his approval to this project - thus he did.

Don L. McCorkle

```
                                          5601 Russell Road
                                          Durham, N.C.  27712
                                          June 12, 1980
```

The Honorable Strom Thurman
Room 209, Russell Senate Office Building
Washington, D.C.   30510

    Re: SP/4 Jacky C. Bayne, RA 12843692 (Ret.)

Dear Senator:

One of your constituents, SP/4 Jacky C. Bayne, of Ft. Mill, S.C. and I would appreciate your help.

Attached are copies of letters I have sent to Secretaries Alexander and Brown of the Defense Department asking for information on the person who saved Jacky's life.

Jacky and I feel your influence will help speed the Defense Department's and the Army's search. Please let me know if you will help (and how you will help).

Thank you.

                                     Sincerely,

                                     Ronald B. Dunn
                                     (former) First Lieutenant, U.S.M.C.R.
                                   SER #0101020
                                   1st Marine Division (+)
                                   Fleet Marine Force, Pacific
                                   Republic of Vietnam 8/67 to 8/68

Attachments

    cc: Jacky C. Bayne
         Route 1, Box 154
         Ft. Mill, S.C.   29715

He got a response from a member of the Committee on Armed Services. The old gentleman from South Carolina carried enough influence that Ron Dunn got answers to his letters.

THE BUDDY PLAN

```
JOHN C. STENNIS, MISS., CHAIRMAN
HENRY M. JACKSON, WASH.         JOHN TOWER, TEX.
HOWARD W. CANNON, NEV.          STROM THURMOND, S.C.
ROBERT F. BYRD, JR., VA.        BARRY GOLDWATER, ARIZ.
SAM NUNN, GA.                   JOHN W. WARNER, VA.
JOHN C. CULVER, IOWA            GORDON J. HUMPHREY, N.H.
GARY HART, COLO.                WILLIAM S. COHEN, MAINE
ROBERT MORGAN, N.C.             ROGER W. JEPSEN, IOWA
J. JAMES EXON, NEBR.
CARL LEVIN, MICH.

FRANCIS J. SULLIVAN, STAFF DIRECTOR
```

United States Senate
COMMITTEE ON ARMED SERVICES
WASHINGTON, D.C. 20510

June 19, 1980

1ST Ronald B. Dunn, USMCR
5601 Russell Road
Durham, North Carolina 27712

Dear Ronald:

Your letter of recent date has been received.

Be assured it is a pleasure for me to contact the Department of the Army in an effort to assist you. As soon as a reply to my inquiry is received, I will be back in touch with you.

With kindest regards and best wishes,

Sincerely,

Strom Thurmond
Strom Thurmond

ST:uai

Regardless of the fact that Ron now had the ear of such an influential member of the political hierarchy in Washington, there was no guarantee that any of the people he now searched for could be found. Thirteen years had passed and people had dispersed to places and some simply had not left traceable records.

Nonetheless, Ron Dunn wrote the Department of the Army the same day he wrote the powerful Senator about one of his constituents.

5601 Russell Road
Durham, N.C. 27712
June 12, 1980

Mr. Clifford L. Alexander, Jr.
Secretary of the Army
Department of Defense
The Pentagon
Washington, D.C. 20301

Re: SP/4 Jacky C. Bayne
RA 1284369 (Ret.)
D.O.B.: 19 June 1945

Dear Mr. Secretary:

Jacky Bayne's story was transmitted via Associated Press and United Press International wires in August 1967. Jacky needs the sequel. America owes him that.

SP/4 Jacky C. Bayne would like to know who saved his life 13 years ago after he was wounded in action in Vietnam, declared dead by a group of Army surgeons, and sent to Graves Registration. There an alert Army embalmer, the man whom Jacky wants to meet and who is the object of this letter, detected faint signs of life and rushed him back to the surgeons.

Jacky survived, but has spent the last 13 years in and out of military and VA hospitals. Although his right leg had to be amputated and he has lost much of the use of his left arm and leg, he is more of a man than most men I know, myself included.

Jacky was a scout dog handler in Vietnam, 48th Infantry Platoon (Scout Dog), 196th Light Infantry Brigade. He was wounded near Chu Lai on July 16, 1967, three days before his 22nd birthday. Newspaper reports state he was medevaced to the 2nd Surgical (Field) Hospital and from there sent to Graves Registration. The embalmer returned him to the field hospital. From there he was transferred to an Army hospital in Japan and, in August, to Walter Reed Army Hospital. Four months later Jacky was sent to the Veterans Administration Hospital in Columbia, South Carolina. He has been in and out of hospitals since.

Military Unit Diaries are scrupulously kept and it should not be too difficult determining the Army embalmer's name and putting Jacky in touch with him.

We Americans owe Jacky more than just a pension, our thanks, and a Bronze Star with Combat "V" for Valor. We owe him the satisfaction of discovering who saved his life, and the opportunity to shake the man's hand and thank him personally.

THE BUDDY PLAN

Page 2 of R.B. Dunn letter to C.L. Alexander dated June 12, 1980

Morally, we owe Jacky at least this much; but, if this is not enough, then Jacky wants to know (legally) under the Freedom of Information Act.

I am available to act in any capacity whatever if it means helping Jacky. Please be assured that I shall do everything necessary to assure Jacky's discovering the identity of the embalmer. This is what Jacky wants and needs.

Jacky is my friend and I owe him at least this much.

Sincerely,

Ronald B. Dunn

Ronald B. Dunn
(former) First Lieutenant, U.S.M.C.R.
SER #0101020
1st Marine Division (+)
Fleet Marine Force, Pacific
Republic of Vietnam 8/67 to 8/68

Attachment: Newspaper article

cc: Jacky C. Bayne
Route 1, Box 154
Ft. Mill, S.C. 29715

The former Marine was getting someone's attention on the level he felt was necessary in order for him to be successful, the very top level.

Don L. McCorkle

DEPARTMENT OF THE ARMY
OFFICE OF THE ADJUTANT GENERAL
U.S. ARMY RESERVE COMPONENTS PERSONNEL AND ADMINISTRATION CENTER
ST. LOUIS, MO 63132

IN REPLY REFER TO:

AGUZ-PSA-I Bayne, Jacky C.
RA 12 843 692

JUN 24 1980

Mr. Ronald B. Dunn
5601 Russell Road
Durham, NC 27712

Dear Mr. Dunn:

This is an interim reply to your inquiry submitted under the Freedom of Information Act to Secretary Alexander regarding the military service of Specialist Four Jacky C. Bayne, U.S. Army Retired.

A search for Specialist Bayne's record has been initiated. You will be further informed no later than the week of 21 July 1980.

Sincerely,

T. A. ROMANO, JR.
LTC, GS
Director, Personnel Services

The search had started. This was fantastic. This was major progress. He now had the attention of the Army with all of their resources focused on finding records which might help him locate (an) unknown face(s) who otherwise would have faded away never to be recognized for the wonderful deed.

There was no doubt that Ron Dunn's initial thesis was providing results, but still there were no names, and it could still, and very well might, all fall apart. But then, the response he had hoped for came.

THE BUDDY PLAN

DEPARTMENT OF THE ARMY
OFFICE OF THE ADJUTANT GENERAL
U.S. ARMY RESERVE COMPONENTS PERSONNEL AND ADMINISTRATION CENTER
ST. LOUIS, MO 63132

IN REPLY REFER TO:
AGUZ-PSA-I Bayne, Jacky C.
RA 12 843 692

23 JUL 1980

Mr. Ronald B. Dunn
5601 Russell Road
Durham, NC 27712

Dear Mr. Dunn:

This is in further reply to your inquiry submitted under the Freedom of Information Act to Secretary Alexander regarding the military service of Specialist Four Jacky C. Bayne, U.S. Army Retired.

Inquiry reveals that three individuals were responsible for saving Specialist Four Jacky C. Bayne's life. John M. Shumway and Samuel J. Lawrence, Jr., have been discharged from the Army. Staff Sergeant Bruce E. Logan is presently serving on active duty in the U.S. Army.

The disclosure of information contained in the military records of individuals without their consent is an invasion of privacy. Accordingly, the Department of the Army's policy precludes the release of home addresses of individuals not serving on active duty unless an emergency exists or for other extenuating circumstances. Procedures are in effect which provide that correspondence from a third party may be forwarded to the individuals at their latest address of record.

If you desire such service, you should forward letters addressed to John M. Shumway and Samuel J. Lawrence, Jr. in sealed envelopes with a request for forwarding action to the Commander of this Center, Attention: AGUZ-PSA-I. Upon receipt, your letters will be forwarded to the individuals' latest address of record for reply at their discretion.

Since active duty addresses are releasable under existing regulations, you may contact Staff Sergeant Bruce E. Logan at the 364th Supply and Service Company, Fort Bragg, North Carolina 28307.

I am sure that Specialist Bayne appreciates your efforts in his behalf.

Sincerely,

T. A. ROMANO, JR.
LTC, GS
Director, Personnel Services

He now had names, *but was that a guarantee he could contact these individuals?* Two of those who were sought had been released from the Army. They might prove very difficult, if not impossible, to locate. Addresses of record change. The ball had now been passed on to him. The powers that be had performed their jobs and had done so in no less than a magnificent manner.

He would send letters to all of the names which had been given to him. There was a hitch with those who had been released from the military.

The military could not legally supply him with addresses of record. What they could do was to forward a letter from him through their channels to the individuals' last addresses of record. Remind all again that we are still dealing with the 1980s and even though there is information on record about people, it is all hidden away and must be retrieved though processes which, most times, are impossible to provide an access point.

Ron received disappointing news on the two individuals who had been released from the military. The letters he had sent through channels to be delivered were returned to him as undeliverable.

There was one name still on active duty; that should not be so difficult, or might it be after all? The Army could legally provide him with all the information about this man. Ron's best chance was to appeal to this man to answer his plea to contact him and provide whatever information he might be able to provide.

THE BUDDY PLAN

5601 Russell Road
Durham, NC 27712
August 2, 1980

S/Sgt. Bruce C. Logan, USA
Alden Road
Fayetteville, NC

Dear Sergeant Logan:

I have been trying to contact you this week at your home and unit but have not been able to reach you. I am sending a copy of this letter to you at the 364th. If neither Jacky nor I hear from you we'll try not to bother you, again.

We need your help!

According to the attached letter from the Department of the Army you helped save Jacky's life in 1967 while in Vietnam.

Please tell us the circumstances surrounding your having done this. Was it in the bush? At the field hospital? In Graves Registration? Were you the embalmer? Did you know him? The jeep driver who drove Jacky back to the field hospital from Graves Registration? Did you know the doctors?

Jacky needs your help, again, Bruce. Please help him. Thank you.

Sincerely,

Ronald B. Dunn

Ronald B. Dunn, (former)
First Lieutenant, USMCR
First Marine Division (+)
Fleet Marine Force, Pacific
Republic of Vietnam 8/67 to 8/68

Phone: 919-

SP/4 Jacky C. Bayne, USA (Ret.)
48th Platoon (Scout Dog)
196th Light Infantry Brigade
  c/o Route 1, Box 154
     Ft. Mill, SC 29715

Phone: 803-

The Promise Kept?

It seemed there was a real possibility that Ron had gotten so close, but was there to be no brass ring? Or was there? Why was it necessary to make such a plea? Surely a man who had been so instrumental is snatching a life from all the death he had seen around him would want to celebrate with the man whose life he had saved and with this man who had taken it upon himself to put forth this fantastic effort to find him.

Eureka

"Will you accept a collect phone call from a Staff Sergeant Bruce Logan?" the operator quizzed.

Ron Dunn, not knowing what to expect and somewhat startled replied, "Yes, I will."

"I'm the man you are looking for," a polite voice on the other end of the receiver stated.

There was a pause as neither quite knew what to say next. The conversation continued and Ron Dunn filled in Staff Sergeant Logan about the reason he had inquired. He also set in motion the possibility of Jacky Bayne and SSG Logan meeting. He now needed to coordinate that event with Jacky and Patsy.

SSG Logan had left the Army, but later decided to re-enlist and make a career of it. At the time he was located, he was serving at Fort Bragg, NC. That would make a meeting between the Baynes and SSG Logan quite feasible.

Ron Dunn worked to arrange the meeting.

THE BUDDY PLAN

When the two first met, SSG Logan extended his hand to Jacky's.

"No man, this ain't right," Bruce said and proceeded to warmly embrace the person he had saved from death.

The two made small talk. SSG Bruce Logan could not believe the miracle he saw before his eyes. He grinned bigger as he glanced at Jacky each time.

Patsy, just as Jacky's mother, wanted to know the details of what had actually happened at the graves registration site. When the situation provided the opportunity, Patsy got SSG Logan out of earshot of Jacky and asked him point blank, "Sir, I'm his wife and I want to know exactly what happened and what he was like when you found him?"

SSG Logan began, "Well, ma'am, I'm going to be perfectly honest with you. When I first saw that man, he was mangled and just like a new born baby coming into the world. That's how he was. I had never seen anything like it. That's why I never called. I wouldn't have given five cents for his chances. I did what I felt like I had to do. I went to him and grabbed his wrist as hard as I could. I felt a faint beat, it was faint, but it was a beat. I called for the medics. They put him in an ambulance and took him to the aid station. I later heard that he had died."

SSG Logan then changed his demeanor and with a grin from ear to ear, said to Patsy, "I can't believe that boy." Perhaps SSG Logan had underestimated his role in the miracle.

As previously stated: When SSG Logan describes what he knows to have taken place and the makes the statement, *'He had heard that Jacky had died,' it creates another series of questions about all of what actually happened. It clearly leads to the idea that Jacky would have to have been given up for dead twice and to be finally brought back to life after the second pronouncement.*

The accounts are such that an embalmer (not Bruce Logan) had actually begun to prepare the body and felt a pulse in the artery in the groin. SSG Logan's account was that he heard sounds from a body which had been placed with others in an area.

Jacky bears the scar he claims was caused by an incision to begin draining the remainder of his body fluids.

Too many years have passed and the circumstances under which the initial actions took place won't permit further investigation. Exactly what actually happened may never be known. But the eyewitness account, in my opinion, trumps any other account. As stated, it also brings into question whether or not there were two incidents of "death".

Sometimes, records are not available because they were not made. Other times, records which are available are not accessible because no one can link them to the particular person. Whatever the reasons, this has become a point of speculation as to exactly what did take place. The best information which is available strongly points to the idea of a second pronouncement of death and then a recovery.

THE BUDDY PLAN

SSG Bruce Logan, Jacky, and former Marine Lieutenant Ron Dunn at Fort Bragg

One of the best stories carried about the reunion at Fort Bragg was written in the local *Fort Mill Times*.
"Jacky Bayne Meets Man Who Saved Him" by Jerry McGuire, Editor, *The Times (August 28, 1980)*.

Excerpts are as follows: "During the last seven years of her life, Mrs. Bunia Bayne's wish was to meet the man who saved the life of her son Jacky 'and pin a medal on him.'

She died in 1974 without getting to meet the man credited with sending for medical help for Bayne.....

'My mother kept saying she wanted to meet whoever it was that noticed that I was not dead and pin a medal on him,' Bayne said in an interview last week. He and his wife Patsy had just returned from Fort Bragg, NC., where they presented Logan with a gold watch engraved with words of appreciation of the deed.

Logan, now 32, was a graves registration specialist at a body collection point at Chu Lai. He received the watch for his efforts during a ceremony attended by his superiors and members of his unit. Also on hand was Ron Dunn of Durham, NC., who had read Jacky's story and spent several months locating Logan.

Logan was first reluctant to tell about the incident, but agreed to at Patsy's insisting and hearing of Bunia Bayne's wish. 'He remembered my case, although he had seen hundreds of bodies in his assignment,' Bayne said. 'Of course, mine was different.'

More reunions with the three men and their families are being planned, said Bayne.

The story of Bayne being almost buried alive circulated around the world. 'I'll never know the full story of the many people who had a part in saving my life,' the Fort Mill Army veteran said. 'There are so many, I'm sure. And among them were my folks, friends and people I didn't know who were pulling for me. They were from Fort Mill, Indian Land, and other places who helped my mother and dad. Most of all, they had faith and prayed for my recovery.'

Indeed, people from all around the world prayed and sent get well wishes."

A Special Thanks

SFC Bruce Logan, thank you, sir, for what you did. Thank you for your service.

A very special thanks to Lieutenant Ron Dunn, USMC, for completing a mission many thought impossible. Maybe Jacky Bayne should reconsider again what he was told in basic combat training by our drill sergeant about Marines.

Chapter Twenty

SFC Bruce Logan
An Amazing Career
(2011)

◆

"The old neighborhood is so different than when I was last here short years ago. The guys are just not the same. Or is it me? There is a new world full of wonder to which I feel I must return."

◆

A knock on the door and we were greeted by a cheerful Patsy Bayne who escorted us in to the living room which was already lively with discussion. My wife Linda and I had gone there to meet two very special people. We could not fathom just how extraordinary the experiences of one had been. We already knew about the other.

"Who's that guy," I jokingly asked as I made reference to Jacky.

He looked up at me and we both grinned and laughed as though we were teenagers. I looked at Bruce Logan and introduced myself as my wife introduced herself to his charming wife.

We joked about the seating arrangements and I asked Jacky if he was going to face in another direction as I reached out and turned his wheelchair and looked at his contagiously grinning face.

He quipped back sharply, "I guess I'll face the other way."

I looked over at Bruce and jokingly said, "Bruce, don't cut him any slack." This of course, got a remark in the background from Jacky.

Bruce started, "I was just bringing Jacky up to

snuff on some of the things that had happened to me in the Army. Some of the things that were totally unforeseen. A lot of things I've been involved in. I stayed in the service."

Me: "Yeah, I saw the 'Retired Army' tag on the back of your car."

Bruce continues, "I came on special assignment in 1976 and the DOD (Department of Defense) handpicked a team, 19 enlisted and three officers. We were assigned to the United States Central Identification Laboratories, the forensic side of the House dealing with MIAs and POWs. I had access to the records of every soldier, Marine, sailor, airman, and Department of Defense civilian that perished in Vietnam. I could never have foreseen that."

With these pronouncements, everyone pulls in a little closer so as to be sure we hear all he is saying. He has our attention.

"Less than a year later in 1977, we all had diplomatic clearances; we had diplomatic passports, ahh, we came under the U.S. State Department, the whole team. So all of our orders came directly out of the State Department."

"One day we got a heavy duty message, we called it a 'TWITCH'. It said 'move your team into Subic Bay in the Philippines.' Now we were based in Hawaii. We got off the C-141 and picked up a C-130 and we flew into North Vietnam." (They had flown a larger C-141 jet from Hawaii to the Philippines to board a smaller C-131 turboprop which could better land at smaller airstrips).

"We flew over Cambodia and Laos and got almost into Vietnamese airspace and a North Vietnamese interpreter came on the radio and told the pilot to change his heading. This brought us into a major airfield they used during the war. And, as we were coming down, I looked out the port holes in the side of the aircraft and on each side of the runway there were

THE BUDDY PLAN

children and I got butterflies in my stomach. I was telling Jacky I thought I was never going to see that place again. The other guys on my team, except for one, never had that experience, so they didn't have a clue as to what I was feeling."

"So anyway, the plane came to a halt and cut his propeller blades off. Immediately when the ramp came down, the heat came up in there and the odor, you never forget that smell."

Jacky and I concurred and I said, "Just like the first time."

Jacky added, "It's like, what am I doing over here?"

Bruce continued, "You never forget that smell. Uhh, I didn't get to see Hanoi during the war, because, you didn't want to see it during the war because it meant you were a POW or an MIA. Anyway, we settled over by some strange looking vehicles. It looked like it might have been a 1950s version of a Russian automobile. They took us over to a meeting area. Immediately, their official staff started talking about aid and, ahh, logistics and funding for the U.S. Government to rebuild their country. Our senior man, Colonel Harvey said, "We are not here to discuss politics, the name of the game is MIAs. That is what we are here for."

"And I'm saying to myself, man, I hope he ain't too harsh, they might decide to put us in the Hanoi Hilton. I thought about all of that, trust me, I thought about all of that."

Everyone in the room laughs loudly because he seems to have been genuinely scared and felt he might have become a prisoner of the Vietnamese government.

"I just couldn't believe, this was a nightmare, this hellhole. Anyway, when they finally decided to do something, they offered to take us on a tour and the senior man thought about it for about 30 seconds and that was the end of that. We didn't get to go on a tour."

"So then, he (the senior North Vietnamese official) took Colonel Harvey and one of our senior people and went into another holding area. About 35 or 40 minutes passed and some Vietnamese came out with some plywood boxes. On top of the box was a paper, white background with black stenciling lettering. It was a person's name. You know we called them a BTB, a 'Believed To Be person.' And everything related to that case matter, personal effects, and other things related to the case were crammed into these little plywood boxes. The lids were nailed down and they had put that stencil I was just talking about on top of it."

"Okay, this is how we received it. This is what the public don't get to see. Now, we knew at that particular time, we were going to get thirteen MIAs. So we brought all our flags accordingly. We brought them ourselves. And, so, after creating our own ceremony, respectful ceremony on the ground there, marching one at a time, two men, one on each side of the plywood remains until we got the last one loaded." (onto the C-130 Aircraft)

"Once the last one was loaded, there was maybe five minutes worth of discussion and we were back in the sky headed for Subic Bay in the Philippines. From there, we transferred them over to a 141 (C-141 aircraft) and flew into Clark, which is in a place called Los Angels, in the Philippines. You have a U.S. Army mortuary in the Philippines. We transported them to the mortuary and there we had to change clothes again, get out of the dress uniforms and get into the work clothes again."

"What I was telling Jacky, people think we have caskets, but what they are is heavy duty aluminum transfer cases. We transferred the remains over and had them tied down in the aircraft so they couldn't move, they were stationary. We put the top on and seal the lids and then put a customs seal on it and can't nobody open that case except authorized immigration people and us. That's it."

"Then we took off to fly back to Hawaii. Once we are there, we have our own little ceremony on the ground waiting for us. We radio ahead so everything will be set up. The public, the press, the whole nine yards is there. And we transport them by hearse, Cadillac hearses, to the Central Identification laboratory where I worked at."

"Once we have everything secured inside, at that point, the commander dismisses the team so you can go, you know you have been deployed a long time."

"When we come back to work, the actual forensic side of the identification procedures start. Okay, now it don't end there, but once you go through all your scientific stuff and kinda narrow it down, we always use what we call the 'X' number, X 1, X 2, or whatever, based on how many you have and it's still BTB or Believed to Be. You don't use names. The reason for that. Now once you have all your findings together, you present that to a guy named Dr. Rourie. He has worked for the government since 1959. He's a Physical Anthropologist. He's the most senior man. He's a world renowned respected individual. I'm proud to have been associated with him."

"When he attaches a name to it, all of this goes to what we call 'The Summary Court Board' in the Pentagon in the highest level of government. That board gets together and they look at all the findings, at all the evidence and the personal effects and anatomical chart and all the other things pertinent to the case and then they vote. People don't know this, but that panel votes on whether we should attach that person's name to those remains or is there enough evidence to say that 'John Doe' is truly 'John Doe'. Only then is it established."

With that announcement, every other person present makes remarks. "Wow." "Lord of Mercy." "That's a lot." "That's really involved."

Bruce continues, "Now, I had left and spent five

years at Fort Bragg and came back in 1984 to the same assignment."

"You had that background," someone spoke out.

Bruce replied, "Yep, I had that background."

Bruce Logan and Jacky in December 2011 at Jacky's and Patsy's Home

"This time, I was telling Jacky earlier, we went into Laos. In 1972, there was Air Force version of a C-130 modified gunship known as 'Puff the Magic Dragon' based at the biggest strategic bombing base that they used to make the strikes in Vietnam. It was in Thailand and it was called Utapao. Okay, it took off from Utapao and went over Cambodia and Laos airspace into North Vietnam. It was supporting U.S. Special Forces that were on the ground. On the way back, when they got over Laos, it was hit with a SAM missile in 1972. There was a crew of 12 on there and they were MIA. There were 12 people MIA for 12 years.

THE BUDDY PLAN

Then In '84, we were ordered into Laos, my team."

"We spent a month inside Laos. We were the first Americans in Laos since the end of the war. Since the end of the reign of the Khmer Rouge. All that same area where they made that movie they call *The Killing Fields*, we were in that same basic location. Okay, we were the first Americans there and spent a month there trying to do whatever we could as far as recovery of whatever was left. What was mostly left was fragmentation of skeletal types of remains and stuff like that."

"The 29th day of the mission, well the last day of the mission, I was telling them, NBC showed up in an old Russian antique helicopter."

Everyone makes inaudible remarks and seems very amused that such helicopters were still used.

"Yeah, they sure did. I don't know what they did or paid to get in there, but the Laotian government gave them 20 minutes and wanted them out of the country. By then, we were ready to go. We were kinda beat."

"So we took one of the craters, not the crash site crater, one of the other craters that was there and put all the guns, Gatling guns to 30 caliber to 50 caliber guns, and gathered it all into this big giant hole. I got pictures of all of this I brought up here, by the way, and we lined the whole hole with C-4 plastic explosive. Believe it or not, we took a pallet of C-4 from Subic Bay in the Philippines all the way into Laos. But it was authorized by the Laotian government because we had to produce a manifest list of things we were bringing into the country."

"We couldn't wear no military uniforms. We worked in J C Penny coveralls we had bought. You get to see that too. That's what we worked in. Couldn't bring no weapons in this country. All the tools and equipment we had on the itemized manifest; the Laotian government eliminated through our state department, fifty percent of it. That made the mission that much tougher."

"So after that, let's see, NBC left, and then, yeah, on the 29th day, and on the 30th day, we lined all that stuff up in that hole and lined it with C-4 and we detonated it. That was to destroy any form of a weapons system so it could never be used again. That was the logic behind the C-4, and so much of it. One package of it is dangerous."

"When we detonated it, all the strange looking wild birds in that part of the world that was singing, you could hear a Church Mouse when that detonated. Because C-4 has a strange sound to it. It's not like dynamite. If you ever hear it, you will never forget the sound of it."

"After we did that, we took off with what we had gathered from those 12 MIAs and brought it back to U.S. soil."

"The same year, in '84, the Summary Court Board in the Department of Defense decided that one of the skeletal remains that we had in the lab in 1984 would be designated as 'The Unknown Soldier' designee of the Vietnam War. I had something to do with all of that. I was involved in all of that."

"Then they set a date which was going to end in Arlington Cemetery. It started at the lab I worked at in Hawaii and then to Pearl Harbor and we loaded the remains on, I think it was the USS Enterprise, I think that was the ship we loaded them on, anyway, the formal ceremony took place there. Then it went by ship until it got to Norfolk, Virginia, and then from Norfolk, you know, that's another ceremony, and from there, and the rest was on national television. Those were some tiring times. Everything had to be 'dress right dress', there's so much procedure, so much this, so much that, so sometimes you kinda get on each other's nerves. The stress level and the professional level, all of that rolled into one."

THE BUDDY PLAN

In the background all are commenting and agreeing.

"You can't volunteer for that. Everyone, everybody on the team is handpicked. I guess they got me the second time because of the job I did the first time. But, you can't volunteer for them outfits."

Each of us interjects more comments.

"I guess you can say I grew up in the Army. I guess 'Nam' had a lot to do with that."

Me: "Now you say you are originally from Detroit? You didn't want to go back up there?"

"Well, I went back up there," Bruce pauses to collect himself. "This thing with Jacky in Vietnam, I was 19 years old when I came home from that God forsaken place, my peers that I grew up with - I didn't realize how mature I was until I got back and got around them. Their conversations and the same interests absolutely did not interest me."

"It was hard for me to believe that I used to be like that. I was somewhat different. I was still Bruce now. I was still me. That was the good part."

Everyone in the background agreed.

"I had the same heart, but I took a lot of things more serious about people and life. I'm still like that to this day. So, Uh."

I quickly changed the subject as I saw Bruce was getting bogged down from the long verbal presentation, "Now where did y'all meet, Brenda?" referring to him and his wife Brenda.

Brenda speaks up, "In Windsor, I'm from Canada. We met back before he went to the war."

Bruce: "Believe it not, we met four days before I departed to go to Vietnam."

Brenda: "But we didn't get married. We've only been married 20 years."

Patsy: "You got married, what were you telling me?"

Brenda: "We got married in 1991."

Patsy: "They're young chickens, aren't they?"

Linda: "Yeah."

Jacky: "Don got married and then went in the Army."

Patsy: "They got married one week and went into the Army the next week, didn't you?"

Linda: "We got married on a Thursday night and he left on Monday morning. We had been engaged. We had been dating. We dated through college. Then the draft got him."

Patsy: "You took both of them down there, didn't you?"

Linda: "Well, I took them to meet the bus, and then I went to work."

Patsy: "You went down to Fort Jackson?"

Linda: "Well, I went on the weekends when they got passes."

Me: "I tried to sneak out the backdoor and they wouldn't let me."

Jacky: "Me too", as he giggles and continues, "we went into Columbia, wasn't even sworn in yet and got back about two hours late. The cab driver kept driving around and around until we ran out of money and he found out where we were supposed to be. We were about two hours late, or more than that, and they put on our records that we were trouble makers."

Everyone giggles.

Jacky tells this story quite often and it still remains one of my favorite, for obvious reasons.

The conversations continue about the various topics until we finally decide to go to eat at a local restaurant.

The conversation, as expected, is lively at the restaurant. The meal was good and when we got back to Jacky's and Patsy's, Bruce stopped by his car to pick up his scrap book.

THE BUDDY PLAN

If there had ever been any doubt, and there had not been, about anything Bruce had said not being accurate, anyone could clearly see the proof of his adventures in his scrap book. Not only did he have pictures, but there were citations for and army records of his fantastic career.

He had not initially talked about his mission to New Guinea to search for the remains of a WW II B-17 bomber which had crashed into a hillside there. The pictures were there and when he saw us looking at them, he did tell us the intricacies about the mission. Just as the other stories, it was extraordinary.

Needless to say, SFC Bruce Logan, Retired, had experienced an amazing career in the U.S. Army. There is no doubt that his second look at a young U.S. Army Specialist in Vietnam, in spite of all the other accomplishments, proved to be one of the most extraordinary things he had ever done.

For all of this, many people give their heartfelt thanks. I only wish Bunia Bayne had been able to look into the eyes of this man. No words would have been necessary, but there would have been many, and from deep within Bunia Bayne's being.

Bruce Logan grew up in the suburbs of Detroit, Michigan. When he went back after his initial stint in the Army, he felt he had grown apart from the old crowd he previously hung with.

He decided to return to the Army. It was a very fortuitous decision for Ron Dunn and Jacky Bayne.

After my conversations with Bruce Logan, I am convinced, just as he is, that he is a man of destiny. Right away he made it known to me that he thought every person had a reason for existing on this Earth. I hope he was convinced that I felt the same way.

He told me of all the things that had happened to him during his time in service. Many of the stories were beyond incredible.

SSG Logan, as PFC Logan, was supposed to have shipped from The United States in 1966 with the recently activated 9th Infantry Division. But none of that happened. His orders were revoked because he had not finished his Advanced Individual Training. Instead, he was assigned to McCord Air Force Base near Fort Lewis, Washington. From there, he became a replacement in a unit in Vietnam in Chu Lai with the 23rd Infantry Division.

Jacky was assigned to the 196th Light Infantry Brigade attached to the Americal Division.

SSG Logan had taken Basic Training at Fort Knox.

Jacky Bayne had taken Advanced Individual Training at Fort Knox.

Chapter Twenty One

Jacky's Faith

♦

The brightness of the spirit shines although the days' light could be dim. It asks, "What can I do, forsaken by my body, what can I do to prove the spirit is still well and can reach out to others?"

♦

Each having a right of bitterness still proclaimed no such bitterness would be found within him.

♦

Mr. Luke Williams had been crippled by the horrendous disease of Rheumatoid Arthritis. His fingers and toes were gnarled and twisted. Even holding a coffee cup and eating were problematic. His mobility was greatly affected by the loss of his leg to the disease. Each and every movement had to be calculated. As he sat in a chair, if you looked closely, you would see the small grimaces as he changed positions even ever so slightly. But each time, the grimace was turned into a smile or a grin. He wanted to bear each pain silently. People were considerate.

He had become a self-made scholar of the Good Book and believed it literally, chapter and verse, as he so often quoted it. He was a testament of his faith. He found his strength there.

In spite of all the physical shortcomings, his brilliant memory allowed him to recollect and say things in a manner that positively affected others. He spread a message verbally as well as he knew how. His mere existence, which put a smile on every situation, was as strong a testimony, if not stronger, that his Biblical quotes.

As I look at Jacky in his wheelchair, I see a strong parallel between the two. Mr. Luke had been the victim of a terrible disease. The cause of Jacky's circumstances was quite different, but the resulting status is similar. Though each suffered/suffers the physical injuries, each was/is an exemplary spiritual being. There is absolutely no doubt that each had/has a message to deliver. The message will help others who often lack the spiritual strength or guidance they need.

If people were to say they understood the miracle of Jacky's recovery, I would protest vehemently. It is still beyond the human realm to know exactly what had to take place to maintain all the memory of events and sharpness of mind. The thoroughness of his recollections far exceeds what the very learned would ever expect. That fact alone makes the enormity of the miracle take on an even greater dimension than one could ever comprehend.

The body has never fully recovered, but the mind with all the wonderful wit he possessed survived and works as well today as any mind I know.

When I first visited Jacky in the summer of 1968 after he had made it home to Indian Land, I cowardly had reservations in my own mind about what to expect when I saw him. I had been at Fort Sill fulfilling my military commitment and was now on leave back to South Carolina.

My brother Dean, his wife Brenda, my wife Linda, and I went to Jacky's home on Barberville Road in the small community of Indian Land. There he lay in his bed while being cared for by his mother. As we walked into his bedroom, he noticed me and the others. It was not the Jacky I knew from high school in times when we had enjoyed all the pleasures of youth and playing sports together.

I had last seen him as we left basic training headed to our other assignments. He was fit and stood tall and erect. Now, he was just a shadow of what he had been physically.

He gazed up at me and with a spontaneous smile began to talk with the same boyish grin I had seen in him years before. It was difficult for him but he was determined. As if he knew I was very concerned, to alleviate my fears, he began, "Do you remember the taxi ride we had before basic training?"

He went on to tell of the details about the journey into town and back and exactly what had happened and what he had told the taxi driver. He still remembers that story even today. It is among his favorites, if not his most favorite. We all laugh each time he tells it. It is ageless to him and to me.

Whatever concerns I had about his mind were gone.

His body was frail but within it was a spirit with the strength ordinary persons such as I could not understand. As seemingly helpless as he was physically, he reached out to comfort others spiritually.

Jacky loves sports and had planned someday to be a coach. He still gave that much consideration even during the time he was recuperating in the Veterans Hospital in Columbia. He might still have coached, except he felt he might be more able to serve in another capacity.

"I believe my son will get better. I believe he has come back home for a reason". Bunia Bayne, 1967, as she faced down the medical staff at Walter Reed Hospital.

Jacky's Testament to His Faith

Before we start our own story, there is another story which must be told, After all, isn't that the beginning of any good sermon. It is true. No one has ever determined why this happened. But like so many other things he has told me, I have to rib him about it. I simply call it **"The Kiss"**.

In the early 1980s, Jacky was invited to talk at a church in Rock Hill. Of course, he accepted. He and Patsy made plans to go by Winthrop College on the way to the church and pick up a young female acquaintance who wanted to hear the speech.

As usual, the people who listened to him were captivated as he gave the details of his ordeal in Vietnam and how his faith was then and still remains the strength of his being.

After the event, he, Patsy, and the young acquaintance decided to stop at Ryan's restaurant in Rock Hill. Some of the church members from where he had just given his speech had decided to eat there as well. The following is an exchange as we discuss the "incident" in Jacky and Patsy's home:

Patsy: "I noticed the young waitress was real friendly to Jacky, but I didn't pay much attention to it. I mean she made sure he had whatever he needed. She came up to him and said 'I'm so glad to see you.' Of course we didn't know what she was talking about."

I look at Jacky and he blushes as he gives a "who me grin".

Patsy continues: "When we are about to finish the meal, she, the waitress, all of a sudden says, 'well are you going to do it or am I going to have to do it?' Jacky told her he didn't know what she was talking about. And with that, I'm telling you, she laid one on him like you have never seen. I'm not talking about just an ordinary kiss, she really laid one on him."

Patsy giggles and says, "That poor Jacky didn't know what to do. And that poor little girl with us said, 'Mrs. Patsy, is Jacky in the dog house?'"

Patsy laughs again and continues, "I told her, no honey, that don't bother me, I'm not that jealous."

I cut my eyes to Jacky and quiz him, "Well, do you have anything to say?"

Not to be outdone, he quips back, "Well, she was a good waitress."

All of us cannot help but laugh as we look at one another.

I started to say more, but I didn't. After some more discussion and laughter, we all agreed that it had been a mistake in identity.

I still might ask him, "What do you think the people from the church thought of your little escapade?" There is no doubt the answer would be fascinating.

Jacky's Testament to His Faith (continued)

There is little doubt that the faithful household in which Jacky was raised had great influence on the strength of his convictions. Bunia and Eb Bayne were people who attended church each Sunday and at other times when there were services. It was their strong beliefs which had given them strength to endure the hardships of Jacky's struggle.

Jacky had been involved as a youth leader in the church as well when he was young.

Even with an often dysfunctional father, Patsy was raised in a home which had maintained a strong faith throughout their ordeal. No doubt this also reinforces the strength of Jacky's and Patsy's faith.

They have an understanding that if they are called to speak, regardless of circumstances, if they can make it, that is where they will go. There is no charge. They pay their own expenses, but they will accept a meal. One speech I listened to in 2011 was delivered to a Wednesday evening church gathering. Many in the crowd knew him from high school. There were also many in the crowd who had never heard of him. Most of those had moved into our area over the last twenty years.

Before he begins to speak, there seems to be a transformation from his jovial demeanor to an almost trance-like state. I don't speculate on the reason for the change, but he is absolutely convinced about what he says.

One of his speeches follows:

"My story is not a fairy tale. It is true. I was pronounced dead, but God determined for me to be yet alive. I became a poor cripple with only the use of my right arm and hand, but God sent me someone who makes me complete - my adorable wife, Patsy.

In Vietnam I worked with the scout dogs. I had Bruno - a German Shepherd. He was with me on my first mission and my last. He stepped on or tripped a mine and they found me not to be alive and later I understand I 'died' again and was found alive. I died twice in Vietnam.

I do not remember. I had no out-of-body experience, nor did I see the so-called light at the end of the tunnel. God is merciful in making our bodies react to severe pain by going into shock or coma. I was in a coma for almost a month.

Then, I lost my dad in 1970 and my mother in 1974. I prayed and tried to keep my faith in God and also prayed that surely He must have something good for me. He sent Patsy just before my mother died.

If you hit bottom - when we hit bottom, we can reach up from the depths and take time for Jesus Christ. The Bible is our way and through it you can understand what life is all about.

First Corinthians plainly tells us that the preaching of the cross, the way of Christ, is foolishness to those who perish in sin, but unto those of us who are saved, it is the power of God. When you are down, find strength in His teachings.

When I was in Vietnam, I felt that I was going to be tested. I felt strange. I felt that God had a plan for me, but I did not know what it could be. Not me.

Now I would like to spend my life – what there is of it – in helping other people."

Some minutes after the speech was over, the handkerchiefs were finally put away.

As Patsy Bayne sat listening to Jacky conclude his speech and I finally gathered my emotions again, I looked over and smiled as Jacky said, "I'll be glad to answer any questions."

I had to raise my hand and as I did, he looked at me and knew exactly what I was going to say. I had already told him I was going to ask two particular questions.

"While you were in the Army, did you pull K P?" I quizzed. I had done so as I had promised.

The question got a chuckle from the crowd.

I had also told him I was going to ask about sleeping on the top bunk, but I didn't.

After we had all gone home, it seemed as though it was times we had shared together in high school. But it wasn't. So many things have changed. We were obviously older and had our own experiences in the world. No doubt those experiences have shaped us for better or worse; we have been forever affected. None of our experiences have been like those of Jacky. Hopefully, we all have hung on to our faith to some degree and no doubt Jacky's speech had served to remind us that we should have. He is an example of that commitment we all need.

Jacky recalls that during the time he was locked in the dismal coma, he had tried to keep his mind active by reciting Bible verses. As previously stated, he had been brought up practicing a strong faith. He found comfort in the words he had learned before his tragedy and perhaps he found enough strength in these words to help him awaken to the world again.

As we sat one day and discussed baseball, Jacky told me about the day in 1976 when Bobby Richardson and Mickey Mantle came by his house. Bobby Richardson was running for U.S. Congress and decided to pay Jacky a personal visit.

Coincidentally, that same year, I was coordinating the Chester County campaign for Bobby. Maybe Bobby was too honest to be involved with such. I actually had a good friend and good man who had been a high ranking state official confirm that assessment. But a political party had convinced him to run and he did.

During the visit with Jacky, Mickey confided in him that people should not worship athletes such as himself. As Mickey grew older, he came to realize his mistakes and was showing remorse for them.

Jacky told me that Mickey had kneeled down to take a few pictures of the two of them and Mickey could hardly get back to his feet. It was sad for someone who had been such a great athlete. Jacky was concerned about Mickey's physical condition and his spiritual situation as well.

Jacky had promised to keep in touch with Bobby Richardson and, in a future response, Bobby informed Jacky that Mickey had seen the errors of his ways and had been saved before he died. No doubt Jacky was as proud of that as he had been with the unexpected visit.

THE BUDDY PLAN

Jacky's memories are beyond miraculously. He can recall it all. He tells of the circumstances of his injuries and then is able to joke intelligently about them. He has accepted them as part of a life he now feels can be of great purpose to others. He finds no time for self-pity. He has blessed throughout his ordeal by the presence of strong faith people.

The graces of God had been given to them to help each through his struggle. That is perhaps what none of us understand. The greatness of God is displayed in ways about which we have no comprehension.

Me, trying to get a rise from Jacky one day, "Patsy, don't you ever get tired of hearing the same old stuff?" as I made reference to Jacky speaking.

"No, it's always a new experience."

Jacky remains quiet, but looks up and gives me a grin as if to say, "gotcha."

There is no doubt that he means what he says. I have heard him speak on more than one occasion and there is a difference in the atmosphere each time. It's very hard to explain, maybe not explainable at all.

When Jacky was asked by a minister friend to speak at a church in Rockingham, he gladly accepted. He also planned to have Mrs. Sarah there as well. Mrs. Sarah, who spent a great deal of time with Jacky and his mother at Walter Reed, had been on leave when the plans were made to send Jacky to Columbia. She had also been the nurse present when Jacky awakened from his coma. Not to be outdone, she found out where Jacky lived and gave him a call. Her presence at Walter Reed had given Bunia Bayne strength to hope when others in the hospital had written her son off.

This is Jacky's and Patsy's account:

"I went to speak at a church in Rockingham. My friend was a pastor there. They also set up a meeting so I could meet with her (Mrs. Sarah) up there -she hugged me and kissed me."

"She came to church that day," he continues as Patsy now comes into the room and begins to listen to the conversation.

"Mrs. Sarah was on the back row," Patsy interjects. "One of the deacons made a remark about a Black lady sitting in the back of the church."

Jacky continues, "When they called me to the front, I said I want my wife and a friend of mine to come up here with me. When she came up to the front of the church, the deacon turned a bright shade of red."

Patsy: "When Jacky got to the place in his speech about finding life, Jacky said, 'I got somebody to tell you all about it,' and he turned the speech over to Mrs. Sarah. Boy, she got up there and talked and talked."

There is no doubt that one with such experience as Mrs. Sarah had things to say that should be heard by everyone. In the course of her service, she had seen wounds that would shock even the hardiest individual. She had seen hopelessness and she had seen seemingly hopelessness turn into miracles.

She was a spiritual being of the highest order.

Mrs. Sarah is now 88 years young. She still keeps in contact with Jacky and Patsy.

Even when people do devious things that could harm Jacky and Patsy, anger does not appear.

In the late 1980s, someone reported to the Veterans Administration that they had separated. Because the benefits received from the VA are based on family status, it would have meant that a considerable amount of money would have been taken from their monthly stipend.

Like many situations with the government, oftentimes, you are assumed guilty until you prove otherwise. Patsy and Jacky eventually proved that they had never been separated and there was never any intent to do such.

Even though someone later informed them who had made the ridiculous accusation, neither decided to confront the individual. Nor did either of them think they should hold a grudge.

It is typical of their attitude toward this life and the people in it. They have the strength and courage through their faith that they are always forgiving. They are always upbeat about whatever obstacles they encounter.

Chapter Twenty Two

In Memory and Honor of Scout Dogs
(2012)

♦

"With eyes upraised his master's look to scan,
The joy, the solace, and the aid of man:
The rich man's guardian and the poor man's friend,
The only creature faithful to the end."
George Crabbe
(1754-1832)

♦

The Service and the Shame
(Two Accounts of Vietnam)

American war dogs logged tens of thousands of missions in Vietnam. Some 325 died in the line of duty along with 261 handlers. The Vietnam Dog Handlers Association estimates that dogs saved 10,000 soldiers' lives during the war.

Dogs have been serving in military conflicts since World War I, returning home after the conflicts ended. Thousands of dogs were left behind during the Vietnam War. Of the roughly 4,900 dogs that the United States used in Vietnam, around 2,700 were turned over to the South Vietnamese Army, and a staggering 1,600 were euthanized, according to veteran and former Marine dog handler Ron Aiello.

THE BUDDY PLAN

Our Platoon Dog, Vietnam

Recently, I received an e-mail from a man who had been one of my squad leaders in Vietnam. He asked if I remembered him and I was quick to reply that I certainly did. He was somewhat amazed when I told him about the things he had done while we served together.

He was even more amazed when I told him I remembered him writing his Congressman about the base commander shooting our platoon dog. It got enough attention from the Congressman that the base commander was reprimanded and was soon replaced. I'm not sure if the replacement was due to the incident with the dog or was due to his natural rotation because of time served.

I do remember the dog was well-loved and cared for by the soldiers who knew him. As far as I know, he never did harm to anyone or anything.

The gentle stroke of the hand to the hairy creature who responds with an affection known from few living things; and for the moment, the young soldier is again home in the safety of his youth. But, it is only for the moment.

The beloved animal brings pleasure by his mere presence. Other soldiers, who are curious, but fearful, want to reach out and touch the four legged friend. For the moment, it will connect them, too, with their boyish feelings of years past when they ran and played in the sunshine of their summers.

Jacky and Bruno

Of the thousands of dogs who served unselfishly in Vietnam, there were seven dogs named Bruno. Jacky Bayne handled one of them out of Chu Lai. He personally knew the original unit commander from Fort Benning, Georgia.

According to the 48th Infantry Platoon Scout Dog web site: "The 48th IPSD (Infantry Platoon Scout Dog) was activated at Fort Benning, Georgia, on 2 September 1966 with Lt. Ian L. Jones in command. After training at Fort Benning, the unit deployed to Vietnam on 11 January 1967 with a strength of 1 Officer and 14 Enlisted men and 26 dogs. After arriving in Vietnam on 15 January 1967, the platoon moved to Tay Ninh on 23 January 1967 to join the 196th Light Infantry Brigade (LIB).

On 12 April 1967, the 48th moved with the 196th LIB to Chu Lai to become part of Task Force Oregon, which later became the 23rd Infantry Division (Americal). In December of 1967, Lt. Gerald W. Vosbury assumed command. The unit moved again in February of 1968 to LZ Baldy. For a four-week long period during April and May of 1968, the 48th was located at Camp Evans near the A Shau Valley in northern I Corps where elements of the 196th LIB and 101st Airborne Brigade had gathered to support the 1st Cavalry Division - Air Mobile (operation Lam Son 216).

The 48th IPSD was deactivated on 30 March 1972. It had served in the war for 5 years, 2 1/2 months. Only one other Scout Dog Platoon, the 1st Cavalry Division's 34th IPSD, had a longer tour in Vietnam. The 48th received the Valorous Unit Award on 3 March 1971, a Letter of Commendation from the

THE BUDDY PLAN

Commanding General of the 196th LIB on 6 December 1971, and several letters of commendation from various U.S. Army Infantry line units that the 48th worked with over the course of its tour in Vietnam."

It was in the early part of 1967 when Jacky volunteered to become a scout dog handler. It was one of these dogs that Jacky partnered. He already had a love for dogs and was told he could make rank faster and would be given additional incentive pay. Once again, the old rule of not volunteering for an assignment in the Army was violated. I never miss an opportunity to tell Jacky. In spite of what I say now, had I been in the same situation and had a dog such as Bruno look at me, I, the coward that I am, might have done the same.

"And what rule did you violate when you volunteered?" I ask him, of course I'm joking, "And we learned that in basic training."

He always remarks with quick wit, "Yes, that's what Daddy told me too."

We grin and laugh and continue the conversation.

He still has a deep love for dogs. While this was being written (2011), his small dog died. Both he and Patsy loved the dog dearly. I thought I had spoiled dogs, but maybe their little dog was considerably more spoiled. The only consolation was that the dog was old and had lived a charmed life and in the end, there was no suffering.

When Jacky awakened form his coma, he wondered what had happened to Bruno. The last thing he remembers about Bruno was walking with him and approaching the edge of the jungle.

People around Jacky wondered if they should tell him. They finally did and he handled it well. Still today, as he talks about Bruno, there's a special tone to his voice. The picture of the two is prominently displayed on his wall along with other memories captured in newspaper articles or framed memorabilia. How can someone forget such a friend? He or she doesn't!

War Dog Memorials

In the United States, there are two memorials to the fearless friends who gave their all in service to the United States: One at March Air Force Base, CA and the other at The Infantry School, Ft. Benning, GA. Californian Jeffery Bennett put the War Dog Memorial project together. There are two identical enormous bronzes of a dog and its handler in Vietnam-era combat gear.

The dedication of the pedestal to honor the K9 heroes of World War II, Korea, Vietnam, and Thailand was held on May 8, 2004, at Sacrifice Field, Ft. Benning, Georgia. Approximately 100 people attended the ceremonies. Jesse Mendez, with a lot of assistance, coordinated and planned the event. On a beautiful Georgia day, canine heroes who so bravely gave their lives were honored for their service and sacrifice by handlers, friends and the general public.

At 1:00 pm a pedestal with the names and Preston Brand numbers (serial numbers) of all dogs KIA (killed in action) since World War II was unveiled. A naval bell rang as each name was announced. The bell tolled over 400 times.

Bronze Dog and Handler Pedestal

The dynamo behind the pedestals is SFC Jesse S. Mendez (USA Ret.), a 21-year army veteran who served three tours in Vietnam. Mendez, now, as he was when on active duty, is obsessed with training. "Realistic combat training" is the phrase the military uses and the sergeant made sure that the men and dogs that he trained were combat ready. No government money was used in the memorial or the pedestals. Each group, representing various dog handling groups raised the money for their pedestal. Mendez organized and put together the twelve pedestals and their content.

Jacky, as well as many other former dog handlers, attended this ceremony. They have grayed and grown pudgy around the middle. Many of the memories of their service have grown dim. What has not dimmed is the love for the dogs with whom they worked. Along with his own service number, each handler can still recall the service number of their four legged friend from years past.

Better Treatment Today

According to a recent article by CNN:
"Today, dogs are no longer left in war zones. In 2000, President Bill Clinton signed a law that allowed the dogs to be adopted by former handlers, law enforcement agencies, and civilians. But Debbie Kandoll, founder of 'Military Working Dog Adoptions', says this law didn't go far enough and is pushing for an amendment to include the reclassification of war dogs.

U.S. Rep. Walter Jones, R-North Carolina, agrees that a new classification is needed to elevate the 'soldier dog'. Jones has been working on a bill that would reclassify the dogs as 'K-9 members of the armed forces' and provide a way for the Defense Department to honor the dogs with official medals.

'Those who have been to war tell me that the dogs are invaluable,' he said. 'That they are just as much a part of a unit as a soldier or Marine. They are buddies.'

Jones has submitted the proposed legislation to the Congressional Budget Office for a cost review. A response is expected by mid-February.

Despite the classification, the military says the dogs are respected. 'While there is a proper, legal classification for a working dog, we know they are living things, and we have great respect and admiration for them,' said Lackland Air Force Base spokesman Gerry Proctor. The dogs are trained at Lackland. 'A handler would never speak of their dog as a piece of equipment. The dog is their partner. You can walk away from a damaged tank, but not your dog. Never.'"

Comments from the CNN Blog

Janelle

"When I was in Afghanistan, a dog handler would walk by and you could see an instant change in all the service members who happened to be nearby. People would sheepishly approach the handler and ask to pet them, or would stare, often not even aware they were doing it. Military working dogs, especially overseas, conjure up feelings of home, loved ones, and safety. These dogs are not only a comfort to people during some of the darkest times of their service, but they serve in some of the hardest capacities that soldiers can and deserve the same respect and treatment as their human counterparts."

GMO

"Auburn University is currently training and has in service in war zones several dogs whose job is to sniff out IED's and warn our soldiers of the danger. Given that these dogs have increased the detection rate of IEDs in the area they are servicing from 50% to 80%, they deserve to be called something other than equipment, don't you think?"

Hollander

"It saddens me that America so often looks at everything as a commodity. It does not matter what is the right thing to do, just what is the cheapest. Too much trouble to bring home animals who have saved American lives, too expensive to keep cattle on grass, too much effort to slaughter animals humanely, this horse is too old to race, send it to Mexico to be made into dog food. We pretend it does not happen, but when forced to confront the fact that we are so casual with living creatures, we say 'this is wrong!' Then we hear the response, 'you are too emotional' and the old 'they are just animals,' or here, 'they are equipment.' We should live up to our responsibilities. But who am I kidding, Americans live in a disposable society – look around - our relationships are disposable, our children are disposable, our environment is disposable. Why should I be surprised that these brave dogs are disposable? This is depressing."

JW

> "To get a better understanding of the bond between soldier and dog all one has to do is read the story of British soldier Liam Tasker and his K9 partner Theo from March 2011. Shortly after Cpl. Tasker was killed in a firefight in Afghanistan, Theo suffered a seizure and passed as well. Broken heart? BTW, The Brits award medals to K9's."

Brian

"Fact Check: The first recorded use of dogs by the United States Army was during the 2nd Seminole War, and not as previously thought - the Spanish American War. 33 Cuban-bred bloodhounds were bought at a

THE BUDDY PLAN

cost of several thousand dollars and 5 handlers were used by the US Army to track the Seminole Indians and the runaway slaves they were harboring in the swamps of western Florida and Louisiana. At the time, there were a few petitions filed and recorded with the United States Congress by the Quakers living in New Jersey, Pennsylvania, and Indiana, strongly protesting the use of these bloodhounds by General Zachary Taylor against the Seminole Indians in the Florida War.

Also, there is Sallie the War Dog who fought with her regiment (11th Pennsylvania Volunteer Infantry) during the Battle of Gettysburg in the Civil War. There is a statue of Sallie in Gettysburg National Park at the base of the 11th PVI Monument.

Sallie, a Brindel Bull Terrier, joined the regiment as a puppy in the early days of the war. Through it all, she provided a source of comfort, pride, and inspiration for her fighting comrades. Sallie would hold her position on the line and bark fiercely at the enemy. One thing was clear; a bond of unconditional love and loyalty existed between Sallie and the men.

At Gettysburg, the gallant little dog became separated from her unit in the confusion of the first day's battle. Refusing to pass through the Rebel lines, Sallie returned to her unit's former position atop Oak Ridge, staying among her fallen comrades, licking wounds of the injured and watching over lifeless bodies. Days later, after the Confederates retreated from the field, she was found weakened and malnourished amidst the dead and debris. A compassionate soldier recognized her and returned Sallie to her unit. No doubt, the reunion was joyful!

Miraculously Sallie had avoided being shot at

Gettysburg, but on May 8, 1864, the same day Captain Keenan was killed; she was shot in the neck by a minnie ball. After being examined at the field hospital, a surgeon pronounced she would live but the bullet could not be removed. After a few days recuperation at the hospital, she returned to the unit with the painful and annoying wound, eventually becoming a battle scar. Upon reporting for "active duty" she felt it necessary to tear the seat out of the pants of a young soldier from another unit running away from the battle line as he crossed along the back of the 'Old 11th.'

Fatefully, Sallie was in her usual position on February 6, 1865, at Hatcher's Run, Virginia, when a bullet struck her in the head, killing her. Heartbroken over the loss of their beloved mascot, the men buried her on the field of battle under heavy enemy fire."

Remembrance Day, 2004, Fort Benning, Georgia

Ron Aiello

"Congressman Jones is also the congressman who had a resolution passed by congress and signed into law authoring a National War Dog Monument to be established in the Washington, D.C. area.

He has been an outstanding supporter of our Military Working Dogs for many years - we (USWDA) do thank him."

Epilogue

"Dante-ish"

Joe Vallely, my OCS cube-mate and friend moved from the bustle of New York City to a small town in the foothills in Eastern Virginia. One day as he walked about looking for a quiet place to enjoy a cup of coffee, he stepped into a quaint little restaurant. While giving the place an official "once over", he noticed a tired looking elderly man eating alone in a small booth.

"Is it possible?" was his initial thought. Joe studied the man intently to be sure it was who he thought it might be. *It was! He was certain.* How odd it seemed to meet such a once powerful man in this remote setting. There was no doubt, it was him.

Years before, this now weary looking elderly man's advice had caused the most powerful men in the world to make decisions that affected the most powerful armed forces in the world.

In geographical distance, he was still only a hundred miles from his former throne of power. But his status of power and influence were now light years in the past.

Fate had taken him from obscurity to fame in the political circles of the Washington D.C. power structure and, just as it had done to so many before him and has done to many since, delivered him back to the original status of obscurity from his pinnacle. The descent from power is often cruel, but even crueler still in this instance was the fact that he was delivered back as a shamed, a very shamed, man.

He had been a leading character on the "power stage" in a play for which he had written the script. Each act unfolded worse than the previous. Dante's impish spirit seemed in control. The curtain could not be drawn to save the actors from their unalterable performance. Each character was bound to play out his part in its entirety. Each was being reviewed by an ever increasingly hostile audience.

Robert McNamara had authored the expansion of the war in Southeast Asia called Vietnam and the final reviews of his work had made a lasting impression on the nation and the leaders who had followed his script.

None of the reviews bore any semblance of kindness. He must now wallow alone in the failure of his writings and deeds. Hopefully, for his own sake, his face would be lost in the fog of forgetfulness, as would his deeds.

He was correct. He has been all but forgotten, except to the generation he had so dramatically affected.

Misty Images

So called progress exacts its price on all things. The student area near the back campus of Winthrop College where I stood that August day, met Wayne Beard, and was told of Kenny Griffin's plight has become foundations for large buildings. Hopefully, the wonderful granite bleachers which lined the field below were carefully disassembled and the granite blocks were put to some good use. Whatever memories were stored in them remain hidden away from anyone to know.

Football is still discussed, but my particular crowd has given way to others. The meeting place has changed. Bill Culp, the man who scheduled the building for our use, a WW II veteran himself, passed away several years back.

I have lost contact with Wayne Beard. He is no longer the Veterans Affairs Officer for the county.

I have had the good fortune to find or to otherwise re-establish contact through the wonders of modern technology with many of those who were dear friends.

They have aged. Even with the contact, the misty images of the youthful experiences bring an understandable sadness.

A Special Note: Kenny Griffin's brother Sam, a retired U.S. Army Colonel who served two tours in Vietnam, now sits disabled in a wheelchair. He, too, is a victim of the war. He wasn't seriously wounded there by a bullet, artillery, or a mine, but the scourge of Agent Orange followed him home. It hid away in his body only to attack him later in life. It was an assault as vicious as any enemy he had ever confronted in Vietnam.

Mr. Luke, Jack Ghent

The prophetic truths of Mr. Luke have been true to form for the U.S. and other nations about the world since I first awakened and heard his quote from the Bible (Matthew24:6). I have since become educated enough to know that it has always been that way and with little doubt, I can understand why it will continue.

Since Vietnam, the U.S. has been involved in three wars in the Middle East. Two of those were with Iraq and one still goes on in Afghanistan in 2012. There have been smaller, less-involved military actions that dotted the pages as well. The rumors of future involvements and saber rattling among political adversaries as they jockey to appease political constituents to the extreme right of their party seem endless. The war mongers still attempt to make the case that any other position is Un-American and any leader who might assume a different stance is weak. Little have we learned from History.

There are still the Jack Ghents who carry out the wishes of the power brokers. They, and others like them on either side, return home scarred from battle.

Their physical bodies remain intact, but they are never whole again. They will wallow for the remainder of their lives in the pain hidden deeply away in their psyches.

Howey's Store

Howey's Store was lost to the progress of the new road that was widened to handle all the vehicles that now zip through like traffic on an interstate. His home located near where the old store was still stands, but it has been relegated to a storage/store of sorts. The portion of the corner property remaining has had a variety of car lots located there in an attempt to make a living for the proprietors. A stoplight attempts to control the exceptionally busy intersection which once had only a stop sign.

The old buildings near the store are all gone. They became eyesores after they were abandoned years ago. The area now gets all sorts of attention from the county government. They know that each new house or business built means money (in the county treasury) which is spent to make things better?

Slagle's Happy Acres

Slagle's Happy Acres remains only as a misty thought in the minds of the older generation of those who ever knew about it. Some can identify with those who came to the place seeking some sort of comfort they could not find any other way. Even the young people who were patrons of the place are now older and settled.

Sugar Creek still flows and the last remnants of the old bridge are barely visible. Catfish still swim in the muddy waters and the grand old trees still reach out for God's grace and mercy knowing they too will someday fall into the murky waters which helped them flourish to glory. Water bugs still skate along in the summer time. Whatever concern they had for any of the happenings remains hidden. When I cross the new bridge near where Harry and his buddies used to roam, I often look for people sitting along the creek banks fishing, but none are there.

The characters are gone from the "Happy Acres". The final curtain call was made many years ago for most. They are at peace with a world in which they experienced the violence, hatred, and evil that lust for power and greed can bring. The effects of it were so great on them, they never recovered to a normal state of being. Hopefully they are in a better place. They spent their days in hell on an earth where such things should never have happened.

But the new generations will do no better. The ominous warnings of Mr. Luke live on and should never be forgotten. It was written long ago and remains in stone; therefore, it won't be altered.

History of Vietnam

Vietnam remains in conflict today. It is not in a shooting war, but the battle for the hearts and minds to control them as a source of slave labor continues. It is not the communists who offer the greater harm. It is something far worse; it is an agreement between the socialist government and the global corporatists who enslave them. The blood of all the former combatants shed in Vietnam was all in vain, regardless of the side on which they fought.

The people will still work in the bloodied fields contaminated by unexploded bombs and Agent Orange and know only a meager existence. The History books will favor the side who writes them. The Vietnamese people will be forgiving to the intruders. The intruding soldiers will be forgiving to those against whom they fought in the fields and jungles. The homeland of the people there is united.

The November 4, 1967, edition of *the Stars and Stripes* newspaper features an article about Jacky on the front page. It recalls the original discovery that he had been found to be alive by an embalmer. Ironically, the lead story in that same paper was **"LBJ Glum on Taxes, Optimistic on Vietnam."** Also on the same page were other lead stories about the recent major successes the United States was having against the communists in South Vietnam.

From those articles, one could surmise that the United States was doing well there and the light was about to shine at the other end of the tunnel. Little did anyone know that in less than three months, the whole of South Vietnam would be raging in full scale combat because of a general offensive launched by the communist forces from the DMZ to deep into the delta region. It was as if the war had started in earnest all over again.

The new communist offensive further tore the U.S. apart politically. It was a time when American people would so closely associate the soldier with an unpopular war that he, along with the politician, would suffer their wrath. For the soldier it was undeserved, not so for the politician.

OCS

What became of all the young officers who graduated from Officer Candidate School? I talked with many of them personally. Some had really grand stories to tell. We lost four out of a class of 125. Statistically, that means we had a bunch more wounded. I know of some who were. I didn't get in contact with all who graduated. I still don't know about 20 or so. Unfortunately, by the time I had found out about many, 40 years later, some of them had already died - the exact cause is not known.

Like all who served, there is no doubt they were affected in some way, whether it was for better or worse.

There is always sadness when you are successful contacting some of the ones who caused a special memory. Our TAC Officer, Lieutenant Hosey Maxwell, passed away ten years before we started the search for our comrades. We were able to establish a friendship with his daughter. We found out things about him that broke our hearts further still.

He had been a victim of the war. He wasn't physically scarred there, but his psychological scars were deep. I suspect that helped speed his early death.

Lieutenant Two, one of the best instructors we had in Artillery, also had died by the time we contacted his wife. She thanked us graciously for our concern.

Return to Fort Sill

A single building is all that remains of the once proud area set aside at Fort Sill, Oklahoma, for training Artillery Officers. Thousands had gone through the process there and then to hostile environs from which many would not return alive and others would return with the scars of war. My generation made its own contribution.

There is sadness all about. The streets where hundreds assembled each morning with the purpose of preparing to go to war are silent and lonely. Only memories are left to blow in the Oklahoma winds.

In the year 2008, a small group from my graduating class returned there. The older pudgy bodies were a far cry from the slim physically fit specimens from the 1960s. It was apparent that too many had enjoyed the good life of food and drink.

Tour of Duty

Maybe the real duty of a soldier is not complete until he or she reflects on the real reasons each was subjected to the experiences which were exacted upon them. The after action report, if you will, that can provide so much insight into *who, what, and why must be told.* No doubt the emphasis should always be on the *why.*

The duty of anyone who has witnessed what war can do is never finished until they look back and convince others that there is no beauty to any of it.

Cry For the Children

Those who never had a chance to enjoy the life that should have been rightfully theirs to enjoy have been silenced forever by man's indifference for other living things. The toothy smiles and grins which brightened the world are lost to the inhumanity of insane political ideology.

Mother's hearts are torn from their chest by the agony and their screams are heard only by the few who listen, but that, too, is forgotten. The insanity continues.

The Coma

Jacky said he recited Bible verses as he lay silenced from the world. He lived there for thirty days. His mind was alive though his body was almost lost to the tragedy of war. He felt the presence of his mother and the nurse, Mrs. Sarah McKenzie, a spiritual Black lady, as they entered his room. He said he never experienced an out of body consciousness. He had no need for that. His consciousness was committed to his body, regardless of the condition of it. He would awaken in it to be with his mother. It was a promise he had to keep.

He felt he was AWOL. He was that duty bound.

The Medical Journey

Jacky is sure that he received the best medical care anywhere. He gives the medical personnel praise for their actions in Vietnam and ever since. The doctors were quite talented and concerned for each wounded soldier who came into the aid stations and hospitals.

The doctors in Tan An, where I was first headquartered, were first rate. The lead doctor was older, 36 at the time I was there. I've seen them work on patients until there was absolutely no hope at all. Even then, they were disappointed that they could not have done more.

A Mother's Faith

Until her last breath, Bunia Bayne held true to her beliefs. She knew in her heart that her son would recover. She again witnessed his contagious smile and listened to his wonderful sense of humor. Her son was never made physically whole again, but then, she saw no imperfections.

She somehow knew she could leave and all would be well.

Mothers Everywhere

The mothers of this earth still cry for those born of their womb. The connections are strong as they suffer the pains and sorrows of those to whom they gave life. Old men commit mother's children to wars which need not be fought. Old men are numb to the feelings of sorrow their actions bring unto others. They aren't among the dead and lame. They won't spend their lives crippled by the ravages their decisions have wrought.

The Medical Journey Continues

Jacky Bayne is as sharp mentally today as any man I know. This takes into account many much younger. He can verbally quip with the best. Physically, he remains confined to a wheelchair. He has a smile on his face each time he greets you. He has found strength though a faith that, unfortunately, most of us don't know.

The Adoption

Henry Stegall was a man who knew the sorrow of losing a son to war. It opened a cruel chapter in his book of life that could never be closed properly. Try as he might, he could never change that which had been written.

Jacky was the beneficiary of whatever good came from the situation. Jacky, in turn, provided what comfort might be derived from the whole of the situation. Whatever stage they were on, the roles were played extraordinarily well.

Jacky Meets Another Angel

With the loss of his father and his mother, Jacky faced the real possibility that he was destined to be a ward of the VA from that time forward. Unable to do all the things necessary for himself, he would have been bound to remain where he would receive proper care.

The soft smile of the young lady who stood before him 4 days prior to his mother's passing was Angelic in every respect. Who had sent her and just at the proper time? It would take a super special person to replace his mother, but the baton had been passed; it's just that we never saw it happen. She was chosen to anchor the race and she has never thought of anything but to give it her best.

The Wedding

Could there ever have been a better union of the spirits than that which took place on August 28, 1977, in Lancaster, SC? Maybe. But this special one is certainly among the best I know about. Why were there so many tears at such a happy occasion? You know the answer.

The honeymoon had to have all the events in it to make a splendid story. The laughter it generates is the perfect ending to that day.

Lieutenant Ron Dunn, USMC

How does anyone explain a Marine coming to complete a mission? The answer is obvious - he is a Marine. There need be no other answer, but there is. *It is called Fate – in the truest meaning of the word.*

There still remains the question: "Why was he chosen to complete that mission which he never knew existed?" The answer is: "He was/is a man of destiny."

SFC Bruce Logan

Bruce Logan retired from the military as a Sergeant First Class after an amazing career. Who could ever have imagined that a young male from the streets of Detroit was destined for such adventures? But he was. He, a man of faith, feels he had a mission, and there was a purpose for his life.

Indeed, he was cast into a role which he played exquisitely.

Jacky's Faith

What more can be said other than the man has strong faith and he lives it each day? Whatever was taken from him has been replenished in ways not understood except by those fortunate enough to sit and talk with him. There is genuineness to it all. There is inspiration to others in it.

In Memory of Scout Dogs

It was too late for the "Dogs of Vietnam", but the attitudes have since changed and we now have humane thoughts about how service dogs ought to be treated.

There is much to be realized about people and nations in viewing the manner in which those creatures who are at their mercy are treated. We are a better nation when we show compassion. We are weaker when we don't. Moral fibers have always made this nation what it is.

And What Was It Really All About _____?

The war finally ended in 1975 and the remaining troops were brought home. There were no great celebrations in the streets. Discussions about the pros and cons of our involvement finally stopped as the main topic of conversation.

It disappeared from the radar screen, except in the minds and bodies of those who had been there. And yes, it never went away for those who had lost dear ones there.

Did Communism win the deciding battle for the entire world to finally begin an irreversible slide down the slope to domination? The answer is a resounding NO!

Terrorism is now the new catch word. With that in mind, we can now mass our troops and invade nations based on questionable information doled out to the mindless masses. To be skeptical is to be unpatriotic. The Military Industrial Complex can afford the propaganda complex which controls the hearts and minds of the people. After all, isn't that what it is all about _____?

The Buddy Plan

When two good friends receive letters inviting them to serve their country, they are drawn closer together for all sorts of reasons. Admittedly, fear of the unknown is one of them.

In retrospect, it is hard to believe my Buddy Plan partner was overly cautious about sleeping in the top bunk during our stint in basic training.

There was never a thought… it would be the last summer Jacky would enjoy the red convertible he had recently bought and enjoyed driving. Nor did we ever have any ideas that the pool room partnership idea would never come to fruition.

"And when were you more nervous," I asked him, "the first day you and Bruno walked point in Vietnam or on your wedding day?"

It has been a long time since Linda told me of your injury. Seems like yesterday, as do so many other things.

I don't think I ever told you welcome home and thank you for your service. "Welcome home and thank you for your service then and now."

"Most of all, thank you for your courage and the inspiration you have given and continue to give to others."

ABOUT THE AUTHOR

The author grew up in the panhandle area of Lancaster County, SC, and graduated in 1962 from, what was then, a small rural school named Indian Land. Starting in the 1980s, the area experienced some of the most rapid growth in the state.

Don's formal education included graduating from North Greenville College, Newberry College, and Winthrop University. He earned degrees in History/Political Science and Psychology and post graduate degrees in Education Administration. His career as a high school teacher in Chester County, SC, teaching Psychology, History, and other related subjects lasted 31 years.

He served in the U.S. Army, active duty, for three years. One year of his service, 1968-69, was spent as an Automatic Weapons Platoon Leader in Vietnam. He received a Bronze Star for his service during his tour of duty there.

The author has retired and moved back to the area where he grew up in Indian Land, SC.

Made in the USA
Columbia, SC
22 May 2019